Developments in Islamic Banking

Palgrave Macmillan Studies in Banking and Financial Institutions

Series Editor: **Professor Philip Molyneux**

The Palgrave Macmillan Studies in Banking and Financial Institutions will be international in orientation and include studies of banking within particular countries or regions, and studies of particular themes such as Corporate Banking, Risk Management, Mergers and Acquisitions, etc. The books will be focused upon research and practice, and include up-to-date and innovative studies on contemporary topics in banking that will have global impact and influence.

Titles include:

Yener Altunbas, Blaise Gadanecz and Alper Kara
SYNDICATED LOANS
A Hybrid of Relationship Lending and Publicly Traded Debt

Elena Beccalli
IT AND EUROPEAN BANK PERFORMANCE

Santiago Carbó, Edward P.M. Gardener and Philip Molyneux
FINANCIAL EXCLUSION

Violaine Cousin
BANKING IN CHINA

Franco Fiordelisi and Philip Molyneux
SHAREHOLDER VALUE IN BANKING

Munawar Iqbal and Philip Molyneux
THIRTY YEARS OF ISLAMIC BANKING
History, Performance and Prospects

Kimio Kase and Tanguy Jacopin
CEOs AS LEADERS AND STRATEGY DESIGNERS
Explaining the Success of Spanish Banks

M. Mansoor Khan and M. Ishaq Bhatti
DEVELOPMENTS IN ISLAMIC BANKING
The Case of Pakistan

Mario La Torre and Gianfranco A. Vento
MICROFINANCE

Philip Molyneux and Munawar Iqbal
BANKING AND FINANCIAL SYSTEMS IN THE ARAB WORLD

Philip Molyneux and Eleuterio Vallelado (*editors*)
FRONTIERS OF BANKS IN A GLOBAL WORLD

Anastasia Nesvetailova
FRAGILE FINANCE
Debt, Speculation and Crisis in the Age of Global Credit

Andrea Schertler
THE VENTURE CAPITAL INDUSTRY IN EUROPE

Alfred Slager
THE INTERNATIONALIZATION OF BANKS

Palgrave Macmillan Studies in Banking and Financial Institutions
Series Standing Order ISBN 1–4039–4872–0

You can receive future titles in this series as they are published by placing a standing order. Please contact your bookseller or, in case of difficulty, write to us at the address below with your name and address, the title of the series and one of the ISBNs quoted above.

Customer Services Department, Macmillan Distribution Ltd, Houndmills, Basingstoke, Hampshire RG21 6XS, England

Developments in Islamic Banking

The Case of Pakistan

M. Mansoor Khan and M. Ishaq Bhatti

Forewords by Rodney Wilson and Agil Natt

palgrave
macmillan

First published 2008 by
PALGRAVE MACMILLAN
Houndmills, Basingstoke, Hampshire RG21 6XS and
175 Fifth Avenue, New York, N.Y. 10010
Companies and representatives throughout the world

PALGRAVE MACMILLAN is the global academic imprint of the Palgrave Macmillan division of St. Martin's Press, LLC and of Palgrave Macmillan Ltd. Macmillan® is a registered trademark in the United States, United Kingdom and other countries. Palgrave is a registered trademark in the European Union and other countries.

ISBN-13: 978–1–4039–9877–4 hardback
ISBN-10: 1–4039–9877–9 hardback

This book is printed on paper suitable for recycling and made from fully managed and sustained forest sources. Logging, pulping and manufacturing processes are expected to conform to the environmental regulations of the country of origin.

A catalogue record for this book is available from the British Library.

A catalog record for this book is available from the Library of Congress.

10 9 8 7 6 5 4 3 2 1
17 16 15 14 13 12 11 10 09 08

Printed and bound in Great Britain by
CPI Antony Rowe, Chippenham and Eastbourne

Say: Behold, my prayer, and (all) my acts of worship, and my living and my dying are for God (alone), the Sustainer of all the worlds

(*The Holy Quran* 6:162)

Contents

List of Tables and Figures

Tables

Figures

Foreword

Pakistani Islamic scholars and economists were amongst the earliest advocates of *shariah*-compliant finance and have made important contributions to the academic literature on the subject, yet their country's record in developing its own Islamic banking system has been very disappointing. In this study Mansoor Khan and Ishaq Bhatti attempt to explain the paradox of how successive Pakistan governments have failed to undertake the necessary practical steps to introduce Islamic finance despite widespread popular support for *shariah* compliance in banking and opposition to the present largely *riba*-based system. Rhetoric from politicians who were supposedly supportive of Islamic finance has not matched the reality, and indeed it has often been left to Pakistanis living abroad and foreign financial institutions to take the initiative rather than local banks that continued to promote loans with interest.

Fortunately today, despite political uncertainties, the climate is more favourable to Islamic banking, with Pakistan following the lead of the Gulf States and Malaysia in introducing a dual banking system where Islamic finance plays an increasingly significant role. The State Bank of Pakistan is very supportive and the Ministry of Finance was enthusiastic about the country's major sovereign *sukuk* issuance.

Yet the history of Islamic finance in Pakistan gives reason for caution. The Council for Islamic Ideology recommended as early as 1980 that a comprehensive Islamic economic and financial system should be established, but despite years of dialogue little was achieved, a situation criticized by the Federal *Shariah* Court in 1991. Subsequently the Commission for the Islamization of the Economy attempted to get the process started, and in 1998 a detailed *Blueprint for an Islamic Financial System* was drawn up by the International Institute of Islamic Economics of the International Islamic University in Islamabad following a workshop on the subject. This important work was unfortunately largely ignored by Pakistan's policymakers.

The documents produced by the Council for Islamic Ideology, the Commission for the Islamization of the Economy and the *Blueprint for an Islamic Financial System* are analysed in detail by the authors, and the debates surrounding their publication are reviewed. This is the first comprehensive appraisal of the obstacles faced in the introduction of Islamic banking and finance in Pakistan. It is evident that legal support, as handed down in the Supreme Court judgement prohibiting *riba* in 1999, has not been sufficient to bring about the transformation of the financial system. Pakistan seems fated to follow the dual system approach, which means in practice that conventional interest-based finance will continue to dominate for the foreseeable future.

The book will interest not only those concerned with Pakistan, but also those interested in Islamic finance more generally. It is an important contribution to the empirical literature on Islamic banking and finance, not least because the case of Pakistan, an almost entirely Muslim country with a population exceeding 160 million and a GDP exceeding $130 billion, deserves serious attention.

Professor Rodney Wilson
Durham University, UK

Foreword

Islam is a religion of righteousness and beliefs predicated on the Quran and the Hadith. It encompasses all aspects of human life including economics and commerce. It is not surprising then that there is a strong connection between values and practices and these are the very foundations that has built the Islamic financial services industry. It started off as an alternative being offered to Muslims who want to ensure that they lead an Islamic way of life, as vicegerent of Allah, but has now blossomed into a full-fledge industry, replete with entire suite of products and services which the ummah can avail themselves to. Indeed it is currently globally recognized as a very viable alternative to conventional banking and finance.

As a country, Pakistan started with the introduction of Islamic banking and Finance in the early 80s. There were some early successes and setbacks too, especially with the 1991 ruling by the Federal Syariat Court. However, the country was undaunted by such an event and pulled itself together to chart a new route for the Islamization of its financial services sector.

Other countries like Sudan and Malaysia also made an early start. In Malaysia, Islamic banking and financial services have been embraced by all and despite its early start as an alternative to the conventional system, it is currently being accepted as a very viable alternative. Malaysia currently adopts the dual system. Incidentally there are more non Muslims availing themselves to Islamic banking and finance than Muslims in Malaysia. This is indeed a good sign. Even the largest Islamic capital market players globally are banks from non Islamic countries and they are attracted to this industry less for the spiritual aspects which Muslims crave for but more for the monies to be made, its ethical overtones and the abundant liquidity to be tapped. We have seen the recent introduction of Islamic banking in London and Singapore and both countries are vying to be Islamic financial centres.

The authors Mansoor Khan and Ishaq Bhatti have researched thoroughly the historical development in Pakistan and also provided a critique of some of these initiatives. However the object of this book remains clear and that is to illustrate that Islamic banking and finance can be a genuine alternative to the conventional system.

This book will be of immense value to scholars, industry practitioners and regulators alike and I congratulate the authors for undertaking this task. At INCEIF, with its vision to be the knowledge leader in Islamic finance we believe that the work of the authors will greatly contribute to this expanding body of knowledge.

Agil Natt
President & Chief Executive
INCEIF
The Global University in Islamic Finance
Kuala Lumpur
Malaysia

Preface and Acknowledgements

Islam offers a full code of conduct enlightening every aspect of human life. In the economic arena, Islam expresses the basic thrust to establish a system based on justice and equality, ensuring the harmonious and well-balanced physical and spiritual growth and general welfare of human beings. Islam rejects the interest-based conventional financial system because its very nature is to bring unfair gains to a handful of capitalists and to harm collective human rights and well-being. The conventional system clogs up the wheels of economic growth and impairs the process of distributing wealth and resources fairly among societies at both national and international levels. Islam presents a more ethical and efficient alternative to the conventional system. This book explores that Islamic paradigm.

This work builds on the Islamic vision of business and economic ethics and then goes into the finer details of establishing an Islamic banking and finance (IBF) system in the modern world. IBF is a relatively new and rapidly growing phenomenon in contemporary global finance. It replaces the interest-based relationship between the borrower and the lender with equity-based and interest-free arrangements. This work covers two important aspects of the contemporary IBF world. First, it takes stock of the conceptual and institutional developments in IBF since the 1970s and of its prospects for future growth in the face of the globally dominant Western market and socio-economic environment. Second, it explores the episode of IBF in Pakistan that was once recognized as the hallmark of Muslim world.

This research has benefited from the invaluable work of many theologians and practitioners of the IBF discipline. We have duly acknowledged and referenced all such sources throughout this work. Many people have made invaluable contributions behind the scenes towards the completion of this book. First and foremost, we are extremely grateful to our spouses and children, who sacrificed a great deal to give us all the time and comforts we needed for completing this work. We give our heartfelt thanks to our academic institutions for providing us with highly conducive working environments. We owe thanks to Leonard J Pullin, Janet Sawyer, Mary Oliver, Brian Cheers and Julie McGuigan of the University of South Australia, to Gary Magee and Raymond Harbridge of

La Trobe University, Australia, to M M Al-Awan and Saiful Rosly of INCEIF, Malaysia, and to David Graf of UAE University for their support for this intellectual venture. Finally, we wish to thank Michael James for copy editing our original manuscript.

Mohammad Mansoor Khan
Mount Gambier Regional
Centre University of
South Australia, Australia

Muhammad Ishaq Bhatti
Economics and Finance,
School of Business La Trobe
University, Melbourne,
Australia

List of Abbreviations

AAOIFI	Accounting Auditing Organization for Islamic Financial Institutions
AMAN	Dubai Islamic Insurance and Re-insurance Company
BCD	Banking and Control Department
BCO	Banking Companies Ordinance
CII	Council of Islamic Ideology
CIE	Commission for Islamization of Economy
DIB	Dubai Islamic Bank
DIFC	Dubai International Financial Centre
DIFX	Dubai International Financial Exchange
EGIBL	Emirates Global Islamic Bank Limited
ETFs	exchange-traded funds
EU	European Union
FSA	Financial Services Authority (UK)
FSC	Federal *Shariat* Court
G-8	Group of Eight
GCC	Gulf Cooperation Council
GCIBFI	General Council for Islamic Banks and Financial Institutions
GDP	Gross Domestic Product
HBFC	House Building Finance Corporation
IAS	International Accounting Standards
IBF	Islamic banking and finance
ICCI	Islamic Chamber of Commerce and Industry
ICP	Investment Corporation of Pakistan
IFIs	Islamic financial institutions
IDB	Islamic Development Bank
IFSB	Islamic Financial Services Board
IIFM	International Islamic Financial Market
IIIE	International Institute of Islamic Economics
IIRA	International Islamic Rating Agency
IIT	Insurance Islam TAIB
IJI	Islamic *Jamhori Itehad* (Islamic Democratic Alliance)
IMANX	Dow Jones^{SM} Islamic Fund
IMF	International Monetary Fund
INCEIF	International Centre for Education in Islamic Finance

IRTI	Islamic Training and Research Institute
IT	information technology
LMC	Liquidity Management Centre
LIBOR	London Inter-bank Offered Rate
MCCA	Muslim Community Co-operative Australia
NAIT	North American Islamic Trust
NIT	National Investment Trust
p.a.	per annum
PBC	Pakistan Banking Council
pbuh	Peace be upon him (the holy Prophet Mohammad)
PLS	profit and loss sharing
PTCs	Participation Terms Certificates
R&D	research and development
ROE	return on equity
ROR	rate of return
Rs.	Rupees (Pakistani currency)
SBP	State Bank of Pakistan
SC	Supreme Court
TBs	Treasury bills
UAE	United Arab Emirates
UK	United Kingdom
UBL	United Bank Limited
USA	United States of America
US$	US dollar
WB	World Bank

Glossary of Arabic Words and Terms

This glossary contains Arabic words and terms used in this study. Arabic words or terms are shown in *italic* font and are explained at appropriate places in the study. Here they are briefly defined for the convenience of readers.

Allah	God the Almighty.
Ahadith	The sayings of the holy Prophet Mohammad (pbuh). They may be defined as the narration of words and actions of the holy Prophet Mohammad (pbuh) and also of actions of his companions about which he remained silent and thereby tacitly approved them.
Al-Hisba	The institution of the Islamic state to supervise the economic and social dealings of the polity.
Bai	Trading
Bai Istisna	A trading contract involving advance payment against manufactured goods.
Bai Muajjal	Sale of goods on a deferred payment basis payable in a lump sum or by instalments.
Bai Salam	A sale in which the buyer pays the price of goods (generally farm produce) in advance.
Falah	Eternal salvation: spiritual and physical success in this life and the life hereafter.
Fatwa	A legal opinion or verdict given by a jurist or a panel of jurists.
Fiqh	The science of *Shariah*.
Gnawing	*Mudarabah* is also known as *gnawing*.
Grarar	Uncertainty, ambiguity or speculation.
Ijarah	An Islamic leasing contract.
Ijarah-wa-Iqtina	A form of hire purchase or lease contract in which the lessee gradually acquires ownership of an economic asset by paying its total value by instalments.

Ijma	A consensus among Islamic scholars on a legal issue, which is not explicitly covered by the text of the holy *Quran* and *Sunnah* of the holy Prophet Mohammad (pbuh).
Ijtihad	A legal interpretation undertaken by the Islamic jurist or jurists in the light of the holy *Quran* and *Sunnah* of the holy Prophet Mohammad (pbuh) for resolving a new problem in Muslim society.
Khamr	Alcoholic beverage.
Maslahah	A juristic activity, to be invoked to decide about an act or thing in the light of holy *Quran* and *Sunnah* of the holy Prophet Mohammad (pbuh), with the objective of promoting the public welfare.
Mudarabah	A joint venture between a fund manager and a fund provider.
Mudarib	Fund manager.
Murabaha	A deferred sale on a cost-plus profit basis. The terms *Murabaha* and *Bai Muajjal* are almost synonymous and interchangeable.
Musawamah	A general sale at a specified price.
Musharakah	Equity participation under Islamic principles.
Mutashabahat	The holy *Quranic* injunctions whose meanings are not clear to a common Muslim.
Qard	Loan.
Qard-e-Hasanah	Goodly loans or free of charge loans for helping the poor.
Qiyas	Interpretative reasoning on the basis of the holy *Quran* and *Sunnah* of the holy Prophet Mohammad (pbuh).
Quran	The divine message revealed by God to the holy Prophet Mohammad (pbuh).
Riba	Interest in compound or simple form.
Riba al-fadl	Interest on trading or barter transactions.
Riba al-nashi'ah	Interest on loan or financial transactions.
Rab-u-mal	Fund manager in a joint venture.
Sadaqah	Charity for the sake of God.
Shariah	The Islamic canonical law based upon the teachings of the holy *Quran* and *Sunnah* of the holy Prophet Mohammad (pbuh).

Sharikah	Sharing or partnership.
Sharikat-al-Inan	Participatory financing.
Shirakah-almatanaqish	Redeemable or decreasing-participation arrangement. It is a form of hire purchase or leasing contract.
Sukuks	Islamic financial papers of debt or securities holding claims and rights for the owner/holder.
Sunnah	Actions and deeds of the holy Prophet Mohammad (pbuh) and also his tacit or explicit acknowledgement of statements for the purpose of explaining the holy *Quran* in simple terms to promote popular understanding.
Tabarru	Gift or charity.
Takaful	Islamic insurance and assurance services (free of interest, gambling and speculation).
Ulema	Islamic jurists.
Usher	The levy of *zakah* on land produce.
Waqaf	A religious institution created by the donation of property for charitable purposes and in the public interest.
Zakah	An obligatory religious transfer paid by wealthy Muslims to poor Muslims.

1
Introduction

1.1 Preamble

There is no denying the fact that the institution of interest is the backbone of the conventional economy and finance. The overwhelming domination of the interest-based system in global economic and monetary affairs, however, does not necessarily mean that it is the best mechanism, or that any future attempt to replace it with another system would seriously disrupt the prospects for business, investment and economic growth worldwide. Nothing succeeds like success, though conventional finance falls far short of perfection. There are some grave reservations and strong caveats concerning the moral and market-based credentials of the conventional system. In general, conventional banking and finance institutions tap funds from small-time investors and provide them to big borrowers for undertaking multi-billion dollar projects. They overlook the finance and venture capital needs of middle- and lower-income groups who want to initiate projects, ensuring more sustainable resource management and enhancing the socio-economic welfare of the people.

The conventional borrower–lender relationship contains unworthy elements such as compulsion, mistrust, vested interests, greed and exploitation. The lender enjoys an exclusive right to get back his rented capital along with a predetermined interest income, whereas the borrower or entrepreneur bears business risks out of all proportion to his abilities. On off-days, if he suffers a huge loss, he has yet to pay his dues and debts all alone, whereas in good times, even though he makes a lucrative profit from the borrowed money, he needs to return only a small portion of it to the lender. Quite often the lender increases the rate of interest on seeing that the borrower is making a good profit.

Sometimes, the increasing cost of borrowing obliges business entities to curtail or shut down their production, which is unfair to workers and society. Furthermore, interest-based loans and grants to impoverished countries across the world have proved to be a great curse, which sends them ever deeper into hunger, deprivation, abject poverty and wretchedness. By all means, the conventional system favours a handful of people, corporations and nations, maximizing their gains at the cost of humanity as a whole (Ahmad, S M, 1952; Mannan, 1970; Berger and Udell, 1990; El-Ghazali, 1994; Welch, 2000; Shah, 2007).

The conventional system does not possess an inbuilt mechanism to ensure the optimal utilization of funds and resources. It allows capital to be priced a priori rather than on the basis of its real demand and supply, actual productivity and investment outcomes. This encourages hoarding and the speculative use of capital, which sabotages the natural and efficient market mechanism. Furthermore, the conventional system indulges the individual's and society's desire for excessive borrowing, extravagance and living beyond their means. The booming conventional economies, based on reckless credit expansion and unrealistic business and finance operations, sometimes become exceedingly exposed and vulnerable to inflationary pressures, higher interest rates and internal and external shocks and eventual collapse. Nevertheless, conventional planners tirelessly use numerous monetary and fiscal measures to artificially create and control the demand for and supply of capital in the market. The inherent deficiencies of the conventional system cause inflationary and deflationary pressures, unemployment, boom-and-bust cycles, overproduction, dumping and growth without distributive justice. Some Western economists and scholars argue that the conventional system delivers few solutions and creates more problems (Keynes, 1936; Robertson, 1937; Fisher, 1945; Simons, 1948; Weber, 1958; Perlman, 1976; Collard, 1978; De Meza and Webb, 1990; Wilson, 1997).

The underlying situation raises at the very outset a crucial question: since the conventional system has such a controversial legacy, why has it been allowed to dominate global economic and finance affairs? As a matter of fact, the conventional system promotes materialistic well-being as advocated by the secularist world view. Secular humanists believe that moral and spiritual values should dominate only in the religious arena, whereas other walks of life should be based on purely materialistic and scientific considerations. This fallacious thinking invokes a dichotomy between the 'church' and the 'state' and thereby replaces the historically established religious paradigm of economics with the new paradigm stressing efficiency, profit maximization and self-interest.

Materialistic people use economic or financial activity as a tool to secure more wealth, belongings and comforts, and the conventional system fervently helps them to do so (Bell, 1976; Kahf, 1978; Howell, 1981; Sen, 1987; Ismail, 1989). Perhaps it is inconceivable that the conventional system could carry out its operations on the basis of risk-sharing, mutual co-operation and universal brotherhood. By its very nature it is devoid of truly humanitarian solutions in the economic and financial spheres.

A growing majority of people worldwide feel the need to implement more ethical and efficient economic and financial solutions. Islamic economics offers itself as an ideal candidate in this regard. It has a religious-based paradigm. It is an integral part of the Islamic philosophy of life that holds that all spheres of human life should be streamlined under divine guidance – unity of command – to ensure the true welfare of human beings in this life and hereafter. The Islamic system ensures a more ethical, social and efficient utilization of wealth and resources worldwide. It bans interest and other exploitative elements from all jurisdictions of the Islamic world, and performs intermediary functions on the basis of equity-sharing, risk-participation and business ethics (Wilson, 1997).

The contemporary Islamic banking and finance (IBF) movement is over three decades old. However, the conceptual development of IBF took place between the late 1940s and the mid-1970s. The huge influx of petrodollars into the Middle Eastern economies in the 1970s and 1980s provided a major impetus to the establishment of several big Islamic banks in the region. Other Muslim countries imitated these breakthrough developments and gradually established their own IBF institutions. Furthermore, conventional financial institutions such as ABN AMRO, Citigroup, Goldman Sachs, and Kleinwort Benson HSBC started to offer Islamic products and services by establishing their own window or subsidiary to serve a Muslim clientele in international markets (Wilson, 1995; Warde, 2000).

IBF made steady progress over the decades. However, it has emerged as the fastest-growing segment of global finance over the recent years due to consistently high oil prices in international markets and increasingly favourable socio-political and economic conditions across the globe. It is now flourishing in Africa, Asia, Europe and North America. The Middle East, South Asia and Southeast Asia are the main emerging hubs of IBF. The IBF market has grown considerably in banking products, *Sukuks, Takaful* services, equity funds, hedge funds, assets and wealth management, risk and liquidity management, real estate and corporate finance. Increasing numbers of ethically based business and finance organizations and individuals worldwide have been coming into the folds of IBF. There are about 300 IBF institutions across 70 countries, holding capital investments of US$500 billion–US$800 billion, with an average annual growth rate of 15 percent over the years (Arekat, 2006). It has been estimated that the IBF industry will have a market value of US$4 trillion by 2010 (Cader, 2007), and will capture 40–50 percent the total savings of the 1.3 billion Muslims worldwide by 2015 to 2017 (Alam, 2006).

IBF has grown into an academic discipline with the passage of time. It has opened new vistas of research for academics and practitioners in Islamic economics and finance. Increasing numbers of MA and Ph.D. dissertations have been devoted to the theoretical and empirical underpinnings of IBF over the decades. The International Monetary Funds (IMF) has extended increasing support to IBF and constantly brings out working papers and research studies on the subject. The Harvard Islamic Finance Forum and other Western academic and research institutions have been playing a vital role in promoting IBF in their regions. Thus it is the first and foremost objective of this book to let the citizens of the world know IBF as a value-based discipline contributing more ethical, competitive and diversified solutions into the world of economics and finance.

In the early 1980s, Iran, Pakistan and Sudan decided to restructure their national economies and financial sectors on Islamic lines. The case of Islamization in Pakistan attracted a great deal of attention worldwide. Pakistan is an ideological state which has made a religious and constitutional commitment to restructure its personal and social institutions in the light of Islamic teachings. All three constitutions (1956, 1962 and 1973) adopted so far in Pakistan contain a clause making the elimination of interest an objective of the state. This represents the supreme objective and commitment of the Pakistani polity to truly achieve financial independence, prosperity and equitable sharing of the benefits of growth by means of the Islamization of its economy. Efforts to provide an institutional shape for Islamic economic teachings were initiated in 1977, when the president of Pakistan, General Mohammed Ziaul Haq, assigned the task of preparing a blueprint for an Islamic economy to the Council of Islamic Ideology (CII). The CII relied on help from top economists and bankers in Pakistan to develop a theoretical model of the Islamic economy by June 1980. The CII model was supposed to be fully adopted in Pakistan by 1984. At first, some initiatives were taken to transform the economy and financial sector of Pakistan along Islamic lines, but the impetus waned and everything was eventually discarded. Over the decades the country struggled through committee after committee and model after model, but the outcome of all these efforts was confusing, to say the least. In 2002, the government abandoned its Islamization policy and instead started to patronize private IBF institutions in the overwhelming conventional market environment of Pakistan.

Apart from driving its proponents to great dismay, the botched attempt at IBF in Pakistan poses a crucial challenge: why, when the overwhelming majority of people in Pakistan are Muslim, and when the government itself initiated the process of Islamization and spent huge intellectual, monetary and material resources on it over the decades, was the whole process aborted? Why did it eventually lead to a dead end and some nonsensical solutions? The literature on IBF in Pakistan is scattered, somewhat old, and does not capture the core developments that have taken place since the mid-1990s that might help us obtain a real insight into the issue. What is missing at the moment is an analytical study shedding light on every aspect of the IBF episode in Pakistan. This book attempts to fill the gap. It deals with all intellectual, practical, political, constitutional and legal developments in regard to IBF theory and practice in Pakistan from 1980 to 2007. The conclusions and lessons derived from this study may be useful for policymakers in Pakistan, researchers, academicians, financial experts, *Shariah* scholars, bankers, regulators and those Muslim countries that wish to undertake an IBF experiment similar to the one attempted in Pakistan. This book may also help acquaint Western economic thinkers and practitioners with the contemporary theory and practice of IBF.

1.2 Outline of the book

This book is composed of ten chapters, including an introduction and summary and conclusions, which fall into three parts. The first part contains Chapter 2 only. It explores the real essence of economic activity in the light of the Islamic philosophy of life. It explains that the foundation of the economics and finance aspects of the human polity rests on each person's faith in God, his accountability before Him (God) and his social responsibilities. It elaborates the ethical principles of Islamic economics that represent the drive to establish distributive justice, without which the supreme ideals of humanity cannot be realized. It singles out interest as the biggest obstacle to establishing a fair and equitable order among human beings. It explores Islamic injunctions and ethical arguments concerning the prohibition of interest, and its economic rationale. It takes a brief account of modern theories on fairness and justice in order to highlight the fact that Islam offers the most accomplished and realistic solutions to issues of socio-economic justice in the contemporary human polity. This part lays down the *Shariah* framework for taking stock of the contemporary theory and practice of IBF.

The second part of this book is composed of Chapter 3. It explains that IBF is a normative discipline that differs from conventional finance in its origin and its conceptual and practical approaches. It performs intermediary functions between the borrower and the lender on the basis of equity participation, risk-sharing and entrepreneurship. This part explores the main characteristics, operative mechanisms, performance, challenges and prospects of future growth of IBF in global finance.

The third part of this book encompasses the discussion from Chapter 4 and onwards. Chapter 4 takes stock of the conceptual developments of IBF in Pakistan. In this context, it thoroughly appraises the recommendations of the Council of Islamic Ideology (CII) developed in 1980 for establishing an Islamic economy and financial system in Pakistan. This chapter is believed to be the first attempt of its kind to provide a comprehensive and objective analysis of the CII's recommendations. Chapter 5 provides an insightful account of the institutional developments and practice of IBF in Pakistan during the period 1981–91. It tries to extract the real essence of previous efforts to capture the adoption and operations of IBF in Pakistan. Chapter 6 explores critical features of the 1991 Federal *Shariat* Court (FSC) judgement on *riba*, which resolved that the IBF system had not yet been adopted in Pakistan, despite the attempts over the previous decade. It assesses the FSC judgement's impact on the IBF movement and its future in Pakistan at that time.

Chapter 7 deals with the attempts made by the Commission for Islamization of Economy (CIE) to revive IBF practice in Pakistan. In this context, the 1992 Report on Banks and Financial Institutions and the 1998 Blueprint of Financial System of the International Institute of Islamic Economics (IIIE) are carefully examined and evaluated. This makes a valuable contribution to the contemporary literature on IBF because no such effort has been made before. Chapter 8 deals with the initiatives taken by the highest judiciary of Pakistan in shaping the course of IBF developments in the country. It takes account of the 1999 Supreme Court (SC) judgement on *riba* and the 2002 SC judgement on the *riba* case review, which have had far-reaching impacts on the IBF movement in Pakistan. This chapter provides a critical assessment of the present and future prospects for IBF in Pakistan. Chapter 9 takes stock of the factors that caused the nationwide IBF experiment in Pakistan to fail. The final chapter presents the summary and conclusions of this study.

2
Islamic Economics: Divine Vision of Distributive Justice

2.1 Introduction

According to the Islamic faith, life on earth is a temporary phenomenon and there is another life hereafter.[1] The life hereafter is everlasting and far superior to this worldly life. Success in the life hereafter is based on leading this life in full compliance with Islamic tenets as enunciated in *Shariah*. Islamic canon law or *Shariah* is based upon the teachings of the holy *Quran* and *Sunnah* of the holy Prophet Mohammad peace be upon him (pbuh). The true and supreme success of human beings is called '*falah*' or 'eternal salvation' – success in this world and the life hereafter. Wholehearted submission to the Islamic faith brings a revolutionary change in human beings. Reliance by human beings solely on divine guidance – unity of commands – for managing their personal and social institutions ensures their growth in material and spiritual spheres, and success in both worlds (Naqvi, 1982; Choudhury, 1998).[2]

Islamic Economics is an ideological discipline that primarily aims at fostering equality, justice, fairness, brotherhood, mercy, compassion, solidarity and freedom of choice in human society. The guiding principles of Islamic Economics only provide a framework for undertaking economic activities; they do not ordain rigid patterns which might become irrelevant with the passage of time. The origin of Islamic Economics can be traced back to the seventh century, when holy Prophet Muhammad (pbuh) laid the foundation of the first Islamic state in Medina, in the Arabian Peninsula. He personally undertook the responsibility to monitor market and business activities in the nascent Islamic state. Later on, his pious successors and Islamic jurists administered the state's economic affairs on the basis of Islamic principles. The renowned Islamic scholars and economists of the early and medieval periods include

Abu-Yusuf (731–798 AD), Al-Shiabani (750–804 AD), Ibn-Hazam (994–1064 AD), Tusu (1201–1274 AD), Ibn-Taimiya (1262–1328 AD), Ibn-Khuldun (1332–1406 AD) and others. In the contemporary age, Islamic Economics has emerged over the past few decades as a result of the efforts of Muslim economists and scholars who are keen to bring the economic and financial affairs of the Muslim world into compliance with Islamic teachings. The scholars who have made major contributions to the literature of Islamic Economics include A Qureshi (1946), S M Ahmad (1952), Uzair (1955), Maududi (1961), Al-Arabi (1966), M N Siddiqi (1967), Al-Sadr (1974) and Kahf (1978), to mention but a few. The worldwide growing Islamic banking and finance (IBF) movement is the hallmark of Islamic Economics in contemporary times (see Chapter 3).

This chapter is divided into five sections. The second section highlights the ethical dilemma of Conventional Economics. The third section explores the guiding principles of Islamic Economics, with its thrust to establish socio-economic justice in the human polity. The fourth section takes stock of modern theories of equity and justice from an Islamic perspective. The final section presents a summary and conclusions of this chapter.

2.2 Ethical dilemmas of Conventional Economics

The global economy and financial markets have made unprecedented progress over the years under the Conventional Economic system. Conventional Economics holds the materialistic world view, however. It believes that human beings are exclusively rational beings, driven by a strong ambition to acquire more and more wealth and to serve their self-interests. The roots of modern Conventional Economics can be traced to the Adam Smith's work. In the most famous and frequently quoted words of Adam Smith (1776),

> It is not from the benevolence of the butcher, the brewer, or the baker, that we expect our dinner, but from their regard to their own interest... led by an invisible hand to promote an end which was no part of his intention.... By pursuing his own interest he frequently promotes that of the society more effectually than when he really intends to promote it.

The Adam Smith's vision of seeking the welfare of society by relying on the individual's selfishness is based on the pre-money barter system of trade. An individual produces better or higher-quality goods or services in order to exchange them for high-quality products and services for his own sake. So he does not mean to serve his fellow beings, but only himself. The self-serving behaviour of individuals ensures greater productivity and thereby promotes public welfare. What ought to be the best for the welfare of the individual as well as society should be determined in light of selfish considerations. Every individual should be keen to seize an opportunity to maximize his wealth, utility and material welfare. Two selfish beings should interact with each other when they believe that they would be better off by undertaking the deals at hand. They pursue economic activities for the purpose of making themselves better off rather than society.

Indeed, Conventional Economics has little interest in promoting benevolent economic behaviour in market. It relieves the market and its agents of any obligation to assume social responsibilities by contending that economic exchanges should be unfettered and that neither the market nor its agents should pay any cost or make any sacrifice for the communal welfare. It teaches business enterprises to make business and investment decisions on the basis of 'cost-benefit' evaluations. The projects yielding the highest monetary returns should be chosen for implementation, without giving any due regard to their moral, social and environmental implications. The 'general welfare' can be promoted by achieving higher productivity and efficiency. There is a cause and effect relationship between efficiency and the public welfare. It is simply assumed that only greater efficiency can ensure the greater public welfare. Without attaining efficiency targets, the public welfare cannot be ascertained. It is 'market efficiency', not 'the people', that is very dear to Conventional Economics. Market agents need to believe that, by becoming more possessive, self-pleasing and self-centred in pursuing their material goals they are doing great favours to society because that is the only road leading to the highest levels of productivity, efficiency and public welfare. The attainment of higher profitability and efficiency are the only social responsibilities of business enterprises and their owners. There are no ethical reasons for entrepreneurs to be efficient and beneficial for the sake of society. In other words, the objective of seeking people's welfare has been grossly discounted in the face of so-called market imperatives – greed and efficiency (Weber, 1958; Maududi, 1961; Mannan, 1970).

The state of maximum efficiency, however, can hardly ensure a wider and equitable distribution of resources. From the very beginning, or after a certain point, the goal of maximizing market efficiency cannot be pursued or achieved without undermining the goals of the equitable distribution of economic rewards and social welfare. When the market does not bear any inherent quality or have the primary objective to promote the general welfare of human beings, it appears less certain that the 'invisible hand' would ensure that the very 'selfish nature' of human beings can serve society, or that this miracle would occur in each and every transaction without any negative implications. In fact, conventional markets have had been found guilty of promoting economic ills such as cut-throat competition, monopoly, hoarding, black marketeering, conflict between employer and employee, and dumping and burning of products just to maintain demand within the bounds of a high price (Robertson, 1937; Ahmad, S M, 1952; Zarqa, 1983; Ismail, 1989).

The Western concept of seeking the welfare of human beings is very narrow. It unilaterally emphasizes maximizing the material success and utilities of human beings without considering their moral and spiritual development. It teaches individuals and society to aim for materialistic possessions, self-love, economic power, social prestige, productivity, efficiency, competitiveness and suchlike. It divides society with class conflicts and inequality. On the one hand, it contributes to sheer deprivation and starvation for the overwhelming majority of people of the globe and on the other hand it provides a handful of people with the means to enjoy a more and more extravagant life. In the present era of Conventional Economics, humanity has been thrown into vicious circles of poverty, deprivation, hunger, inequities, dependency, indebtedness, unrest, tension, hatreds, terrorism and wars.

The following facts and figures speak for themselves. The GDP (Gross Domestic Product) of the poorest 48 nations (i.e., a quarter of the world's countries) is less than the wealth of the world's three richest people combined.[3] The developed countries, representing 20 percent of the world's population, consume 86 percent of the world's goods.[4] Regrettably, half of the world – nearly three billion people – entered the new millennium with an income of less than US$2 per day; of these, 1.3 billion extremely poor people lived less than a dollar a day.[5] The current statistics show that 985 million people on this earth live on less than a dollar a day, equivalent to 18 percent of the population of the developing world.[6] In this modern age of technology, the world has been transformed into a global village that possesses enormous amounts of food, resources and sophisticated means of communications, but, despite this, the people dying of hunger in Africa, Latin America and other such regions cannot be fed and rescued. Over 850 million people worldwide are suffering from hunger.[7] It is worth mentioning that hunger and poverty are wreaking havoc, claiming 25,000 lives every day.[8]

The rich countries have been making extravagant claims that devastating poverty is being banished from the globe, but in real terms they are doing very little. In the 1990s, global poverty dropped by 20 percent, but at the same time there was a further increase of 18 million hungry people and the number is growing at the current rate of 4 million per year worldwide.[9] The large majority of victims of hunger and malnutrition are children and women. Every five seconds a child dies because she or he is hungry. More than 60 percent of chronically hungry people are women.[10] Each year five million children of the poor die from malnutrition or from preventable diseases such as diarrhea and measles.[11] Every minute, a child under 15 years of age dies of an AIDS-related illness. Every minute, another child becomes HIV-positive.[12] There are over 39.5 million people suffering from AIDS, 90 percent of them in developing countries. Since 2001, over 22 million people have died from AIDS; in 2006 alone 4.3 million people were infected by HIV and 2.9 million died from AIDS.[13]

Under so-called globalization, rich countries are very keen to share and take control of the enormous wealth and resources of the globe, but not its abject poverty. Rather, the dependency of poor nations on rich nations has been agonized over to no effect. The World Bank has miserably failed to curb growing poverty and hunger across the globe. Rather, the Bank has turned into a tool of Western capitalism, with the aim and the policies to punish the world's poor (Smith, 2005; Nicholas, 2006; Shah, 2007). Conventional Economics has divided the citizens of the globe into two separate worlds: the world of winners, the moral culprits, and the world of the losers, the poor victims. Nelson Mandela argued, 'Like slavery and apartheid, poverty is not natural. It is man-made and it can be overcome and eradicated by the actions of human beings.'[14] Arundhati Roy, recipient of the 2004 Sydney Peace Prize, said, 'A world run by a handful of greedy bankers and CEOs who nobody elected cannot possible last.'[15]

Mohammad Yunus, the winner of the Nobel Peace Prize 2006, argued, 'The one message that we are trying to promote all the time, is that poverty in the world is an artificial creation. It does not belong to human civilization, and we can change that... the only thing we have to do is to redesign our institution and polices, and there will be no people who will be suffering from poverty.'[16]

The richest nations have now realized their responsibilities towards global poverty and starvation and have pledged themselves to save more than 500 million from extreme poverty, 300 million people from extreme hunger, 300 million children from death before reaching their fifth birthday and also the lives of 200 million mothers by 2015.[17] This is not the be-all and end-all; rather, it should be regarded as the first step in the right direction. The underlying discussion makes it very clear that Conventional Economics first nourishes and breeds gross socio-economic inequalities across the globe, and then tries to find passive and piecemeal solutions to them. It does not appreciate human values such as mutual trust, co-operation and benevolence to ensure universally beneficial economic and business environments. It subordinates the 'moral' human being to the 'rational human being and leaves him to cry in the wilderness. Indeed, why should the issue of seeking social welfare – a positive value – be left to the mercy of selfish behaviour – a negative value? Welfare is a virtue and it should come from virtue, not from vice: selfishness and greed. Being part and parcel of society, the economic sphere and marketplace should ensure the general welfare of the people by all means.

2.3 Guiding principles and goals of Islamic Economics

Islamic Economics is deeply concerned about the growing disparity and injustice in the global community, and, more importantly, offers truly effective means and measures to eradicate these evils. It ordains the functioning of markets under moral and social considerations. It broadens the horizons of Conventional Economics beyond the materialistic frontier. It explores the moral and spiritual aspects of economic activities and their far-reaching impacts upon human beings. It extends the time-span for seeking utility or promoting self-interest from this life to the life hereafter. It also broadens the horizons of utility from the material alone to encompass also the spiritual. Furthermore, it replaces the 'rational' being with the 'faithful' being who pursues personal interests within social interests and bounds. The Islamic approach deals with self-interest in a very realistic and delicate way. The holy *Quran* refers to human self-interest – people are greedy, impatient and over-possessive.[18] Islam uses moral reinforcements to discipline self-interest. It offers a holistic view of self-interest – enlightened self-interest. It holds that every human being is a member of God's family and enjoys an equitable right to share in God's gift of wealth and resources. The faithful person relies on moral forces such as altruism, co-operation, brotherhood, fraternity, affection and mutual love to rein over his selfish nature and lust for riches (Hasan, Z, 1988; Ahmed, 1991).

The 'faithful being' believes that his every act has moral implications for himself and others. He is both a physical and a spiritual being in very immaculate, delicate and inseparable ways. He cannot achieve true well-being unless he fully recognizes the spiritual part of himself. A quest for material well-being (material fulfilment and satisfaction – utility) without spiritual enrichment is illusory and untenable. If a person does not maintain a healthy relationship between his material and spiritual utilities (well-being), or if he seeks one at the expense of the other, he cannot lead a truly happy and successful life. So human effort and resources are to be used to pursue and acquire utility or satisfaction in both arenas, material and spiritual. The two kinds of utility reinforce each other and together they ensure the balanced growth of the individual and society. One induces a person to achieve material objectives for himself; the other prompts him to give away a part of his material possessions to his poor brethren in the polity. If seeking material utility or well-being is a matter of self-interest, then seeking spiritual utility is a matter of moral and social interests – the divinely inspired state of self-interest. This contrasting means of acquiring a 'composite utility' develops an internal system of checks and balances in a person. In simple terms, the Islamic concept of human well-being is an altruistic phenomenon. A person cannot acquire well-being in a true sense without making contributions towards the well-being of others.[19]

Aristotle argues that the successful life is one which is virtuous and rewarding. Success and happiness amount not only to what we acquire and possess in life but also to what we contribute towards the happiness and success of others.[20] Economic behaviour has a powerful effect on a person's character and his struggle to grow in moral excellence, spiritual enrichment and material prosperity. Such growth should be the supreme goal of humanity for its own sake. Immanuel Kant wrote, 'Act so that you treat humanity, whether in your own person or in that of another, always as an end and never as means only.'[21] From the Islamic perspective, moral excellence comes from pinning one's faith in the supremacy of ethical values. The business ethics of Islam are rooted in faith, which reins in personal self-interest. Adherence to virtue in the business world brings real success and happiness in people's lives. Islamic business ethics embrace an altruistic vision to ensure true welfare for individual and society. So faith – faith in God and His guidance –fills the gap of morality in the marketplace that Conventional Economics leaves wide open.

With general well-being as its supreme goal, Islamic Economics appoints *Shariah*-based moral principles as vanguards in the marketplace and leaves nothing to the invisible hand. It pursues an efficient market mechanism within ethical and social boundaries. It appreciates the Pareto-optimal[22] state by allowing market agents to benefit within framework of *Shariah*, without inflicting any harm on others. However, it does not subscribe to the Pareto's claim that once the optimal state is obtained, any utility-increasing redistribution cannot be achieved by voluntary market exchanges because someone would have to be made worse-off in order to increase the overall level of utility. Beyond the Pareto optimal horizon, Islamic Economics explores spiritual aspects of well-being or utility and self-interest. After acquiring the Pareto optimal state, it pushes utility-increasing redistribution process further. The rich exchange their (extra or spare) material utility (wealth) for enhancing their overall utility (material plus spiritual – the most accomplished form or value of utility). They improve or increase their own spiritual utility by giving away part of their wealth to the poor in order to enhance their overall utility (material utility). It is purely a voluntary market exchange, where value (wealth-material utility) is exchanged for value (spiritual utility – eternal salvation) with mutual benefit and without making any party worse off. The person's act of giving or making a sacrifice for others is a very high-yielding investment in the long run (the life hereafter). It is the most ethical and productive business deal in the market of faith.[23]

Islamic Economics takes an economic activity as a holy responsibility and a 'communal activity' which allows an individual full freedom to pursue his personal goals while fully complying with society's norms, values and expectations. In order to provide true freedom to an individual, it is necessary to place other people under in some kind of restraint. Along with freedom comes equality, which requires that limits should also be placed on the individual in order to let others enjoy the same kind of freedom. The individual enjoys economic freedom and private ownership within social contexts. Individual and society are responsible for contributing towards the each other's welfare. Islamic Economics relies on just means and measures to determine and promote just business relationships and outcomes in the marketplace. It draws on Divine guidance and tools to ensure an equitable distribution of wealth and the balanced material and spiritual growth of the individual and society. The Islamic state is responsible for preserving the Islamic character of personal and social institutions.[24] It ensures that every economic activity undertaken by a person or institution is financially and socially beneficial.[25] It takes strict measures to curb unethical business practices and fervently promotes just and efficient relationships among market players. It collects *zakah* from the rich and distributes it among the poor.[26] It is responsible for providing food, clothes, shelter, education, medical facilities, equal opportunities, freedom of speech, dignity and other human rights to every one of its member (Chapra, 1979; Ahmed, 1991).

Figure 2.1 highlights the means and measures of Islamic Economics to establish distributive justice in the human polity and also ensure its physical as well as spiritual growth. The ethical principles of Islamic Economics are composed of positive and negative injunctions. The positive injunctions are about ensuring wider and sustainable patterns of wealth distribution, whereas the negative injunctions pertain to dismantling the monopoly concentrations of wealth creation and sources of distribution, and further refining distribution systems. The guiding principles and goals of Islamic Economics are explored in the discussion below.

2.3.1 Right of private ownership

Shariah takes an uncompromising stand over the individual's right of private ownership. It appreciates the natural socio-economic differences among human beings which serve the Divine purpose to put them on trial in this worldly life, and also establishes healthy business relationships among them. The right of private ownership is not absolute in Islam. It can be really enjoyed only within *Shariah* bounds. The rich person is encouraged to spend his wealth for others' benefit as well as his own. The ownership right of a wealthy person cannot be validated if other fellow beings are living below the poverty lines. So the right of ownership is an effective tool to protect individual rights, foster market efficiency and promote mutual co-operation among human beings.

2.3.2 Free consent and mutual co-operation

Islamic Economics regards free consent and mutual co-operation as indispensable factors for fostering healthy business relationships.[27] The consent of a person should be obtained by free means. A person should be provided with all relevant information and there should be no element of undue influence, misrepresentation and fraud in seeking his consent to a contract.[28] If economic relations and market mechanisms based on free consent and mutual co-operation are working within moral and social bounds, even the Islamic state is not allowed to interfere with them. However, free consent and mutual co-operation are not legitimate means for undertaking business activities that are prohibited by *Shariah*. If a person co-operates with a wrongdoer then he should be equally punished along with the wrongdoer. If a person in authority perpetrates an immoral act upon his servant or subordinate, then he is guilty and answerable to God for the misuse of his authority.[29] When people enjoy

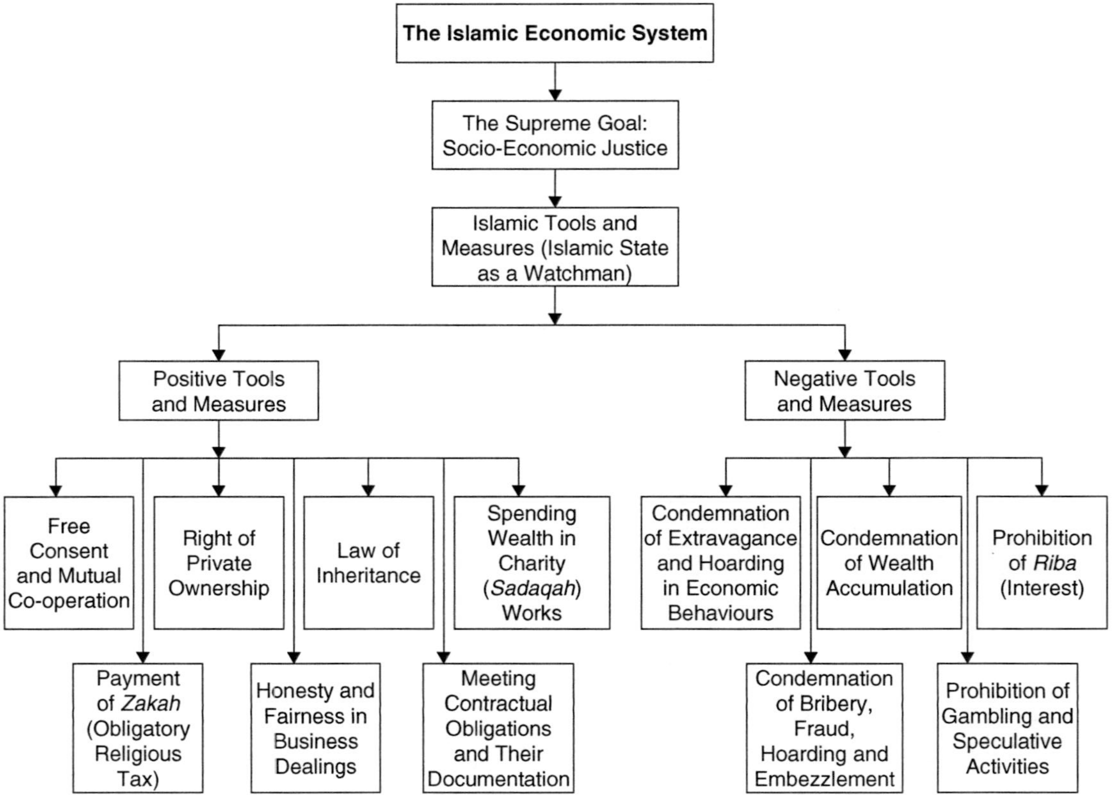

Figure 2.1 Guiding principles and goals of Islamic Economics

true freedom to undertake economic activities on an individual or collective basis, investment and business opportunities are boosted and the market displays greater flexibility, innovation and efficiency, leading to an optimal level of economic growth (Hasan, Z, 1988).

2.3.3 Law of inheritance

The Islamic law of inheritance is a Divinely given mechanism to ensure the wider circulation of wealth in society. Under the Islamic law of inheritance, close and distant relatives of a deceased person, including sons, daughters, spouses, parents, brothers, sisters and others, are entitled to receive a fixed share of his property.[30] The Islamic law of inheritance has far-reaching socio-economic and moral implications for human society. However, where the division on the business enterprise of a deceased person could have negative consequences of, heirs are encouraged to enter into a partnership to run the enterprise. The new management may enrich the business with more human and financial resources, which will most likely rejuvenate its performance and growth. Similar remedies may be adopted to mitigate any undesirable impacts of the division of agriculture land under the Islamic law of inheritance (Ramsey, 1928; Boulding, 1973; Zarqa, 1983).

2.3.4 Honesty, fairness and promise-keeping

Islamic Economics has a high regard for virtues like honesty, fairness and promise-keeping in all walks of life, including the business sphere. The moral integrity of society and the marketplace is based on these values. The holy Quran says that a Muslim should keep his promises whether the other party is a Muslim or a non-Muslim. The holy Prophet Mohammad (pbuh) said that a person has no faith who cannot keep the trust of others.[31] *Shariah* regards commercial contracts as moral and legal promises, and advises the contracting parties to render them in writing and honour them by all possible means.[32] The practice of these virtues enhances mutual trust and co-operation among parties and their faith in the credibility of marketplace. The capitalist or investor shows a greater willingness to enter into joint ventures with the entrepreneur or borrower because there is more transparency in business and profit-sharing matters. A well-established trust among market participants greatly encourages them to pool their ideas, knowledge and experience for exploring more innovative and profitable business opportunities. Business organizations with a good public image can conduct their operations at a lower cost because they gain legitimacy and enjoy strong support from their investors and other stakeholders. They can afford to undertake more risky and innovative ventures, which further boosts the shareholders' wealth and the public welfare. Fair and reliable business and financial reporting ensures the allocation of the national wealth to its most efficient uses. Trustworthy business environments reduce the overall costs of legal disputes, insurance claims, collateral requirements, agency and monitoring, benefits which are ultimately transferred to consumers, shareholders and society. In sum, fairness and honesty in business dealings promote an overall environment that is conducive to investment, venture capital and enterprise. This might evolve into the most accomplished form of market efficiency and economic growth, with greater rewards for capitalists, entrepreneurs and society as a whole.

2.3.5 Benevolence

Benevolence is one of the greatest human virtues.[33] It brings moral excellence to the human character. Muslims are brethren in faith and merciful among themselves.[34] The holy Prophet Mohammad (pbuh) argued that one who gives a destitute debtor more time to repay his debt, or reduces the capital sum owing, is under the protection of God when no other protection is forthcoming. He further said that the upper hand (one who gives) is better than the lower hand (one who receives).[35] Islam regards benevolence as an indispensable feature of the business and finance sphere. It is under the sheer compulsion of benevolence that the rich offer some of their wealth for redistribution to the poor. Economic benevolence promotes thriving and altruistic business environments and strengthens the bond of universal brotherhood and mutual co-operation among human beings.

2.3.6 Payment of *zakah* (obligatory religious tax)

Zakah is a compulsory religious tax levied upon the total net worth of an individual over and above the limits prescribed by *Shariah*. The holy *Quran* ordains that wealth should not remain concentrated among the rich alone.[36] *Shariah* prescribes for the poor and destitute a due share of the wealth of the rich.[37] The holy Prophet Mohammad (pbuh) said that wealth should be taken from the rich and returned to the poor.[38] The rate of *zakah* is about 2.5 percent per annum on accumulated wealth in any form.[39] The *zakah* levy on land produce is known as *usher* and its rates vary from 10 to 20 percent per annum. The holy Quran says that *zakah* purges human beings of the greed for wealth.[40] It is a key tool of Islamic Economics for eradicating inequalities, discourage hoarding and concentration of wealth, and thereby ensure healthy economic and spiritual growth and development of the individual and society (Kahf, 1993).

2.3.7 Spending wealth on charity (*sadaqah*)

God is the real owner of all worldly wealth and resources. If a person is rich, it is God's special favour upon him. To pay gratitude and thanks to God, the rich person should make charitable donations to his fellow human beings. So if a person spends his wealth on fulfilling his own and other people's needs, then his wealth brings him real joy.[41] Charity overcomes a person's love of and greed for wealth, which are the worst enemy of humanity.[42] A rich person can save the poor from economic and spiritual deprivation. The holy Prophet Mohammad (pbuh) said that poverty may sometimes turn into disbelief.[43] So charity brings moral and material benefits for the giver, the receiver and society as a whole. It improves the purchasing power of downtrodden people and has far-reaching effects on overall consumption, production, employment and economic growth. It promotes mutual co-operation, trust and a sense of brotherhood in human society (Shafi, 1998).

2.3.8 Condemnation of extravagance, hoarding and black marketeering

Shariah condemns both extravagant and miserly economic behaviour.[44] Both, spendthrifts and accumulators of wealth reduce the scope for making productive and optimal use of the national wealth.[45] Islamic teachings hold that Muslims should follow the middle way (moderation) in life.[46] It is a very anti-social use of worldly resources to produce luxury goods for a small group of people. These extreme behaviours, ridden by self-interest, are very common in the capitalist and Western worlds. The holy *Quran* also warns about serious punishment for hoarders.[47] The holy Prophet Mohammad (pbuh) strictly forbade Muslims from hoarding.[48] The hoarders of goods create an artificial scarcity of goods for purposes of profiteering at the cost of creating great hardship for society. Similarly, monopoly, black marketeering and other activities which sabotage the fair market mechanism are strictly prohibited by *Shariah*.

2.3.9 Condemnation of bribery, fraud and embezzlement

Shariah holds bribery, embezzlement and misappropriation to be moral and legal crimes.[49] It recognizes every act as a fraud that contains elements of injustice, exploitation and gains for one party at the expense of other. All exposed and hidden frauds committed by a person to take unfair social and economic advantage over others are strictly prohibited by Islam.[50] The powerful and rich can use bribery as a tool to acquire unjust possession of property that belongs to others. These malpractices grossly violate the spirit of distributive justice.

2.3.10 Prohibition of gambling and speculative (*grarar*) activities

Islam strictly prohibits speculative transactions and all kinds of gambling.[51] It accords high honour to one's earnings from hard work. Gambling does not involve any labour or productive activity. It brings gains for one person at the cost of others. Gambling destroys the moral, economic and social fabric of the human polity. Contemporary socio-economic life in Western countries is plagued with gambling and betting, with its ever-increasing numbers of casinos, racing clubs and similar institutions. Present-day stock markets are engaged excessively in speculative activities such as swaps, forwards, options and futures. *Shariah* prohibits all such activities because they encourage the concentration of wealth in the hands of a few and cause gross socio-economic inequalities (Kahf, 1993).

2.3.11 Prohibition of the wine trade

Shariah ordains that the manufacture, transportation and sale of wine (*khamr*) are serious crimes.[52] Similarly, the income earned from the business of prostitution is strictly abhorred and condemned by *Shariah*.[53] These activities destroy moral values such as mutual love, trust, self-esteem and universal brotherhood.

2.3.12 Prohibition of *riba* (interest)

Shariah ordains that a creditor's demand for any increase on capital over and above the principal in lieu of time, as a condition for extending credit, is *riba* or interest, and strictly prohibited. The prohibition of interest is absolute; it does not matter whether the stipulated increase on capital is high or low, simple or compound, taken for personal or private, productive or consumption purposes (Maududi, 1961). The rulings on the prohibition of interest are mentioned in four places in the holy Quran.[54] The absolute prohibition of interest is also well-proven from the holy Prophet Mohammad (pbuh)'s traditions. The holy Prophet Mohammad (pbuh) said that the selling of wheat for wheat is riba or usury unless it is transferred from hand to hand and is equal in amount. Similarly the selling of barley for barley is riba unless it is from hand to hand and equal in amount; selling dates for dates is usury unless it is from hand to hand and equal in amount.[55] He even cursed persons who ate *riba*, gave *riba*, documented the *riba*-based contract or stood witness to it, and added that they were equally guilty.[56] Early and contemporary Islamic scholars unanimously maintain that any predetermined excess or return over and above the loan capital taken for either commercial or consumption purpose is strictly prohibited by all the sources of *Shariah*.[57]

There are two types of *riba*, namely, *'riba al-fad'l* – interest in trading or barter transactions – and *'riba al- nashi'ah'* – interest in loans or financial transactions (Chapra, 1985).

2.3.12.1 Universal prohibition of riba *(interest)*

Other religions and ethical codes have also categorically prohibited interest in all its manifestations. The acts of giving interest-free loans and forgiving loans to the poor are highly valued in the teachings of Christianity: forgive us our debts, as we also have forgiven our debtors.[58] The holy Prophet Jesus said that God approves of the generous person who lends freely.[59] In Biblical times, all payments for the use of money were forbidden. It was, however, not until 1830 that the Church issued the verdict that it is lawful to receive interest on money lent to merchants who are in the business of trade (Khan, G M, 1992). Judaism's precepts hold that if you lend money to any of my people who is poor, you shall be to him as a creditor, and you shall not extract interest of him.[60] The holy books of the Jews, i.e., *Muta* and *Tulmood,* make no distinction between usury and interest. After some time Judaism advised that Jews may recover interest only from people of other faiths, as a special privilege granted to the faithful Israelites (Jews) by God.[61] Aristotle (384–322 BC) also severely condemned money-making on an interest basis as immoral and highly unnatural.[62] The Encyclopaedia of Religion and Ethics holds usury and interest to be one and the same thing. So far, Western economists have failed to provide any viable justification for charging interest on money-lending. However, they argue that the rate of interest should be fair and reasonable. But 'fair interest rate' and 'exorbitant interest rate' are in fact relative terms and interchangeable with respect to time and region (Qureshi, 1946).

2.3.12.2 Rationale behind the prohibition of riba *(interest)*

The Islamic rationale for the prohibition of interest is the exploitative nature of interest. Interest-based transactions violate humans' birthright – free will. Interest-based consumption loans are taken out by the poor in times of hardship. Charging interest on such loans is sheer exploitation of the poor, which further aggravates social and economic disparities in the polity. Commercially based lending holds the borrower solely responsible for bearing all risks and losses and repaying the principal and accrued interest to the lender. Such transactions are labelled as voluntarily and morally justified in the conventional and Western worlds. However, it has much to do with selfishness and little to do with free will and mutual co-operation between the debtor and the creditor.

If the entrepreneur incurs losses, he pledges or sells his personal assets to repay the loan and accrued interest. Sometimes, the borrower earns a very high profit but keeps most of it for himself. So either way, one party gains at the expense of the other. The interest-based business relationship creates a mistrustful and speculative environment. Sometimes, capitalists withhold their wealth to create an artificial fund shortage, which pushes rates of interest further up. The increasing cost of borrowing obliges a large number of businesses to wind themselves up under the threat of bankruptcy. The gravity of the situation may lead to the recurrence of business cycles, greater unemployment, inflationary pressures, budget deficits, debt-ridden economies, overproduction, dumping, low wage rates and growth without distributive justice (Maududi, 1961; Zarqa, 1983; Chapra, 1985; Ismail, 1989).

2.3.12.3 The debt crisis of poor countries

Interest-based dealings within a nation erode its moral and spiritual fabric and thereby promote excessive materialism, dependency, greed, hatred and class conflict, leading to socio-political and economic instability. Conventional interest-based economics and finance have very far-reaching and immiserating effects at the international level. Indeed, mounting interest-based foreign loans to poor countries have posed the most formidable threat to their economic growth, stability, independence, human rights, peace and prosperity. Rich countries and multibillion-dollar financial institutions make loans to developing countries because they have surplus funds and want to profit from the poor and their poverty. There are also political considerations behind such lending, as Western countries recklessly lend to corrupt governments in developing countries in order to capture their vested interests. Loans from World Bank and other conventional creditors have strings and conditions attached which deprive the people at the grass roots from any benefits from them. The poorest and most destitute people have turned out to be victims rather than beneficiaries of loans from rich countries. Debt-ridden countries are obliged to heavily downsize their expenditures on education, food and basic health facilities in order to honour their debt repayments and obligations. Debt servicing leaves poor countries bleeding from abject hunger, poverty, malnutrition, disease, AIDS, and political and social chaos (Bulow and Rogoff, 1990; Claessens and Ishac, 1991; Lassard and Walliamson, 1985).

The UN Millennium Project, 2005, registered, 'Dozens of heavily indebted poor and middle-income countries are forced by creditor governments to spend large proportions of their limited tax receipts on debt service, undermining their ability to finance vital investments in human capital and infrastructure. In a pointless and debilitating churning of resources, the creditors provide development assistance with one hand and then withdraw it in debt servicing with the other.'[63]

Indeed, sub-Saharan Africa is obliged to pay US$13 billion in debt service and allow 7,000 of its citizens die each day due to lack of funding for healthcare. It pays more in debt service than it receives in aid, new loans and assistance.[64] According to the Africa Council of Churches, 'Every child in Africa is born with a financial burden which a lifetime's work cannot repay. The debt is a new form of slavery as vicious as the slave trade.'[65] Dr Adabayo Adedeji, African Centre for Development Strategy, said, 'Debt is tearing down schools, clinics and hospitals and the effects are no less devastating than war.'[66] Julius Nyerere, former president of Tanzania, a debt-ridden country, argued, 'Must we starve our children to pay our debts?'[67] It is no use of giving aid to debt-ridden countries because debt eats up their indigenous and externally generated resources. For every US$1 received in grant aid, low-income countries pay back US$2.3 in debt service.[68]

The poverty in developing countries and their enslavement to Western countries is largely caused by mounting debt. The wealthiest nations, being the lenders, hold the key to the economic freedom and prosperity of the poor and debt-ridden countries in their hands. Through the interest tool, the IMF or the World Bank run the governments in developing countries, and debt has become the modern form of slavery. Edgar (2007) observed, 'the very legal debt slavery still persists and is sanctioned by the same governments who eventually wrote law that constitutionally ended the enslavement of human beings by another human being.'

A number of institutions that include Jubilee USA Network, Oxfam and ActionAid have over the years been courageously fighting conventional lenders and financial institutions for outright cancellation of the debts of poor countries. Their efforts prompted the IMF, the World Bank and G8 to launch the Heavily Indebted Poor Countries (HIPC) Initiative in 1999 for the reduction of the debt of some 41 eligible countries to more manageable levels. In 2000, the leaders of 189 countries pledged themselves to spare no effort to free men, women and children from abject poverty and the dehumanizing conditions of extreme poverty, and to provide freedom to the human race from want – the Millennium Development Goals (MDGs).[69] In 2005, G8 leaders, the World Bank and the IMF agreed to cancel debt worth over US$40 billion for 20 of the world's poorest countries.[70] These steps were taken to enable poor nations to meet the MDGs by 2015. Given the enormity of the debt and poverty problems, these steps are only modest and the real dream of justice is far from realization. There is a dire need to take revolutionary steps to establish socio-economic justice among nations. There should be full cancellation of the debt of impoverished countries. UK Prime Minister Gordon Brown estimates that 67 countries require 100 percent debt cancellation in order to meet the MDGs.[71] Moreover, there is need to provide US$30 billion in aid each year to enable the poor countries to meet Goal One – Eradication of extreme poverty and hunger – and a further US$16.5 billion annually to attain the remaining goals. However, the World Bank is deeply reluctant to allow 100 percent debt relief for impoverished countries on the pretext that it would weaken the creditworthiness and lending operations of the Bank in the long run.[72]

It is a matter of great concern that some conventional lenders and multinational companies – vulture funds and the vulture system – have recently secured debt repayments from the poor debtor countries with the help of the US and European judicial systems and courts. Many financial institutions have cheaply sold off the debt of impoverished countries to vulture funds. From 1999 to May 2007, 14 African nations were sued by vulture funds and commercial and other creditors.[73] These examples of enforced debt collection and massive profiteering by vulture firms are nothing less than a direct onslaught on people who are already suffering from extreme hunger, poverty, dehumanization and death (Watkins, 2007; Nacpil, 2007). The former president of the World Bank, Paul Wolfowitz ,observed, 'It is appalling that a sovereign debt can be bought off on the open market and then the original debtor country made to pay several times what was borrowed.'[74]

Debt reduction can allow impoverished countries to provide food, shelter, clean drinking water, medical facilities and education to their people. It is reported by Jubilee USA that after debt relief and the elimination of school fees, 1.5 million children returned to school in Tanzania almost overnight.[75] The Zambian Member of Parliament Kambwiwi Chisamba said, 'Thanks to debt relief, we have been able to rehabilitate our schools and our hospitals. But we have made many sacrifices and we still have a long way to go.'[76]

The underlying facts and figures strongly support the Islamic contention that interest is the main hurdle to ensuring an equitable distribution of wealth and resources in the global polity. Islam strictly bans interest and related exploitative tools in the economic and financial spheres.

2.3.12.4 Rejection of time value of money and indexation of loans

Shariah repudiates the conventional concept of the time value of money as well. It does not recognize money as an independent agent of production. The money owner or lender is not allowed to claim a time value on his money because money is a medium of exchange, a store of value and a non-rental merchandise, and therefore its self-trading is absolutely prohibited. If money itself becomes a source of its own increase, this might encourage its speculative use, hoarding and concentration in the hands of a few. Abu-Saud (1980) argued that interest is gained because somebody does not purchase immediately on receiving the proceeds of his sales, because this somebody knows that if he abstains from spending, he would gain. However, *Shariah* allows time to hold value in trade-based transactions that include *Murabaha* and *Bai Salam* and others (see Chapter 3).

Furthermore, Islam does not allow the creditor to demand compensation for any decrease in the purchasing power of money due to inflationary pressure under the indexation system, because there are several macroeconomic factors that cause inflation, and therefore the debtor alone could not be held responsible for it (Ghazi, 1993; Hasanuz-Zaman, 1993). *Shariah* holds that money or capital should be combined with human capital and entrepreneurial effort to undertake productive investments. The return on capital is directly linked to market outcomes and the creation of additional wealth and value added goods for society. The value of money is more stable in the Islamic economy because the speculative use of money, its renting and concentration are absolutely prohibited (Mannan, 1970; Zarqa, 1983; Ismail, 1989).

2.4 Modern theories of equity and justice

Islam is known as a religion of justice and its code of conduct is an expression of God's will for justice.[77] It is only through divine guidance that natural justice can be established in the human polity. The doctrine of Islamic justice holds as its first and foremost rule that every person should receive his due from others and give to others what is their due. A person should not be treated with injustice and he should not be allowed to deal with others with injustice. All divine religions and moral codes have duly recognized the importance of justice. Aristotle (384–322 BC) said that justice is not a portion of virtue but the whole of virtue; and injustice – the opposite of justice – is not a portion of vice but the whole of vice.[78]

Islamic Economics is keen on establishing distributive justice among people. It provides a real insight into wealth: it is a means to the ends of physical and spiritual growth of the individual and society. It relies on the Divinely given framework to pursue the goal of equity and distributive justice. On the one hand, it sets up market distribution and efficiency mechanisms within moral and social parameters. On the other hand, it puts forth the redistribution system featuring the tools and measures which eradicate any imbalances and inequalities that may arise from letting the market function freely within the moral framework. In this way Islamic Economics keeps the gap between rich and poor within natural limits. It distributes 'rewards' and 'sacrifices' among people on the basis of their capabilities and market considerations. It takes effective measures to ensure that the disabled and the less talented are provided with all basic necessities and amenities of life. Modern theories of fairness and justice are explored in the discussion below in light of the Islamic principles of distributive justice.

2.4.1 John Rawls's theory of justice

John Rawls sees distributive justice behind the 'veil of ignorance'. He argues that the future is unknown to a person and so is what the future holds for him – success or failure, economic prosperity or deprivation. Motivated by self-interest, a person desires to reserve or ensure a 'secured or better position' in future, even if it comes about by making some economic sacrifice. So uncertainty about future outcomes – the veil of ignorance – obliges rich or talented members of society to surrender their wealth or economic possessions in favour of poor or less talented members of society. The fear – the veil of ignorance – acts as a primary stimulant or source to ensure distributive justice. Rawls establishes the fairness principle that allows economic and social inequities but only if they provide equal rights, opportunities and liberties to all people, and, most importantly, benefit even the least advantaged individuals in society. He does not support strict and fair equality and thinks that talented individuals should be allowed to have greater monetary rewards. The fear – the veil of ignorance – also wins the approval of less gifted people for allowing a greater share of wealth to talented people (Rawls, 1971, 1993).

First, it may be noted that Rawls provides very inadequate information to people about the future and its characteristics, secured benefits or positions, and the bundle of economic sacrifices they are obliged to make. The right of people to make informed decisions with freedom and peace of mind is almost denied. People are not informed what exactly is bargained and at what price. The future appears very bleak and people are made anxious about it, and then their anxiety or ignorance is exploited, though with fair intentions, in order to take away a part of their wealth which they rightfully hold and may not be willing to surrender otherwise. There is only the 'fear', not reality or truth, that they would find themselves in a helpless or unsecured position in the future. So they are subjected to enormous pressures to gamble on their future. The whole deal is not very fair and square.

Rawls claims he is establishing socio-economic equality in the best interest of human beings. But he ignores basic human rights and offers no real incentives, rewards, freedom of choice, motivation and other normative values to human beings to follow his suggested pathway to fairness and equity, which is too hypothetical and ahistorical. People are forced to adopt benevolent or social behaviour under a kind of threat and coercion to their own well-being. If talented people found that the 'risk premium' they have paid to obtain a 'secured position' in future is out of proportion or unjust, they would feel that the system is unjust or over-sympathetic towards less talented people, who are benefited at their expense. They would refrain from giving their best efforts, which may handicap the state of optimal productivity and economic growth. Furthermore, it would trigger mistrust, hatred and class conflicts among people, leading to serious social, political and economic upheavals. These can be the eventual outcomes or consequences of blindly preferring self-interest to developing any form of distributive justice. Reliance on self-benefit and self-serving forces can hardly generate truly benevolent economic behaviour in the individual and society. Rather, these unnatural forces may precipitate highly unpredictable, fragile and unsustainable forms of socio-economic order. Furthermore, Rawls does not suggest a full set of means and measures or well-defined framework to translate his ideals about distributive justice into reality. He simply relies on a single factor – the coercive use of the state power and progressive taxation.

Islamic doctrine offers a more realistic and pragmatic view of distributive justice than does Rawls's vision of fairness and justice. From the Islamic perspective, the 'future' is extended to this life as well as the life hereafter. Faith in the day of judgement and eternal life hereafter is like 'veil of ignorance' or mystery because a faithful person holds an unshakable belief that they will happen in the future. So uncertainty or veil of ignorance prevails for every person in terms of his accountability before God on the day of judgement. In order to get a 'secured position' – greater success or prosperity – eternal salvation – in this life and the life hereafter, talented or rich people voluntarily give away their wealth to poorer and less talented people. The Islamic outlook on Rawls's theory is based on free will and eternal truth, and there is no room for compulsion, fear, uncertainty and speculation. People are provided with all relevant and reliable information about the future, and they are also told about the means and measures that can be adopted to ensure a 'secured or prosper position – eternal salvation' in future.[79] People can rest assured that they are making a well-informed decision with their own free will, and by relying on normative values such as altruism, incentives and rewards.[80] In this way the Divine expression of distributive justice has been laid down for the guidance of human beings seeking true happiness, success and eternal salvation.

2.4.2 Right-libertarianism

The right-libertarian doctrine of distributive justice allows unrestricted freedom to human beings. Right-libertarians contend that the best moral code and ideal form of distributive justice can only be achieved by granting people exclusive rights of self-ownership. Liberty is the sole right of human beings and so they may enjoy it by all means. People may evolve a free society without any real role and powers given into the hands of government. The government may protect people's natural rights, which include their life, liberty and property, against any violence, fraud and trespass in the free society. There may be no government bindings or make free individuals pay tax, give to charity and make any economic sacrifice. All sorts of economic inequities may be allowed to continue in the free society because they are the product of people's free will and actions. So individuals are held solely responsible for bearing all the consequences arising out of their free actions. More importantly, right-libertarians argue that markets may be absolutely free from the government's influence and interventions. They see the government or any other external force as a major threat to socio-economic justice prevailing in the free society (Hayek, 1944; Narveson, 1983).

Right-libertarianism presents over-simplistic and materialistic solutions to the issue of distributive justice, which is rather delicate, moral and spiritual. It absolutely rejects holding anything superior to the freedom of the individual, who is elevated as hedonistic, opportunistic and self-worshipping. This grossly undermines and rather negates the central position of religious, spiritual, moral and social forces in the lives of human beings. This theory holds that the whole or sole prerequisite or recipe for establishing distributive justice is to leave people alone without any inner moral and spiritual guidance or any external social and government influence and control. It presumes that the free society would contain an ideal form of distributive justice or well-being for its people, which would survive provided no member benefits himself at the expense of others. It seems very strange that a person does not need to be concerned about contributing towards the goodness of others. It is hardly possible to achieve any kind of distributive justice in a society whose members are not under any moral and social obligations to intentionally and actively contribute towards the well-being of others. When individuals are allowed to exclusively reserve the economic rewards of their efforts to themselves, without making any sacrifice and meeting any social responsibilities, the distribution of resources would remain grossly unfair and unjust. Dominated by self-interest and love of wealth and power, members of such so-called free society would violate each others' rights and freedoms in real life. A neutral or passive attitude is not enough to establish or restore distributive justice because it cannot cope with a situation in which distributive justice that is diminishing or decaying, which might be the case for ever. Every member should actively and aggressively contribute towards the welfare of society and that should be taken as the foremost and supreme objective of the individual and society – if you are not part of the solution, you are part of the problem. In simple terms, if an individual is neutral or value-free, he is most probably damaging to distributive justice. Frankly speaking, this theory contains a very naïve and myopic vision of distributive justice.

The Islamic doctrine of distributive justice is far superior to right-libertarianism. It is neither neutral nor passive, but very persuasive and motivational. It holds that all human talents, efforts and energies are God-given and so should be used to benefit the whole of humanity. Therefore, it not only forbids a person from making other people worse-off but also advises him to contribute towards theirs well-being. Every person is a part and parcel of society and his happiness and welfare is directly linked with and dependent on the happiness and welfare of others. Every act of a person should benefit him as well as society. Furthermore, Islam places ethical and social checks and balances on the market, which is a value-based institution and primarily aims at ensuring social, moral and material welfare for all members of society. From the Islamic perspective, economic activities have material as well as spiritual, and ethical as well as social, dimensions, aiming to contribute to and achieve the most accomplished form of distributive justice. The Islamic state is responsible for ensuring that the freedom of market and its players is truly preserved within moral and social contexts.

2.4.3 Left-libertarianism

The doctrine of left-libertarianism allows equal rights and ownership over national resources to all human beings at the start of their lives, but then they are allowed full freedom to make their fortunes on the basis of their abilities and efforts (Vallentyne and Steiner, 2000). Left-libertarianism swings between two extremes. On the one side, it aims to establish an ideal form of 'common equality' by putting all individuals of society on a par, without giving any regard to their talents, birth status, fortune, disabilities, etc. On the other side, it promotes 'gross inequalities' by letting individuals acquire as much wealth and resources as they can, without making any contributions towards the welfare of less talented and disabled people in the polity. So it strongly stresses 'fair equality' at first glance and then completely overlooks it. It presents a scenario like a marathon race, wherein all contestants are lined up at the start and are then advised to run as fast as they can to beat their opponents.

Left-libertarianism ignores the fact that the liberty of human beings to begin with equality is neither achievable nor sustainable. In the absence of a well-founded restorative or redistribution system, this theory might create the worst situation in the human polity – the survival of the fittest. Sooner or later, talented people would win the resources placed in the hands of less talented people. Thus, this theory bears in itself the beginning of the end of distributive justice. The concept of treating all members on a par while distributing national economic resources is very myopic and rather scary, invoking bloodshed and endangering human life on earth. To give an equal share of wealth to every member of society, it is required to take away wealth from rich and talented people by force, which might cause serious socio-economic and political turmoil – a civil war – leading to bloody revolution like the Communist Revolution in the early 1900s, which eventually proved unable to deliver (Andrew, 1995).[81]

Islamic philosophy does not subscribe to the left-libertarianism's search for distributive justice within two unnatural, wild and unjust ends. Rather, it holds that economic and social differences among people on the basis of their birth and abilities show the Divine wisdom in putting people on trial in this worldly life. Such differences are a great means to establish and promote a sustainable and efficient economic order based on mutual trust and co-operation; most importantly, they are allowed to operate within normal and social bounds.[82] On the one hand, talented people enjoy economic freedom and the fruit of their labour. On the other hand, poor and less talented people receive an equitable share of the national wealth and resources under the guardianship of Islamic state.

2.4.4 Utilitarianism

Utilitarians believe that distributive justice can be achieved by making a fair and equal distribution of resources to all members of society. They hold that the supreme goal is to ensure the utmost well-being and happiness of society as a whole. They promote the ethically and socially based principle that no one should be excluded from equal and larger benefits. Every person is morally obliged to safeguard the interests and benefits of others. Good actions are those whose outcomes are good in terms of benefiting people. Utilitarians suggest that all wants and preferences of society are to be summed up and sorted out by consulting its members. The available wealth and resources of society are to be used to satisfy its prioritized needs at their highest levels. Utilitarians strongly argue that rich people to give their surplus wealth to poor and needy people. However, they do not demand strict equality; rather they seek a position midway between the extremes of equality and non-equality (Schultz, 2004; Darwall, 2006; Stein, 2006).

The utilitarian approach to distributive justice may be explored in the Islamic philosophy of life. Utilitarians overemphasize the effectiveness and efficiency of goodness. They tend to rank good deeds on the basis of their tangible outcomes. It is most likely that one good deed with greater real essence but lower value in terms of outcomes may be overshadowed by another good deed with lesser real essence but higher value in terms of outcomes. The real outcomes of an act could be either implicit or explicit or both, material or spiritual or both, and over a period of time that approaches infinity. Moreover, moral values such as truth, honesty, benevolence, promise-keeping and fairness have an intrinsic than an extrinsic value, and they provide the foundations of all virtuous and good deeds and their outcomes. Similarly, spiritual acts, such as praying, fasting and worshipping God, are supreme goodness, and the real springs of morality and goodness, but they could not so be classified under the utilitarian doctrine because they have no direct and physical appearance or outcome. Truly speaking, goodness should be done for its own sake. Goodness is a form of human happiness and spiritual enrichment and therefore all extrinsic benchmarks, parameters and references prove to be the wrong tools to achieve it.

Indeed, the human vision in determining good acts and their eventual outcomes can be very narrow and myopic, and all err.[83] The moral conscience and intuitions of human beings can only reflect on established moral values, but they cannot conceive and develop them on their own. Passing judgement on what is good and moral falls outside human faculties and means. The human vision and moral conscience cannot see without divine enlightenment (guidance).[84] The real essence and goodness of every act should be decided under Divine guidance – *Shariah*, as God is all-seeing, all-knowing and the best promoter of goodness for human beings.[85] For example, dealings in pop music or wine may bring apparent goodness to some people but they are immoral from the *Shariah* perspective. Moreover, utilitarians pit the individual's morality against his own self-interest and then provide him with no inner and outer reinforcements to overcome his desire and greed for wealth and power. In this context, Islam holds that moral forces are deeply rooted in faith, which acts as an intrinsic and powerful stimulus to discipline self-interest in human beings along moral lines.

If the ideals of utilitarianism were to be realized, that would require a set of common and universal moral principles of distributive justice. However, when members of society went into the finer details of deciding what is moral and what is immoral, the whole affair would become highly complex, subjective and discriminatory. The people's judgements are always based on their emotions, prejudice, personal preferences, religious beliefs, cultural links, personality, education, training, ethnic and group affiliations, gender and so on. Human society is composed of many heterogeneous groups with conflicting interests. What could be moral and good in the eyes of one group or nation may not be moral and good in the eyes of other groups or nations. It is therefore most likely that moral rules of goodness could be decided only by a simple majority rather than an overwhelmingly majority. The moral rules so established, however, cannot become universal. Rather, they might be alleged to favour the rich over the poor, men over women, the strong over the weak, the opposition over the government, and so on. Any discrimination and unfairness towards weaker persons, groups and nations would kill the utilitarian spirit that takes an uncompromising stand to ensure goodness for all. It implies that there is an indispensable need to remove the issue of determining universally acceptable moral rules of goodness from the hands of human beings and entrust it to divine hands. Indeed, *Shariah* – Divine guidance – provides a full code of goodness and paves the way for humanity towards establishing distributive justice.

It may be noted that human beings largely make decisions with insufficient knowledge and expertise, with uncertainty and with confusion, which impairs the scope for making quality and productive decisions. More often than not, good intentions are found to be too vague to indicate the right pathway to goodness. Moreover, this life and world are mortal and dominated by physical rules, and moral principles are subjugated to them. Physical and scientific rules act as confounding factors to frustrate moral actions and their true outcomes. In real life, most moral and good deeds remain inconclusive, unnoticed, and unappreciated, which might frustrate moral people and lead them to lose their belief in goodness. For such reasons, Islam holds faith in the day of judgement and the life hereafter, where moral acts and their eternal, complete and unhindered consequences and implications would be established and people would be judged and rewarded on the basis of their intentions and moral acts – eternal salvation.[86] This very truth persuades human beings to remain moral and to continue doing good deeds without worrying too much about their outcomes, and with even stronger and unshakeable conviction.[87]

The utilitarian approach does not hold any deeper faith than that in moral and good deeds, and consequently rich people would feel little urge to spend their wealth on the poor. Richness cannot be defined in definite terms and no cap can be placed on it. There is no end to greed for money and possessions. The rich person sees his wealth as too little, and he wishes to have more and more of it. The more he gets, the more his hunger for it grows. So the thirst for wealth always remains unquenched. Most likely, utilitarian concepts should be enforced by the active support and involvement of the state. If the state placed a cap on the riches or wealth that one person could possess, all individuals, dominated by self-interest, would make no effort beyond the point where the fruits of their labour would be regarded as an 'extra wealth' that might be surrendered in favour of poor people. If talented people could not take away the whole package of their wages, it would impair, partially if not wholly, their rights of private ownership and the free market mechanism, leading to serious socio-economic imbalances. In simple terms, utilitarianism does not offer any viable and pragmatic road map for establishing distributive justice. It sincerely intends to establish distributive justice, but it lacks the soul and the heart of it, i.e., faith – faith in Divine guidance and the Islamic philosophy of life.

Under the Islamic doctrine of distributive justice, moral rules are held supreme in human life, business and market. *Shariah* provides very powerful, clear-cut and universally applicable guidance to ordain personal and social institutions to establish the most accomplished form of distributive justice. Islam ordains socio-economic life on the basis of universal brotherhood, altruism and benevolence. All human beings are from the same parents, and constitute one family. Muslim society is like a body and every member is like a limb, and if he is in trouble the whole body is affected and responds with pain. Islam relies on normative values and moral reinforcement to educate people that every dollar given to a needy person is a high-yielding investment for the giver and contributes towards his betterment and salvation in this life and the life hereafter.[88] It persuades people to donate more wealth even by curtailing their own needs to help those people living below the poverty line.

2.4.5 Pluralism

The doctrine of pluralism holds that unique and different criteria should be used to distribute different types of goods and resources in society. For example, rewards and punishments should be distributed according to desert, professional positions according to credentials, medical treatment according to need, and so on. So people in different spheres should be rewarded on the basis of their abilities. Furthermore, an individual should not use his privileged position in one sphere to secure privileged positions in other spheres. In this way even highly gifted individuals would not be able to acquire undue benefits in different spheres or most of the spheres, because of the natural limitations on his abilities and time. So inequalities would prevail but not on a very large scale (Walzer and David, 1995).

This theory envisages competitive market environments that might create better chances of establishing distributive justice. In the real world, however, people use their privileged position in one sphere to acquire benefits in other spheres. Like an investment portfolio, people diversify their self-interest portfolio. It is most likely that a person with economic power would use his wealth to acquire social and political power – power corrupts and absolute power corrupts absolutely. The lust to acquire more and more privileges and power is an egotistic and empire-building game. When a person is allowed to pursue self-interest by some means and in some spheres, he may pursue it by all means and in all spheres of life – every thing is fair in love and war – the war of greed to acquire and possess endless benefits and resources. Furthermore, all personal and social institutions are interlinked in such complex ways that it is hardly possible to divide them into isolated and independent compartments with their own unique and different criteria for fair and meritorious distribution of resources.

The doctrine of pluralism does not aim to impose any checks and balances on the individual and society. It does not truly count on moral and motivational measures to develop a system of self-discipline among human beings. Greater or sole reliance on strict rules and procedures cannot restrain or prevent people from pursuing their vested interests. The more rules we enforce to achieve distributive justice, the more likely we are to fail to do so. By developing many and varied criteria for distribution, pluralism makes the issue of establishing distributive justice highly cumbersome and complex. It also promotes polarity, divisions and conflict in human activities and institutions.

Islam ordains personal and social institutions under the principle of unity. All departments of human society, as per the Divine vision, are strongly interlinked and have very profound effects each other. They are subjected to the Unity of Command (Divine guidance for a full code of conduct) in order to observe the best internal and external governance and harmony. The moral and spiritual beliefs and training of Islamic market players evoke in them a high level of self-awareness and sense of social responsibility. They strive to match or justify their privileged position with their responsibilities towards their fellow human beings, not to take unfair advantage of them. So the moral consciousness based on faith – the person's faith in the life hereafter and his accountability before God to seek eternal salvation – acts as a driving force to translate the high Islamic ideals of distributive justice into reality.

2.4.6 Strict egalitarianism

In a very simple and strict version, strict egalitarianism holds that all members of society should be given equal amounts of resources, power and happiness, irrespective of their abilities or any other considerations (Carens, 1981; Nielsen, 1979). The main objection which can be made against this theory is that it nullifies the right of private ownership, economic freedom, and the spirit of competition and entrepreneurship. This theory ignores the fact that mentally and physically retarded people require a greater amount of wealth and resources to meet their needs. It also tends to develop a culture of economic parasitism. Wealth and resources would be mostly produced by hard-working and talented people, but lazy and less talented people would obtain an equal share in them. Without special reward, talented people would not put their utmost effort into their work. This may cause inefficiency, low productivity and poor economic growth. From a broader perspective, strict egalitarianism inevitably poses a powerful threat to the concentration of powers and resources in the hands of a tyrannical minority. Indeed, the failure of government to implement its fairly attractive plans would be taken to indicate its lack of resources and powers, and therefore more powers will be transferred to the state. Eventually, power would be concentrated in the hands of a group of morally corrupt people at the expense of the overwhelmingly majority, who would be grossly victimized, powerless, dependent and hapless. In simple terms, the effort to realize distributive justice under strict egalitarianism might lead to unprecedented examples of socio-economic injustice (Hayek, 1944).

If human beings are too pressured to surrender their right of private ownership and freedom, they become more committed and rebellious in pursuit of their self-interest. Indeed, strict egalitarianism embodies the Marxist vision of distributive justice, which was attempted in the 20th century in the former USSR and its allied Communist countries. However, the Marxist quest for distributive justice remained a wild goose chase over 70 years until it met its natural death with the demise of the USSR in the early 1990s (Elster, 1985; Andrew, 1995). The beginning of the so-called Marx's era of distributive justice inflicted death and suffering on millions of human beings; its practice registered the worst type of injustice, corruption, inefficiency; and its failure or end caused colossal socio-political and economic disasters.[89] Islam, by contrast, offers a highly educational, motivational and self-disciplinary approach to establishing an order of distributive justice. The Islamic vision regards private ownership rights, freedom of choice, market efficiency and economic benevolence as the central pillars in establishing distributive justice among the people of planet Earth.

2.5 Summary and conclusions

Shariah lays down basic guidance for all departments of human life. Islamic Economics adheres to the divine objectives and principles to manage the economic and financial affairs of human society. Life is composed of physical and spiritual dimensions, and economic activity, being part of life, should serve both dimensions. Islam guides human beings to ensure both material and spiritual gains in the economic and business field. It is the basic thrust of Islamic Economics to establish distributive justice. Islamic Economics relies on given tools and measures to evolve ethical and efficient channels for creating and distributing wealth and resources. It embodies moral values and rules such as free consent, mutual co-operation, the right of private ownership, the law of inheritance, fairness, promise-keeping and honouring contractual obligations, making charitable donations and payment of *zakah* as the main building blocks in establishing distributive justice. Furthermore, it bans immoral and anti-social elements that include interest, gambling, speculation, hoarding, monopoly, profiteering, black marketeering, speculation, bribery, embezzlement, misappropriation and fraud, because they militate against the fair and equitable acquisition and distribution of resources, and instead cause the concentration of wealth in hands of the few. The Islamic sate assumes a supervisory role in enforcing the Islamic economic system in both the spirit and the letter.

Islamic Economics presents a holistic view of socio-economic justice that stands head and shoulders above all modern theories of fairness, justice and equity. The globally dominant Conventional Economics and finance has divided the human polity into two extreme poles of wealth and poverty. The elite enjoys material excess and luxury, whereas the overwhelming majority of people suffers from extreme poverty and deprivation. Man-made rules and systems have miserably failed to ensure the sharing of God-given wealth and resources under the supreme principle of justice and universal brotherhood. Islamic Economics resolves this serious ethical, social and economic dilemma of modern humanity. The guiding principles of Islamic Economics ensure an equitable share of wealth and resources for all the citizens of the globe, and also enable them to achieve moral excellence, spiritual happiness and eternal success in this life and the life hereafter.

3

Islamic Banking and Finance Movement Worldwide: Performance and Prospects

3.1 Introduction

Islamic banking and finance (IBF) is an ideological discipline that draws on *Shariah* principles to expunge interest and other exploitative elements from the economic and financial spheres of human society. It is an equity-based system that primarily relies on profit and loss sharing (PLS) modes, namely, *Mudarabah* (joint venture) and *Musharakah* (equity participation), to perform borrowing, lending and investment functions. However, it may use some other interest-free instruments, such as *Murabaha* (deferred payment sale), *Ijarah* (leasing), *Bai Salam* (advance payment) and *Bai Istisna* (procurement engagement), to replace the interest-based banking and finance system in its entirety.

This chapter articulates the case for IBF in a simple and comprehensive fashion. It aims to depict IBF as adding more ethical, competitive and diversified tools and systems into global finance. It highlights the core credentials, theory and practice of IBF. It looks at recent developments in IBF in the Middle East, South Asia and Southeast Asia. It captures some breakthrough developments of IBF in Western markets in recent years. It takes stock of the problems and challenges facing IBF and its future growth prospects in global financial markets.

3.2 Evolution and growth of IBF

The contemporary IBF movement reflects the persistent efforts made by Islamic scholars and institutions to find *Shariah*-compliant means and measures for eliminating interest from economic and financial dealings in the Muslim world. Islamic scholars such as A Qureshi (1946),

N Siddiqi (1948) and S M Ahmad (1952) pioneered the idea of practising Islamic banking in modern times. Uzair (1955) made a major breakthrough by developing a more accomplished IBF model that explained the depositor–banker and banker–entrepreneur relationships under the *Mudarabah* principle. His work laid the foundation for the development and growth of IBF on modern lines. Maududi (1961), Irshad (1964), Al-Arabi (1966), M N Siddiqi (1967) and Al-Sadr (1974), amongst others, profiled other functional aspects of the IBF model to further crystallize it into reality. Meanwhile, the Kuwait Investment House Project and some periodical literature contributed by Huda (1964), Mannan (1970) and Udovitch (1970) elaborated a mechanism thoroughly to replace the conventional banking model with the Islamic banking model. The Conference of Finance Ministers of Islamic Countries in Karachi, Pakistan, in 1970 and Egyptian Study in 1972 appeared to be milestones in IBF history. These conceptual developments led to the adoption of the charter of the Islamic Development Bank (IDB) in 1974, which is the first-ever high-profile financial institution of the Islamic world (Siddiqi, M N, 1981).

The Mit-Ghamar Social Bank, established in Egypt in 1963, however, may be regarded as a pioneer of the contemporary IBF movement. The bank's operations were in trade and industry on a PLS basis. The bank appeared to be very successful due to increasing community support. Within a short time, its business developed into nine branches, managing funds to the value of 1.8 million Egyptian pounds deposited by more than 250,000 depositors. However, this experiment was abandoned in 1967 for political reasons (Scharf, 1983). The Pilgrimage Management Fund Board undertook a similar experiment by establishing the Tabung *Haji* in Malaysia in 1963. The shareholders of Tabung pooled their funds to invest in business and trade activities on the basis of risk-sharing. The core objective of the creation of Tabung was to provide financial assistance for its members' pilgrimages to Makkah, Saudi Arabia (Ahmad, A, 1987).

The practice of IBF had acquired significant shape and momentum by the end of 1970s due to increases in the general economic prosperity of the Middle Eastern countries from the huge influx of petrodollars. The Middle Eastern Islamic financial institutions (IFIs) received increasing socio-political and economic support for their growth and prosperity. Many reputable Islamic banks came into being, including, Nasser Social Bank Cairo (1971–72), Islamic Development Bank (1975), Dubai Islamic Bank (1975), Kuwait Finance House (1977), Faisal Islamic Bank of Sudan (1977) and Dar Al-Maal Al-Islami (1980) (Presley and Wilson, 1992). The IBF movement attracted a great deal of attention worldwide when three Muslim countries, namely, Pakistan[1], Iran[2] and Sudan,[3] decided to implement *Shariah* principles in their national economies and banking sectors.

A number of Western market players, including ABN AMRO, Citibank, HSBC and others, established their own Islamic window or subsidiaries to attract petrodollar deposits from the Middle East and their Muslim clientele worldwide. At the time of writing (2007) there are about 300 IBF institutions across 70 countries, holding capital investments worth US$500 billion–US$800 billion, with an average annual growth of 15 percent over the years (Arekat, 2006). It has been estimated that the IBF industry will have a market value of US$4 trillion by 2010 (Cader, 2007) and will capture 40–50 percent of the total savings of the 1.3 billion Muslims worldwide by 2015 to 2017 (Alam, 2006).

The IBF industry is the fastest-growing segment of global finance. It aims to offer truly viable and ethical solutions in the retail and corporate sectors. It started with retail-based lending and investment operations and after a decade or so made progress in corporate financing and syndications, equity and leasing. Since 2001, the Islamic capital market has maintained annual growth as high as 15–20 percent due to rapidly growing trading in *Sukuks* (Islamic bonds) among Islamic business and finance organizations. Malaysia is the largest issuer of *Sukuk* – there they are worth more than US$32 billion. *Sukuks* constitute about 85 percent of the Middle Eastern capital market: US$13 billion of them have been issued there with an average growth rate over 45 percent during 2002–7. The Middle East and Asian regions would primarily rely on *Sukuk*s to meet their US$1.5 trillion infrastructure needs over the next five years.[4] There are also over 350 Islamic equity funds managing assets in excess of US$4 billion with an annual growth rate about 15–20 percent. These include Dow Jones Islamic Index (DJGI).[5]

Takaful or the Islamic insurance industry has experienced annual growth of 20 percent in recent years. There are more than 250 *Takaful* companies managing premiums worth US$2 billion in 2005 which are expected to grow to US$7.5 billion by 2015.[6] *Takaful* instruments have added much-needed risk cover for Islamic business and finance and also provided long-term investment opportunities for Islamic investors and institutions. Other growing areas of IBF include assets and wealth management, hedge funds and treasury and risk instruments. Yet considerable scope remains for Islamic solutions in derivatives, swaps, options and futures markets. The growing IBF discipline offers common ground for collaboration and partnership with conventional finance. The main players from both Islamic and conventional streams may pool their expertise and resources to devise more ethical and efficient solutions in business and finance.

3.3 The IBF infrastructure

An increasing number of supporting bodies have been working to develop a well-integrated infrastructure and regulatory framework for the IBF industry. Islamic Financial Services Board (IFSB) has been assisting the industry to secure strong governance and regulatory frameworks. Accounting Auditing Organization for Islamic Financial Institutions (AAOIFI) has been engaged over the decades in devising universal and internationally competitive Islamic accounting and auditing standards and practice. International Islamic Financial Market (IIFM) has taken upon itself to develop well-regulated and efficient Islamic financial markets. Liquidity Management Centre (LMC) has been working to devise a wide range of instruments and tools of Islamic money and capital markets with a special focus on providing excess liquidity avenues to IFIs. International Islamic Rating Agency (IIRA) and other international rating agencies have been engaged in streamlining IBF regulatory frameworks, systems and products in light of efficient market principles. General Council for Islamic Banks and Financial Institutions (GCIBFI) has been promoting better understanding and awareness of the IBF industry among market players, stakeholders and the general public. An increasing number of training and research institutions, including Islamic Training and Research Institute (IRTI), Institute of Islamic Banking and Insurance London, Islamic Finance Training and International Centre for Education in Islamic Finance (INCEIF) and Islamic Finance Training, are acting as a nursery to develop best-of-breed human capital resources, management and strategies that can truly promote the research and development (R&D) in IBF that is much needed and desired in the contemporary world of business and finance. Islamic Development Bank (IDB) has been promoting socio-economic developments in Muslim countries under Islamic Economic principles. Along with IIFM it has devised a ten-year roadmap to ensure the systematic growth and development of an IBF infrastructure. The increasing sophistication of information technology (IT) and the Internet has been enhancing the resourcefulness of IFIs in organizing their operations on a more efficient basis across the globe. International and offshore financial centres in Southeast Asia (Labuan) and Middle East (Dubai International Financial Centre, DIFC) are playing a key role in promoting Islamic finance services worldwide.

3.4 Factors contributing to exponential growth in IBF

The unprecedented growth in IBF has been triggered by some core developments on socio-political and economic fronts worldwide. In general, Muslims' economic conditions have improved markedly over the decades, and Muslims now control enormous economic resources and wealth. The increasing globalization of business and financial markets has made it incumbent upon Muslims to utilize their economic and financial resources in the most efficient and faithful manner; otherwise other nations may exploit them largely for their own benefit. Above all, the Muslim world needs to cooperate with the rest of the global community in the economic and financial realms in order to enjoy real political autonomy, peace and prosperity. In the contemporary age, world politics has become incredibly proactive in the field of economics and finance. Superpowers like the United States of America (USA) have the strongest and biggest economies and financial markets. The international community now applies economic sanctions and boycotts as their best tactics against the countries which they think pose a threat to global peace and security. The European Union (EU) and Group of Eight (G8) have acquired a great deal of significance in shaping and shifting the dynamics and dimensions of international politics.

There are growing concerns in the global Muslim polity over the increasingly dominant role of the USA and its Western allies in global politics after the 9/11 episode, the war in Afghanistan, the war in Iraq and its subsequent ramifications, and the grim situations in Palestine and Lebanon. These events have acted as a catalyst to rejuvenate the Islamic resurgence in the Muslim world, which urges Muslims to ordain their personal and social institutions under *Shariah* principles and establish a strong bond of universal brotherhood among their ranks. Muslim countries have come closer together to offer a common front against the challenges and threats posed to their ideology, their territorial and political integrity and their global reputation. They aim to develop and reinforce business, trade and financial links among themselves. In particular, the Middle Eastern countries are becoming very keen to pool their human and economic resources to secure greater integration, efficiency, economies of scales and bargaining power in international markets. Furthermore, they plan to evolve common financial and monetary systems. The first dedicated Islamic Index – Global GCC Index – comprising 66 listed companies has been promoting Islamic *Shariah*-compliant business and investment in the Middle Eastern markets. The Gulf Cooperation Council (GCC) countries, which include Bahrain, Kuwait, Oman, Qatar and United Arab Emirates (UAE), have decided to establish a joint central bank in the near future. By 2008, they will also establish a World Islamic Bank – Eamar International Bank. Both these giant institutions will strive to tap regional wealth and resources on a more efficient basis and thereby enhance the efficiency and breadth of Middle Eastern financial markets. Most importantly, the GCC countries will achieve monetary integration by introducing a common currency by 2010 (Kamil, 2007). IFIs are highly proactive in undertaking real economic and business activities in the Middle East region. They can play a crucial role in integrating the regional business and financial forces and thereby transform the Middle Eastern region into an Islamic economic bloc. Such patterns may prevail in other parts of the Muslim world in coming years (Khan M M and Bhatti 2008c).

3.5 Salient features of IBF

IBF differs from its conventional counterpart in its origin, aims and mechanisms. It has adopted a *Shariah* paradigm and operates as a value-based system aiming to promote market efficiency with justice. It conducts lending and borrowing operations based on core principles such as equity-sharing, entrepreneurship, risk-taking and innovation. The very distinctive nature, functioning and market-based credentials of IBF are highlighted in the discussion below.

3.5.1 The value-based paradigm

IBF draws on divine guidance to work within ethical and social contexts. Under the holistic world view of Islam, the banker is a trustee and answerable to God for making efficient, ethical and socially beneficial use of the available wealth and economic resources of the community. IBF widens production and distribution channels to reach out to people at the grass roots. It promotes more equitable and innovative business and investment environments by removing the barriers involved in conventional lending, such as the requirements of collateral and creditworthiness.[7] It specializes in financing small- and medium-size business enterprises to ensure sustainable economic growth and social welfare. Thus it dismantles the concentration of wealth and resources in the hands of a few.

IBF opposes all anti-social and immoral activities featuring interest, gambling, speculation, hoarding, monopoly, profiteering, black marketeering, bribery, embezzlement, misappropriation, fraud and making or selling wine. Islamic bankers do not indulge in speculative activities to manipulate markets for their own vested interests. It may be noted that

IBF is also known as a vital part of the wider Islamic resurgence in the contemporary Muslim world, directed at reorienting the socio-political and economic lives of Muslims under *Shariah* principles. Thus IBF provides an opportunity for the contemporary Muslim community to practise more profitable banking without any cost to their religious faith and spiritual selves and belongings (Ahmad, A, 1987).[8]

3.5.2 Banking for the poor

An exclusive feature of IBF is that it engages in doing business with weaker social groups. It promotes fair and equal opportunities by ensuring easy and economical access to financial and technical help for people living in the lower echelons of society. IBF mobilizes *Waqaf* funds, donations, *zakah* funds and benevolent loans or *Qard-e-Hasanah* from its shareholders, clients and others to help needy and downtrodden people.

3.5.3 Market-based credentials

IBF relies on saving and investment vehicles based on risk-sharing in business enterprises. It is primarily an equity-based system featuring zero-based interest, shared economy, joint venture, mutual funds, leasing, innovation and promising rates of return. The PLS system is the heart of Islamic financial intermediation. IBF establishes the relationship between savers and borrowers through PLS instruments rather than interest. It takes funds from depositors under the stipulation that neither nominal values nor predetermined returns on their deposits will be guaranteed. It undertakes business and investment ventures alone and also in partnership with entrepreneurs, and shares the resulting gains or losses with its depositors (Karsten, 1982; Anwar, 1987).

In the Islamic economy, the ban on interest payments and receipts, and the levy of *zakah* (a tax deduction of 2.5 percent on Muslims' wealth that remains out of productive use or circulation for one Islamic calendar year) oblige capitalists to invest their funds on a PLS basis. This ensures a higher rate of capital formulation and investment, greater availability of risk capital and optimal utilization of economic resources. Since IBF does not finance projects under the conventional criteria of the borrower's creditworthiness and strong collateral, the possibility that loan applications for bad projects with strong collateral may displace loan applications for good projects with weak collateral is eliminated, so ensuring a more ethical and efficient use of the national wealth. In other words, IBF promotes a market-based mechanism wherein available investment alternatives are appraised on the basis of their credentials, leading to a marked improvement in allocation and distribution systems. Furthermore, it utilizes existing wealth to produce more wealth, goods and services. In the competitive Islamic economy, prices of goods and services are trending downwards because the supply of goods and services is constantly increasing through innovation and competitive entrepreneurship. Since the return on capital is based on its actual productivity and outcomes, IBF possess a greater capacity to absorb and readjust to external forces, shocks and other such volatile market behaviour. This also allows credit creation and policies of monetary expansion to have a minimal inflationary impact on the Islamic market and economy (Zarqa, 1983; Chapra, 1985; Khan and Mirakhor, 1987; Ahmed, 1994; El-Ghazali, 1994).

The majority of the risk-sharing instruments of IBF have commonly long been applied in the conventional financial world. However, they are always used there only as a secondary vehicle to enhance efficiency, diversification and risk management techniques. In the highly conducive environments of IBF, by contrast, these instruments are designed to play a central role. They are made fully capable of bringing about a truly efficient, ethical and socially desirable utilization of the financial and economic resources of the community.

3.6 Theory and practice of IBF

The IBF model is primarily based on equity-sharing or PLS instruments, namely, *Mudarabah* and *Musharakah*. The model also encompasses *Qard-e-Hasanah*, or interest-free loans to the poor on charitable grounds. The PLS modes and *Qard-e-Hasanah* are ideal means to eliminate interest from the financial sphere and to strive for the establishment of a just socio-economic order. Indeed, some secondary interest-free instruments, including *Murabaha*, *Ijarah*, *Bai Salam* and *Bai Istisna*, are also included in the IBF model to enhance its practical scope, diversification and risk-management capabilities. The basic model of IBF is shown in Figure 3.1.

3.6.1 PLS modes: *Mudarabah* and *Musharakah*

Mudarabah and Musharakah are the central pillars of the PLS banking model. *Mudarabah* is a form of partnership wherein one party contributes money capital and other party devotes human capital to undertake a business activity for mutual benefit. Each party takes an agreed percentage of the profit. If a *Mudarabah* venture incurs losses, then the financier bears all the money losses, while the managing party receives no reward for its efforts. The financier is also named as 'investor' or '*rab-u-mal*' or

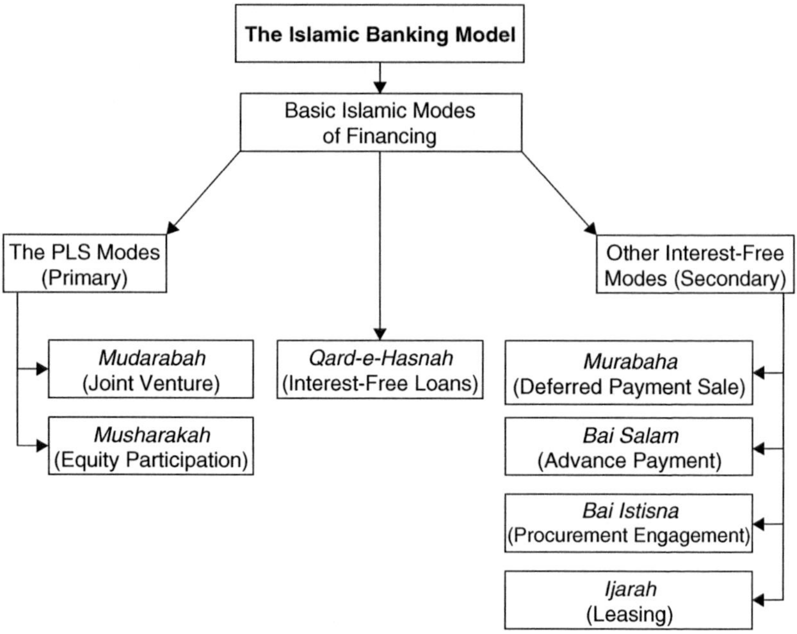

Figure 3.1 The IBF model: basic policy instruments

'commeditaire', while the managing party is called '*Mudarib*' or 'fund manager' or 'commendit'. In general, the financier is not supposed to interfere with the management of *Mudarabah* affairs (Abu-Saud, 1980; Udovitch, 1970).

In the Arabian Peninsula, business dealings on a *Mudarabah* basis were in existence long before the dawn of Islam. However, there is no direct reference to *Mudarabah* in the holy *Quran* and *Sunnah* of the holy Prophet Mohammad (pbuh). Many early jurists, such as Imam Malik (796) and Imam Shafi (820), pointed out that family members and close friends of the holy Prophet Mohammad (pbuh) were engaged in investing the wealth of orphans under their guardianship in *Mudarabah*. The same practice was followed uninterruptedly by their predecessors. *Mudarabah* is similar to the venture capital investment in the Western business world. In the history of medieval Europe, *Mudarabah* was known as 'commenda' and was mainly a marine activity (Udovitch, 1970; Saleh, 1986).

The IBF model based on *Mudarabah* is also known as a two-tier *Mudarabah* system. Figure 3.2 shows the basic functioning of *Mudarabah* banking, in three steps. In the first step, the Islamic bank accepts funds

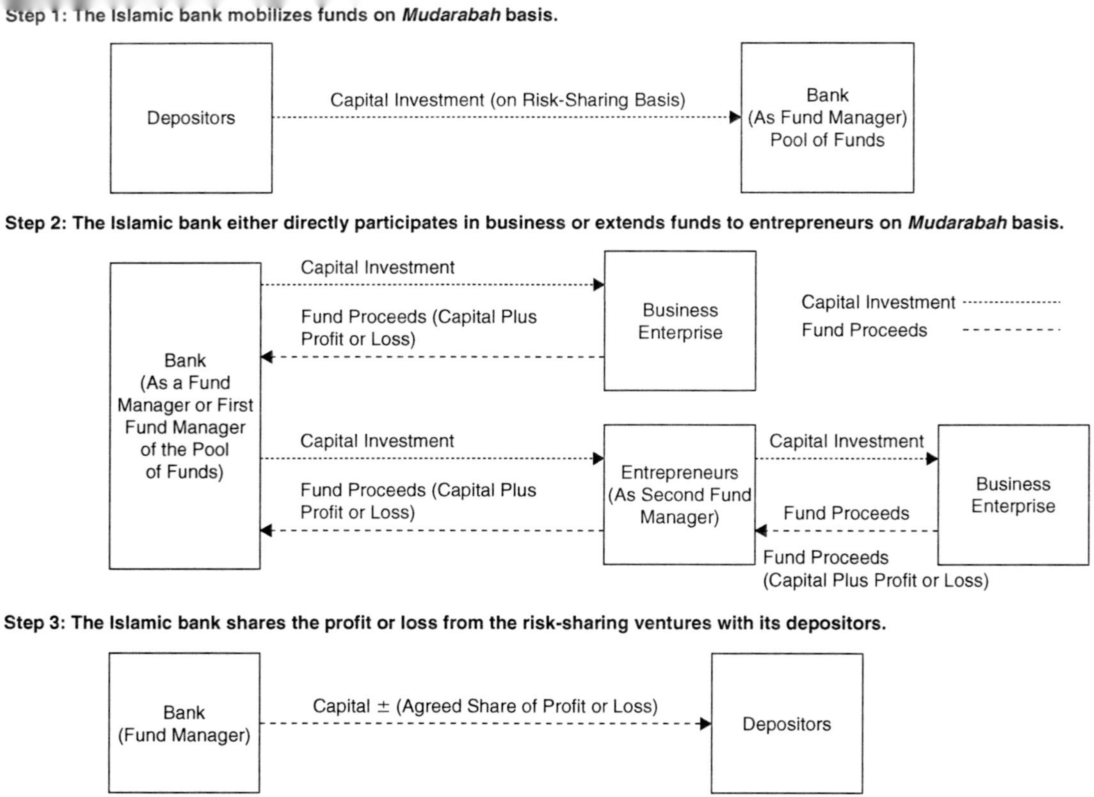

Figure 3.2 *Mudarabah* (joint venture) banking model

from depositors under the risk-sharing arrangement. In the second step, the Islamic bank either directly invests these funds in profitable investments or extends them to entrepreneurs to engage in business enterprises by becoming partners of the Islamic bank on a risk-sharing basis. In the third step, the Islamic bank shares with depositors the profit or loss earned from *Mudarabah* undertakings and investments. This model is also known as the *Mudarabah* banking model or PLS model (Ahmad, A, 1987; Uzair 1978).

Musharakah is another central pillar of the IBF model. The term is derived from the Arabic word *Sharikah,* which means 'sharing' or 'partnership'. Under such arrangements, two or more persons contribute their funds and managerial skills to undertake a business enterprise on the basis of mutual risk-sharing. *Musharakah* was commonly practised in Arabian business life before the advent of Islam. In Islamic history, *Musharakah* remains one of the major modes for investment in business and trade (Anwar, 1987).

Musharakah partners are free to agree on any ratio for profit sharing but they are required to share business losses in strict proportion to their capital contributions. Furthermore, *Shariah* strictly prohibits partners from receiving predetermined and guaranteed returns on their investment. All partners enjoy equal rights and responsibilities to manage a *Musharakah* enterprise but one or more partners can manage it on behalf of others (Anwar, 1987; Wilson, 1994; Ariff, 1988).

Under the *Musharakah* principle, the Islamic bank makes equity contributions towards the client's company or particular project and in return has the right to receive an agreed percentage of the profit. The bank contributes towards losses in proportion to its investment in the client's firm. Both the bank and the entrepreneur reserve the right to manage the *Musharakah* enterprise. However, in actual practice the client exercises the managerial responsibilities of the *Musharakah* enterprise, and the bank scrutinizes and audits its accounts on a regular basis. In corporate *Musharakah* financing, the bank appoints its staff to the boards of directors of the company financed on a *Musharakah* basis (Bendjilali and Khan, 1995).

Figure 3.3 explains the relationship between the fund seeker and the Islamic bank under the *Musharakah* principle. The Islamic bank and the client (entrepreneur) make their financial contributions under a *Musharakah* contract. The Islamic bank allows the client to manage *Musharakah* affairs. The Islamic bank and the client mutually share the profit or loss earned from *Musharakah* investment.

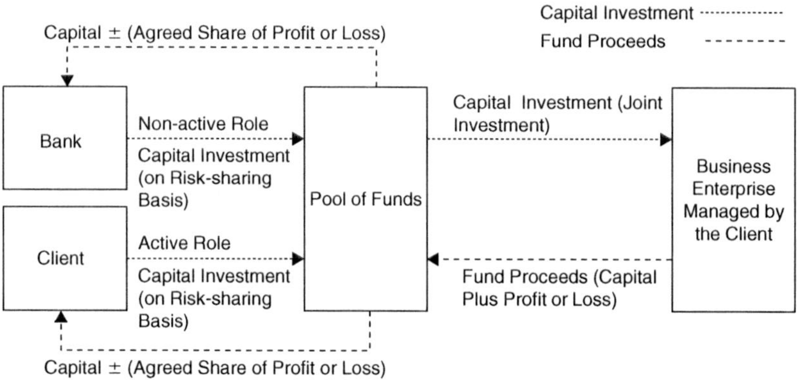

Figure 3.3 *Musharakah* (equity participation) banking model

In IBF theory, PLS modes are the most flexible and efficient financing tools for short- and long-term investments, although in practice their use is always limited. Table 3.1 reveals that on average 6.34 percent of the total financings of Islamic banks in the sample was based on PLS instruments (*Mudarabah* and *Musharakah*) during 2004–6. The given sample comprises the big banks of the IBF industry and so may reflect a general trend of using PLS systems across the board. The weighted average use of PLS instruments by the top ten Islamic banks, representing about 50 percent of the IBF industry, was up to 17.34 percent of their total financing operations during 1994–96 (Ahmad, Khan and Iqbal, 1998). It may be concluded that the use of the PLS system has dropped by an average of 11 percent in the IBF industry since 2006.

The practical scope of PLS instruments has always been restricted by operational difficulties and business ethics constraints in the IBF industry. Not surprisingly, IFIs find that most projects submitted by their clients for PLS financing are bad, risky and with overoptimistic prospective profit figures. They have no special regulatory frameworks, standard procedures, expertise and tools to assess the viability of PLS investment proposals. The IFIs' cost of monitoring PLS projects could be very high. The inefficient tax system and high rate of illiteracy in most Muslim countries have proved to be formidable obstacles to applying PLS concepts in practice. IFIs do not show any enthusiasm for marketing PLS investment products that have ever caused them great troubles and losses. The majority of entrepreneurs maintain two sets of accounts to avoid tax, and others shy away from the idea of entering into PLS arrangements with IFIs because they do not want to share their private details

Table 3.1 Application of PLS (*Mudarabah* and *Musharakah*), *Murabaha* (deferred payment sale), *Ijara* and *Bai'Istinna/Bai'Salam* modes in the IBF industry (US$ thousands)

Name of Islamic Bank	Total Investment and Financing	PLS %	*Murabaha* %	*Ijara* (%)	*Bai Salam/ Bai Istisna* %
Al Rajhi Bank (31 December 2006)	23,884,600	N.T*/Nil	14,079,797 (58%)	9,112,761 (38%)	577,134 (2.42%)
Albaraka Bank Bahrain (31 December 2006)	391,124.766	27,525.244 (7.03%)	289,071.426 (73.90%)	42,187.279 (10.79%)	1,000** (0.25%)
Bahrain Islamic Bank (31 March 2005)	662,978.83	43,443.109 (6.55%)	406,148.59 (61.26%)	38,401.69 (5.79%)	N.T*/Nil
Bank Islam Malaysia Berhad (30 June 2006)	2,439,612.057	20,464.736 (0.84%)	404,956.463 (16.60%)	90,560.104 (3.712%)	181,803.455 (7.4%)
Bank Muamalat Malaysia Berhad (31 December 2006)	1,477,251.957	161.837 (0.0109%)	308,670.702 (20.89%)	376,889.715 (25.51%)	106,125.800 (7.18%)
Dubai Islamic Bank (31 December 2006)	11,044,826***	1,653,457 (14%)	9,248,383 (83.73%)	1,644,437 (14.88%)	1,212,546 (10.98%)
Gulf Finance House (31 December 2005)	1,248,904	61,015 (4.88%)	725,677.00 (58.10%)	N.T*/Nil	N.T*/Nil
Kuwait Finance House (31 December 2005)	15,433,653	N.T*/Nil	8,253,477 (53.50%)	2,076,735 (13.45%)	1,745,666 (11.31%)
Qatar International Islamic Bank (31 December 2004)	1,288,308	6,242.03 (0.485%)	1,007,448 (78.19%)	60,120.6 (4.66%)	42,787.4 (3.32%)
The entire Islamic banking sector of Pakistan**** (31 December 2006)	1,079,594.693	182,786 (17%)	435,271 (40%)	322,417 (30%)	9,108.68 (2%)
Average %		**6.34%**	**54.42%**	**16.31%**	**5.60%**

Source: Summary data taken from the *Annual Reports* of the respective Islamic banks.

* N.T: Not traceable.

***Bai Salam* investments in *Sukuk Salam* (bond).

***Gross total of Islamic and financing assets and investments is shown. Furthermore, property investments are also based on Islamic modes, but are not included in the table because there are no details of their distribution over different modes.

or their profits with outsiders. General depositors are strongly averse to risk-taking and so do not want to commit their funds to IFIs, which have no deposit insurance schemes. Any genuine attempt to adopt the PLS system by IFIs could prompt their depositors to withdraw their funds, leading to a credit crunch in the IBF industry. Consequently, IFIs follow conventional policies and thereby give a full surety to their customers that their funds and fixed returns on them are fully guaranteed (Ahmed, 1987b; Khan, S R, 1987; Al-Omar and Abdel-Haq, 1996; Ashraf, 1998; Bashir, 1999; Ghafoor, 1999; Warde, 2000).

3.6.2 Interest-free modes: *Murabaha* (deferred payment sale)

Shariah recognizes *Murabaha* as a trade-based activity. *Murabaha* refers to a sale wherein the seller does not possess the goods required by the buyer but acquires them from the original source and then sells them to the buyer after adding an agreed profit margin. The legality of *Murabaha* cannot be established from the primary sources of *Shariah*, i.e., the holy *Quran* and *Sunnah* of the holy Prophet Mohammad (pbuh). The early Islamic jurists, such as Imam Malik (796) and Imam Shafi (820), approved *Murabaha* sales but did not refer to price increases in the case of deferred payments. Subsequently, some other Islamic jurists, such as Sarakhsi (1091), Marghinani (1197) and Nawawi (1277), allowed the seller to charge a higher price in a deferred payment sale by calling it a normal practice in trade (Saadullah, 1994; Vogel and Hayes, 1998). The *Murabaha* instrument may be successfully applied in the IBF world. Under the *Murabaha* model, the bank buys the specified goods from the trader or manufacturer at a spot price and then sells them to the client at a deferred price covering the cost and the profit margin (the mark-up basis). The bank cannot thereafter increase the agreed price of a *Murabaha* contract because the client defaults or for any other reason. Figure 3.4 presents IBF operations on the basis of *Murabaha*.

The bank should adopt the following procedure in practising the *Murabaha* mode of financing. When the client approaches the bank and asks for financial assistance towards buying goods on a *Murabaha* basis, the bank or client obtains the required information about the goods from the marketplace. Then the bank lays out all terms and conditions for the future *Murabaha* contract with the client, and specifically informs him about the cost price plus profit which it would earn from him in this particular transaction. Up to this stage, dealings between the bank and the client amount to a moral agreement that cannot be legally enforced. In other words, there would be an agreement or promise between both parties to enter into a *Murabaha* contract in the near future. If the client

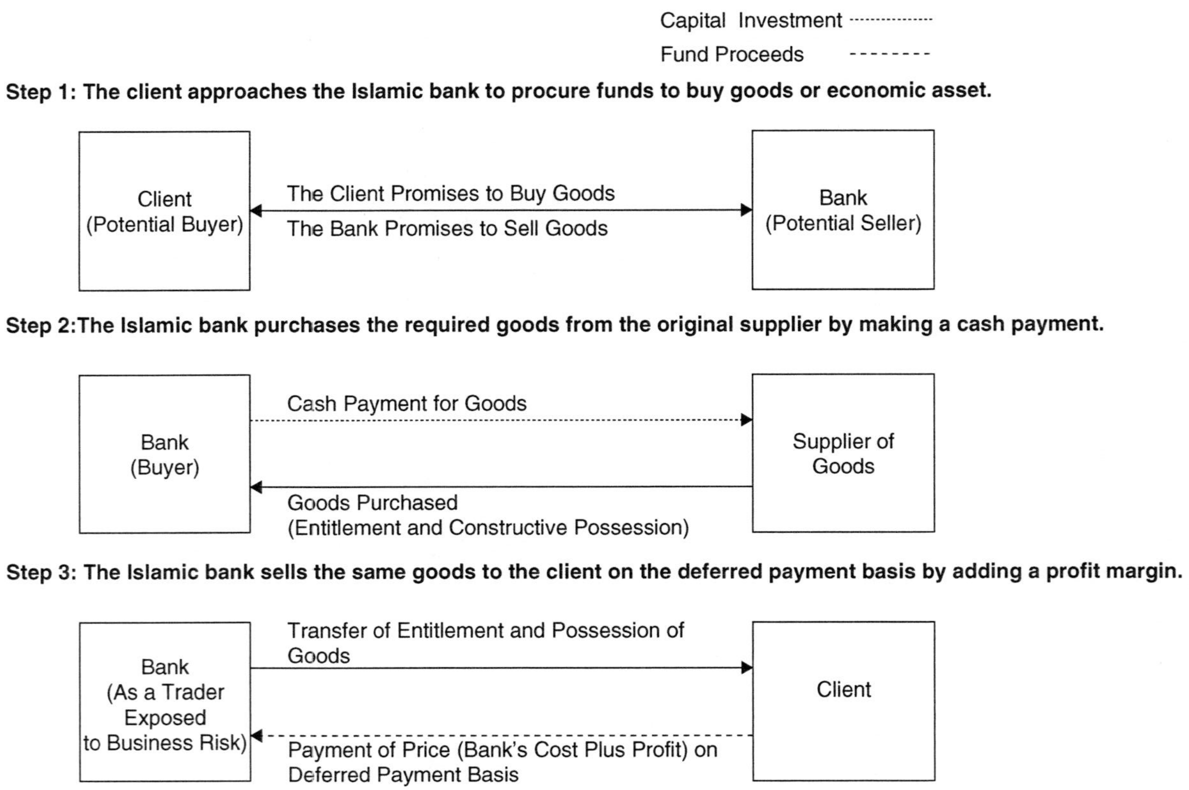

Figure 3.4 *Murabaha* (deferred payment sale) banking model

changed his mind and refused to buy goods, the bank could not claim any financial compensation from him for the loss which it may incur due to his breach of promise.[9] It implies that *Shariah* envisages the Islamic bank as a trader that should bear business risks, such as theft, damage, destruction, non-acceptance of goods and price fluctuations in *Murabaha* transactions (Wilson, 1995; Iqbal, 1998; Vogel and Hayes, 1998).

For the validity of *Murabaha* it is important that the transaction between the bank and the client should be absolutely independent from the transaction between the bank and the supplier or original seller of the goods. Therefore, two agreements or contracts between the bank and the client should be executed. First, the client may promise the bank to buy goods on a credit basis. Second, he may enter into a sale contract with the bank on a deferred payment basis. It is not necessary for the bank to take physical possession of goods in a literal sense. After proceeding with *Murabaha* contract, the bank may advise the supplier to deliver the purchased goods to the client on its own behalf. *Murabaha* has firm roots in *Shariah* as well as Islamic history, though a large majority of Islamic scholars express strong disapproval of its use in the IBF world because by its very nature it tends to degenerate into an interest-based activity (Siddiqi, M N, 1983; Ahmed, 1987b; Homoud, 1994; Khan, T, 1995).

IBF operations are dominated by *Murabaha*. Table 3.1 provides empirical evidence that on average *Murabaha* has up to 54.42 percent representation in the total financing and investment portfolios of ten Islamic banks during the period 2004–06. The weighted average use of *Murabaha* by the top ten Islamic banks, representing 50 percent of the Islamic banking industry, amounted to 65.66 percent of their total financings during the period 1994–96 (Ahmad, Khan and Iqbal, 1998). It implies that IFIs have been adamant in relying heavily on *Murabaha* in practice. Presently about 95 percent of financing is debt-based and only 5 percent risk-sharing at IFIs.[10]

The actual practice of *Murabaha* financing grossly violates *Shariah* principles. For example, IFIs insure *Murabaha* goods for damage, destruction and theft, and impose all such costs on their clients (Bashir, 1999; Warde, 2000). They use interest rates to fix returns on *Murabaha* contracts. They assign higher returns on *Murabaha* contracts with longer periods, just as conventional banking does. They follow the rule 'pay now, pay less principal'.[11] They recover fines and additional charges from clients who delay their *Murabaha* loan repayments. Furthermore, they unlawfully recover losses from clients who breach their promise to buy *Murabaha* goods. For all practical purposes, IFIs earn almost risk-free returns on their *Murabaha* investments (Homoud 1994; Ghafoor, 1999).

3.6.3 Interest-free modes: *Ijarah* (lease financing)

Under the *Ijarah* arrangement, the lessor or owner authorizes another person (beneficiary or lessee) to exclusively enjoy the usufruct of his asset for a specified period in exchange for rent payments. *Shariah* ordains that the lessor should bear all costs of repairs, insurance, depreciation and damages in relation to the leased asset. He should bear the risk of uncertainty attached to the total useful life of the asset, and to the extent to which the asset will remain under the lease. Furthermore, lease payments should not be determined by using interest as a benchmark. Rather, they should be based on the productivity and profitability of the leased asset. The Islamic concept of leasing is explained in Figure 3.5. The Islamic bank or leasing company buys the economic asset required by the client and then enters into a leasing arrangement with the client for an agreed period.

Leasing arrangements can be successfully applied in industrial, manufacturing and other sectors of the Islamic economy for meeting their short- and long-term financing needs. Presently IFIs are engaged in retail finance for home mortgages, cars and household needs. There are some good reasons for the increasing popularity of leasing in IBF worldwide. In fact, IFIs mostly rely on lease financing known as *Ijarah-wa-Iqtina*, which enjoys strong support among *Shariah* scholars. It bears a close resemblance to conventional leasing, and therefore relies on the established conventional infrastructure in practice (Iqbal, 1998; Warde, 2000). Table 3.1 shows that lease financing used by ten Islamic banks accounts on average for 16.38 percent of their total financings during the period 2004–06.

3.6.4 Interest-free modes: *Bai Salam* (advance payment) and *Bai Istisna* (procurement engagement)

Bai Salam is a forward sale in which the seller pays the whole price of the goods that are to be delivered to him at the specified future date. This instrument was widely used in the agricultural sector at the time of the holy Prophet Mohammad (pbuh). Muslim farmers have always met their short- and long-term financial needs, such as for buying seeds and fertilizer, by selling their future produce to the seller at the time of cultivation. It may be noted that a slight variation of *Bai Salam*, known as *Bai Istisna*, involves the sale of manufactured goods at an agreed price at the future date of delivery. Figure 3.6 shows that *Bai Salam* and *Bai Istisna* may involve three steps. First, the bank makes a payment to the client for purchasing the specified farm or manufactured goods from him. Then the client delivers the required goods to the bank and thereby meets his

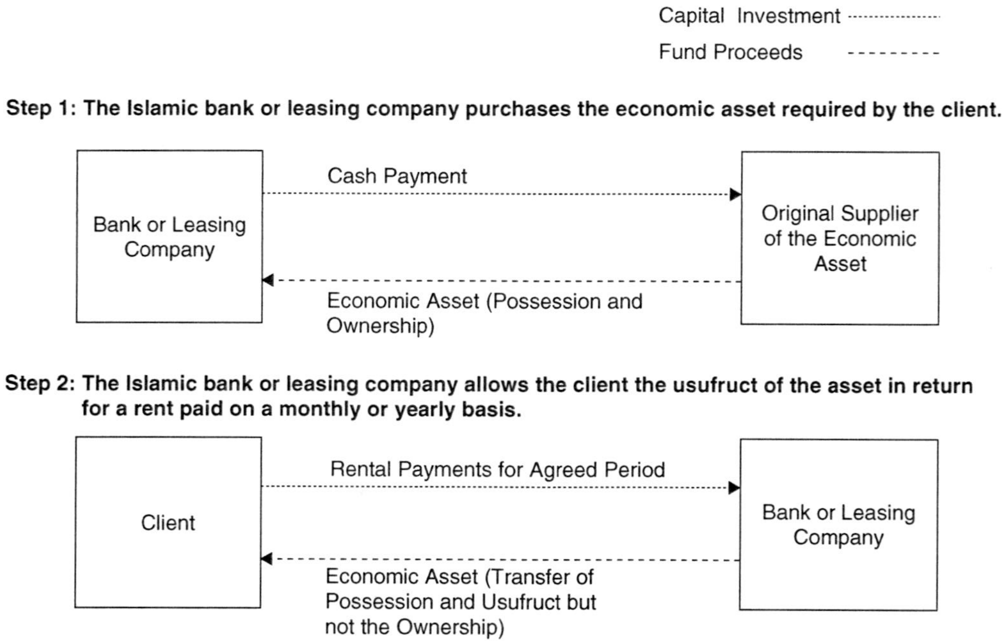

Figure 3.5 *Ijarah* (leasing) banking model

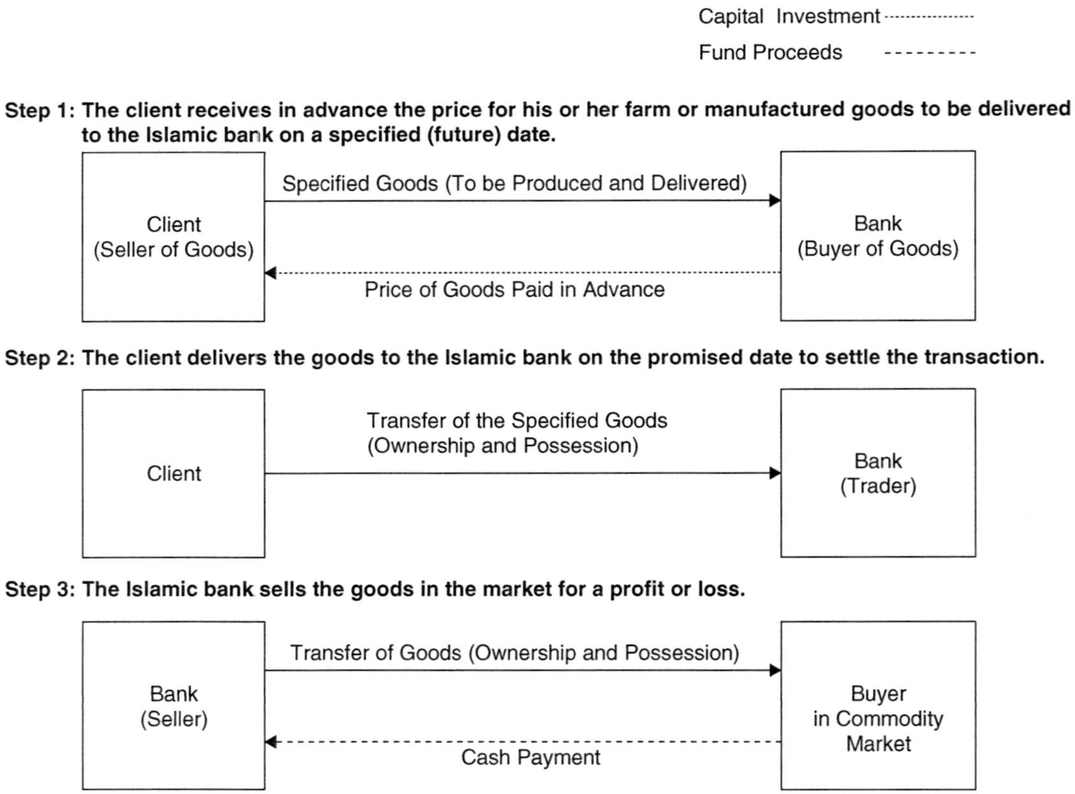

Figure 3.6 *Bai Salam* (advance payment) and *Bai Istisna* (procurement engagement) banking model

part of the contractual obligations. Finally, the bank sells these goods in the market, making a profit or a loss.

It should be noted that *Shariah* does not permit IFIs to sell the goods purchased under *Bai Salam* and *Bai Istisna* before having them in their actual possession. This restriction is imposed to eliminate any possibility that the goods may serve as a proxy for carrying out financial activity that resembles the conventional mode. *Shariah* impresses upon Islamic banks that the terms and conditions of *Bai Salam* and *Bai Istisna* contracts, such as price, quantity and quality of goods, should be determined as precisely as possible so as to ensure that there is no element of *riba, gharar* (speculation) or dubious sale in such transactions (Gari, 1997; see Chapter 2). It may be noted that *Bai Salam* and *Bai Istisna* can be used to develop Islamic future contracts and short-term liquidity investment avenues for IFIs. However, neither instrument has received proper attention from IBF practitioners so far. Table 3.1 shows that ten Islamic banks carried out on average 5.60 percent of their total financing operations through *Bai Salam* and *Bai Istisna* during the period 2004–06.

3.7 Islamic financial market

There is increasing interest on the part of Islamic as well as conventional market players in the fastest-growing segments of Islamic financial market, namely *Sukuks,* Islamic equity investment funds and *Takaful* services. These developments greatly promote *Shariah*-compliant business and economic activities in the Muslim world on the one hand and enhance the overall depth, diversity and flexibility of the IBF system on the other. The following discussion provides a brief account of recent growth and developments in the Islamic financial market.

3.7.1 Islamic capital market: *Sukuks*

Sukuks or Islamic bonds are *Shariah*-based substitutes for conventional securities or bonds. They are derived from trading in or production of real and tangible assets or their usufruct and services. The buyer or holder of *Sukuks* acquires exclusive ownership over the underlying assets, and receives interest-free payments or rentals until the maturity date or sale of *Sukuks*. Among 14 types, *Sukuks* based on *Ijarah, Mudarabah* and *Murabaha* are very common and mostly used in the Islamic world. *Sukuks* have not only created long-term Islamic investment opportunities but also broadened the efficient means of liquidity investments for IFIs. They are widely used for financing infrastructure, development and industrial projects.

The Islamic capital or *Sukuk* market has grown strongly since 2001 in the Muslim world. In 2001, the Malaysian government launched *Sukuks* to lay the foundation of a worldwide Islamic capital market. By the end of 2003, Malaysia had 90 percent of the global *Sukuk* market. In 2005, *Sukuks* represented 52 percent of a total of US$29.18 billion outstanding corporate bonds in the Malaysian market.[12] Presently Malaysia is the biggest issuer of *Sukuks*, worth over US$32 billion (Alvi, 2006). The Malaysian Securities Commission has established a well-regulated *Sukuk* market in the country.

Bahrain first introduced *Sukuks* in the Middle Eastern market in 2001. Qatar and IDB issued US$400 million and US$700 million respectively in *Sukuks* in 2003. The Middle Eastern *Sukuks* market stood at US$1.9 billion in 2003 and then rose to US$6.7 billion by 2004 (ibid). Presently *Sukuks* worth more than US$13 billion constitute 85 percent of the Middle Eastern bond market.[13] Dubai Islamic Bank (DIB) is the biggest dealer in the global *Sukuk* market. So far it has issued US$9 billion of *Sukuks*, which include the largest ever issues of US$3.52 billion. The bank holds US$12 billion of *Sukuks* in the pipeline, of which over US$10 billion would be issued to companies from the USA, Asia and Europe (Razak, 2006b). The LMC and *Sukuk* Exchange Centre have emerged as the main trading centres for *Sukuks* in Bahrain. Dubai International Financial Exchange (DIFX) is the global leader in listing *Sukuks* worth up to US$4.11 billion.[14] More often than not, *Sukuk* issues in the Middle East are heavily oversubscribed, and frequently transacted by international and Western market players.

The first international US$600 million of *Sukuks* were issued by the government of Pakistan in 2005. In early 2006, Wapada *Sukuks Ijarah* worth Rs 11 billion (US$181.36 million) were issued in the Pakistani capital market. In 2007 Emirates Global Islamic Bank Limited (EGIBL) has agreed to arrange Rs 20 billion (US$329.75 million) of *Sukuk* issuance to the Pakistan Development and Management Company for undertaking infrastructure developments.[15] In early 2006, Citigroup Islamic Investment issued the Dow Jones Citigroup *Sukuk* Index, which would provide the universal benchmark for appraising the performance of *Sukuks* and also assist in developing their secondary markets worldwide. Presently the UK government is giving active consideration to amending its tax and regulatory systems to allow domestic *Sukuk* issues and further promote their international operations in the region.

There are major challenges in the Islamic capital or *Sukuk* market. There is a serious dearth of *Shariah*-compliant assets for issuing *Sukuks* of diversified types and time periods. *Sukuks* are valued on the basis of LIBOR, which is seriously un-Islamic. *Sukuk* operations need to be simplified and well-regularized across the board. The development of effective and efficient risk cover for *Sukuk* issuers against interest rate, default, foreign exchange and *Shariah*-compliance is urgently required. To ensure optimal growth and development of the Islamic capital or *Sukuk* market, there is a dire need to win increasing support and participation from Islamic retail and corporate investors and international market players (Alvi, 2006; Hobson, 2006).

3.7.2 Islamic equity investment funds market

Islamic equity investment funds are becoming increasingly popular among Islamic investors, businesses and financial institutions. The companies which are selected for Islamic investments should be consistent in earning promising returns and, most importantly, in not being directly or indirectly engaged in business affairs involving alcohol, tobacco, pork-related products, conventional financial services, gambling, cinema, pornography, music and suchlike. Furthermore, they should have overwhelmingly equity-based financial structures and no more than 5 percent of non-operating income from *Shariah*-prohibited sources. Islamic equity investment funds are managed by financial managers under *Shariah* guidance and surveillance (El-Gamal, 2002).

The first-ever Islamic equity fund – Amana Income Fund – was set up by North American Islamic Trust (NAIT) in 1986. The Islamic equity funds market started to pick up momentum in the early 1990s, and secured high growth patterns after the mid-1990s. The introduction of Dow Jones Islamic Market Index and the FTSE Global Islamic Index Series in 1999 and thereafter provided universal standards and criteria for trading in Islamic equity investment funds worldwide. In June 2000, Wall Street launched the Dow Jones^{SM} Islamic Fund (IMANX), which now comprises over 600 international companies selected from more than 60 indexes from 34 countries and covering 10 economic sectors, 18 market sectors, 40 industry groups and 70 subgroups. The IMANX offers the most competitive, diversified and Islamic ethically-compliant investment opportunities for education, new homes, retirement, etc.[16] The Dow Jones has recently launched Dow Jones-RHB Islamic Malaysia, Dow Jones Islamic Market China, Offshore Indices such as mutual funds and Exchange-Traded Funds (ETFs) composed of *Shariah*-compliant companies listed on the Hong Kong Stock Exchange, the New York Stock Exchange and Nasdaq or the American Stock Exchange. Furthermore, TAIB Islamic UK Equities Index Fund is drawn from the companies listed in UK stock exchange markets.[17]

Presently there are more than 122 Islamic equity funds[18] worldwide, managing assets of over US$5 billion with a growth rate of 12–15 per cent per annum. Particularly since 2000, they have achieved annual growth of about 25 percent (Smyth, 2006).[19] They are now very popular with Middle Eastern investors and business and finance institutions. In 2006, DIB and Dubai World launched private equity funds of US$5 billion (Razak, 2006a). Standard and Poor's (S&P) has recently introduced the GCC *Shariah* Series to attract petrodollar investments from the Gulf and across the Muslim world.[20] Deutsche Bank has meanwhile launched a number of *Shariah*-compliant mutual funds in the UAE and Bahraini markets. It has plans to offer these Islamic funds in other Middle Eastern, Asian and European markets very soon (Stapleton, 2006). Failaka International, established in 1996, has been actively engaged in collecting and analysing information and data on Islamic equity investment funds. International financial investment managers such as Brown Brothers Herriman, Citibank, Deutsche Bank, HSBC and Merrill Lynch are promoting Islamic equity investment funds in global business and finance.

3.7.3 *Takaful* or Islamic insurance market

Takaful is an Arabic term, which literally means 'joint guarantee'. *Takaful* institutions offer *Shariah*-compliant risk management tools to Islamic business and society on the basis of mutual sharing and co-operation in business enterprise. They may be established on either a non-profit-making or a profit-making basis. *Takaful* institutions based on the non-profit-making or co-operative model receive donations – *tabarru* or charity – from their policyholders or members to create a fund to help those who may suffer future losses. The majority of *Takaful* companies in Sudan are based on a co-operative model. *Takaful* institutions established with profit-making objectives are based on either *Mudarabah* or *Wakalah* or both – a mixed model. Under the *Mudarabah* model, *Takaful* institutions act as managers or *Mudarabs* of the funds of policyholders. The premiums paid by policyholders contain two parts. The first part is called *tabarru* – gift or charity – which is used to create *wakfh* – an underwriting or insurance pool to pay off indemnity claims or insured risks. The other part is invested in *Shariah*-compliant avenues. The total income derived from *Takaful* investments is shared by *Takaful* institutions and policyholders under mutually agreed ratios. In case of loss, policyholders bear all financial liabilities, while *Takaful* institutions sustain loss in that they receive no rewards for or returns on their managerial efforts and time. This model is widely practised in Malaysia, Indonesia and other Muslim countries (Kassim, 2006; Tolefat, 2006).

Under the *wakalah* model, *Takaful* institutions act as the agents of policyholders. They charge a fixed fee, known as a *wakalah* fee, to policyholders for managing *Takaful* affairs. Policyholders pay premiums that cover agency remuneration, operational costs and donations to *wakf* funds to meet indemnity claims from policyholders for the given year. Generally, policyholders enjoy an absolute right to any surplus underwriting funds. They are also liable to make further contributions if underwriting funds fall short of indemnity claims for the given year. This model is widely practised in Middle East countries. In a mixed *Takaful* model, the *Wakalah* principle covers underwriting activities and the *Mudarabah* principle allows *Takaful* institutions to undertake financing and investment activities. This model has been adopted by *Takaful* companies working in Bahrain and other Middle Eastern countries (Billah, 2006; Tolefat, 2006). *Takaful* institutions now offer a wide range of substitutes for existing family and general conventional insurance services that are prohibited by *Shariah* for involving excessive uncertainty (*gharar*), gambling (*maisir*) and interest (*riba*).

The *Takaful* industry is one of the fastest-growing segments of Islamic finance at the present time. The first *Takaful* company – Islamic Insurance Company – based on the co-operative principle, was established in Sudan in 1979. In 1985, Malaysia established Syarikat *Takaful* Malaysia Berhad under the *Mudarabah* principle. *Takaful* industry has grown steadily over time, growing as much as 20 percent per annum in recent years. Presently there are more than 250 *Takaful* companies managing premiums of US$2 billion in 2005, which are expected to grow to a value of US$7.5 billion by 2015.[21]

Takaful companies have been a great success in the Middle East. Bahrain hosts 26 *Takaful* companies and three re-*Takaful* companies. The *Takaful* industry is a well-established part of the Iranian Islamic economy and business finance. There are five *Takaful and* one re-*Takaful* companies in Jordon, and four *Takaful* and re-*Takaful* companies in the UAE. Furthermore, *Takaful* operations are making headway in Brunei, Egypt, Kuwait, Qatar, Saudi Arabia and Syria. Standard and Poor's (S&P) estimated that the Middle Eastern *Takaful* market is worth US$170 million and is expected to reach US$4 billion in the near future, while the total potential size of the GCC insurance industry is over US$20 billion.[22]

Malaysia has gradually developed a well-established organizational and regulatory infrastructure for *Takaful* institutions. It has recently announced a ten-year tax exemption (from 2007 to 2016) for the *Takaful* sector. *Takaful* assets in Malaysia have recorded a threefold increase in recent years, rising from US$517.38 million in 2001 to US$1.77 billion in 2006 (Kadir, 2006). The first *Takaful* company – *Takaful* Keluraga – was established in Indonesia in 1994. At the beginning of 2006, there were more than 30 *Takaful* and re-*Takaful* entities in Indonesia, holding a 1.5 percent share of the national insurance market.[23] In addition, Syarikat *Takaful* Company and NTUC Insurance Cooperative offer Islamic insurance services to Singaporean Muslims.

The Securities and Exchange Commission of Pakistan has been working to devise a proper regulatory framework for launching *Takaful* operations in the county. Two Islamic Insurance companies, namely *Takaful* Pakistan and First *Takaful* Insurance, have been recently granted licenses to operate in the Pakistani market. Islamic Commercial Bangladesh Insurance Company offers *Takaful* products and services in Bangladesh, while *Amana Takaful* Insurance serves Sri Lankan Muslims, who represent about 8 percent of the total population in the country.[24] Sudan is the pioneer of *Takaful* services worldwide and presently hosts six *Takaful* companies. British Islamic Insurance Holdings, Insurance Metropolitan Ghana and HSBC *Amanah Takaful* offer Islamic insurance services to over two million Muslims in the UK.

Despite promising growth and developments, it may be noted that the *Takaful* industry is passing through its infancy stage and dealing with teething problems. In this context, it urgently needs to develop its own organization and regulatory infrastructure, R&D facilities and well-qualified management. *Takaful* companies are experiencing a serious dearth of long-term Islamic investment and business opportunities. They are in a do-or-die situation to develop re-*Takaful* or reinsurance services, which would bring their liquidity and insolvency risks within normal bounds. Presently *Takaful* companies reinsure about 80 percent of their risk on a conventional basis which is neither good from a market perspective nor *Shariah*-compliant. There is also an indispensable need to educate market players and Muslim society about *Takaful* services so as to win their strong support (Macfarlane, 2006; Othman, 2006).

3.8 IBF: Worldwide growth

IBF is the fastest-growing industry on the financial world. It has been experiencing exponential growth in three regions of the world, namely, the Middle East, South Asia and Southeast Asia. In the African region, Sudan has been the torch-bearer of IBF affairs over the past three decades. IBF practice has been making headway in North America, Europe and Australia. The forthcoming discussion provides a general review of recent developments of IBF in terms of products, systems, infrastructure and markets worldwide.

3.8.1 IBF in the Middle East

The Middle East, overwhelmingly populated by Muslims, is the home of IBF. The Middle Eastern economies are highly promising, featuring a stable currency and lower interest and inflation over the years. Having gone through radical restructuring in recent times, Middle Eastern markets are now more regulated, transparent and integrated at the regional and international levels. The Middle Eastern region enjoys greater political stability, law and order, and therefore is emerging as a hot spot for international business, finance and investment. The GCC countries have great ambitions to undertake infrastructure developments, which exceeded US$360 billion in the region for the year 2006.[25] Both the Middle East and Asia have budgeted over US$1 trillion for infrastructure developments in the next five years.[26] Middle Eastern markets now offer very lucrative opportunities for international trade, business and investment. The present socio-political and economic conditions of the Middle East represent very fertile soil for the continued growth and development of IBF.

There is ever-increasing support for IFIs in the Middle East from rich individuals, state institutions, market players, governments and other community groups. Most Middle Eastern countries have allowed IFIs to work as distinct entities in the given conventional regulatory environments. IFIs in Middle Eastern markets appear to be more versatile and resourceful than ever in successfully dealing with emerging challenges and opportunities. Big IFIs are making individual and collective efforts to develop a full spectrum of innovative, customer-oriented and competitive products and services. They are tightening their grip on petrodollars, which have a history of slipping away to European and Western financial markets. There is a strong and persistent boom in Middle Eastern economies due to soaring oil prices, which doubled from 2002 to 2006; and if oil prices remain at such levels they could bring US$18 trillion or more in additional revenues over the next 5 years, and at least 60 percent of this additional income might find its way into *Shariah*-compliant banking and investments (Graham, 2006). Furthermore, a research study estimated that Islamic banks' deposits in the GCC countries will exceed US$110 billion by 2010 (Abdulmalik, 2006).

Bahrain is the biggest hub of IBF affairs worldwide. The country hosts 33 Islamic banks and 26 *Takaful* and three re-*Takaful* companies operating at the domestic and international levels.[27] The country is also a hot spot for international trading in *Sukuks*, Islamic equity funds, mutual funds and other instruments. Most of the Islamic institutions, such as AAOIFI, IIFM and IIRA, are located in Bahrain. The country has a plan to establish its own *Sukuk* Exchange Centre in the future. Iran embarked upon nationwide IBF practice after the Islamic revolution of 1979. In the first two decades, Iranian IBF practice remained highly centralized and isolated from Islamic and conventional markets. Since the mid-1990s, however, the Iranian government has been gradually deregulating and privatizing its economy and financial sector. A number of IFIs, which include Bank *Karafarin*, Bank *Eqtesdae-e Novin*, Bank *Parsian*, Bank *Saderat* and Bank *Rfah-e Kargaran*, are now working in the private sector to offer more innovative and competitive IBF products and services to their customers. The Iranian government is keen on increasing its interactions with Islamic as well as conventional financial markets worldwide.

Jordan Islamic Bank has been the pioneer of IBF in Jordon since 1978. It held 10.1 percent of the total investments of the Jordanian banking industry in 2006.[28] Another Islamic bank, International Arab Bank (established in 1997), has been a great success in the Jordanian financial sector over the years. *Takaful* services and *Sukuks* also have good future prospects in the business and finance spheres of Jordon. Kuwait hosts the largest number of IFIs, and ranks third in terms of the Islamic banking assets it holds, which are worth US$22.7 billion (Khojah, 2006). The country hosts the oldest and biggest Islamic bank – Kuwait Finance House (KFH) – which was established in 1977. In early 2006, the Kuwaiti Parliament gave approval for the establishment of three new IFIs, namely *Jaber* Islamic bank, *Jaber* Funds and *Boubyan* Bank. It is estimated that IFIs in Kuwait will manage funds of about US$56 billion by 2010. Currently five *Takaful* and one re-*Takaful* companies hold a 14 percent share of the Kuwaiti insurance market.[29] There is an increasing demand for *Sukuks* in the corporate and real estate sectors of Kuwait, and its government is working on developing proper regulatory frameworks for *Sukuk* issues and trading. IBF is passing through an embryonic stage in Lebanon. During the year 2006, four new Islamic banks have emerged, namely BLOM Development Bank, Arab Finance House, *Al-Baraka* Bank Lebanon and Credit *Libanie*. Presently Islamic banking assets in Lebanon are worth US$60 billion, with a growth rate of 10 percent per annum. The Central Bank of Lebanon expects that Islamic banking will be able to secure 5–10 percent of the total financial market of Lebanon within next 3 to 5 years (Parker, 2006). The Central Bank of Lebanon has plans to introduce *Sukuks* and *Takaful* services in its market over the next couple of years.

Qatar is another hot spot of IBF in the Middle East. There are four major Islamic banks in Qatar, namely, Qatar Islamic Bank (established in 1983), Qatar International Islamic Bank (established in 1991), Doha Islamic Bank (established in 2006) and *Al Rayan* Bank (established in 2006). Other IFIs, which include First Finance Company, Investment House, *Al Jazeera* Islamic Company and Islamic Financial Securities, mainly offer Islamic retail products and brokerage services to the Muslim clientele. Qatar Islamic Bank has decided to establish Islamic Investment Bank of Qatar with a US$1 billion capitalization at Qatar Financial Centre.[30] Presently Islamic banking practice represents a 30 percent share of the Qatari financial industry, and is expected to grow to 50 percent in the coming years (Jaidah, 2006). Qatar Islamic Insurance Company has emerged as one of the leading insurance service providers in the country. In 2003, Qatar issued *Sukuks* for the first time; presently they constitute 20–35 percent of a total project financing in the country.[31] IFIs have been playing a key role in the economic growth and development of Qatar.

IBF activities have achieved rapid growth in Saudi Arabia over recent years. There are two major IBF players in Saudi Arabia, namely, *Al Rajhi* Banking and Investment Corporation and Bank *Al Jazira*. Conventional banks are also serving the IBF clientele by establishing their own Islamic windows or subsidiaries. Islamic banking operations have now captured 64 percent of operations in the Saudi Arabian financial market (Harrison, 2006). Other IBF entities include *Al Bilad, Amlak* Finance and *Dallah Al Baraka* SAAB *Takaful* Company. In July 2006, SABIC signed the underwriting agreement for its debut *Sukuk* issuance for a total amount of SAR 3 billion (US$799.98 million), the first public issue in the Saudi market under the new Capital Market Law (Al-Humaidi, 2006). Saudi Arabia hosts IDB, which is performing a crucial role in promoting IBF in the Muslim world.

The entry of Syria into the IBF club is one of the most recent developments in the Middle East. The Syrian Parliament approved IBF laws in 2005. By the end of 2006, the Syrian government had permitted three Islamic banks, namely *Al-Sham* Bank, Saudi *Dalat Al-Baraka's Al-Baraka* Bank and Syrian International Islamic Bank, to launch their operations in the country. Moreover, three *Takaful* companies, namely, *Aqeelah* Insurance Company, *Al-Nour* Insurance Company and Syrian-Qatari Company, are ready to operate in the Syrian market after receiving their licences from the Syrian Insurance Supervision Committee. IFIs may help in integrating the Syrian financial market into the IBF mainstream in the Middle Eastern region.

The worldwide IBF practice originated in the United Arab Emirates (UAE) in 1975, when the first and biggest Islamic bank – Dubai Islamic Bank (DIB) – came into being. There are now four other fully dedicated Islamic banks in the UAE, namely, *Sharjah* Islamic Bank, Emirates Islamic Bank, Abu Dhabi Islamic Bank and Dubai Bank. Conventional banks also offer Islamic products, through either an Islamic window or an Islamic subsidiary. Islamic banking assets are now worth Dh750 billion (US$204.234 billion) and comprise 10 percent of the UAE's total banking industry; they may grow to 30 percent by 2010.[32] Major *Takaful* companies in the UAE include Abu Dhabi National *Takaful*, Dubai Islamic Insurance and Re-insurance Company (AMAN), Islamic Arabic Insurance and Re-insurance Company and Insurance Islam TAIB (IIT). Most of funding needs for the UAE's real estate sector are met by Islamic mortgage and *Sukuk* issues. DIB is the biggest dealer in the global *Sukuks* market. Demand for Islamic retail finance and private equity funds in the UAE has been increasing over time. Both DIFX and DIFC are encouraging trade in Islamic securities, equities, derivatives, funds, depositary receipts and other instruments.

The Middle Eastern IFIs are deeply involved in real estate financing worth trillions of dollars. The financial planning or wealth management sector has also emerged as the most lucrative and fast-growing area of Islamic financial markets. The private assets are estimated to be worth over US$750 billion in the Middle East. More than 300,000 rich individuals in the Middle East hold wealth of over US$1.4 trillion (Salim, 2006). According to a 2005 survey by McKinsey & Company, more than 75 percent of the top 30 global asset managers are now active in Dubai (Varley, 2006). *Takaful* services and a *Sukuks* industry have been receiving a very warm response from the Middle Eastern business sector and society. Islamic equity funds investments are also growing rapidly in the region. More than 100 GCC companies were set to issue initial public offerings (IPOs) in the year 2006. It is estimated that IFIs can target more than US$1.3 trillion of Islamic investor funds on Middle Eastern markets (Alvi, 2006). The Middle East region hosts an increasing number of regulatory and supporting bodies of the IBF world.

The majority of well-regarded and best-performing IFIs are located in the Middle East. An increasing number of conventional banks in the region are converting their operations partially or completely on Islamic lines in order to serve a wider clientele base and to sustain their existing market share. It seems more than likely that banking and finance institutions in the Middle East may experience a shift from the conventional paradigm to Islamic conventions. These IBF developments in the Middle East may have a far-reaching impact on global financial markets.

3.8.2 IBF in South Asia (Subcontinent)

The South Asian region includes three main Muslim countries – Pakistan, Bangladesh and Afghanistan – and the largest Muslim minority, of 125 million, in India. A number of IBF institutions and rich individuals from the Middle East are interested in pouring funds into infrastructure, real estate sectors and equity markets in India and Pakistan. IBF has been recently revived in Pakistan under a dual banking system. Presently there are six fully dedicated Islamic banks, which have a joint share of 2.2 percent of the total banking industry in Pakistan, with assets worth US$1.3 billion (Al-Refai, 2006). The IBF movement in Pakistan is thoroughly explored in later chapters of this book.

The first Islamic bank – Islami Bank Bangladesh – was established in 1983 in Bangladesh. The IBF system has made steady progress over the decades in the country. Presently there are seven Islamic banks, namely, *Islami* Bank Bangladesh, Oriental Bank Bangladesh, *Al-Arafah Islami* Bank, Social Investment Bank, *Shahjalal Islami* Bank, Export Import Bank of Bangladesh and Bank *Al-Falah*. In 2005, Islamic banking deposits accounted for 13 percent of total banking deposits, and Islamic investments represented 5 percent of total investments in the banking sector of Bangladesh (Rana, 2006). Some Bangladeshi Islamic banks are interested in promoting *Shariah*-compliant securitization financing in the corporate sector of Bangladesh. The government of Bangladesh needs to share the experience and resources of the international IBF industry to further promote truly innovative, competitive and *Shariah*-compliant banking operations in the country.

There are bright prospects of IBF taking root in India and Afghanistan in the future. A feasibility report on launching a full-fledged Islamic bank in India is under the consideration of Indian higher authorities. The entry of IBF institutions in India would enable Muslims there to undertake faithful banking. This would also create more diversified business and finance opportunities for Indian market players. The government of Afghanistan can also tap Islamic business investments by promoting IBF in the region. The top officials of the Afghanistan International Bank (AIB) have plans to add PLS instruments to its existing range of conventional products.

3.8.3 IBF in Southeast Asia

In the Southeast Asia, Indonesia, Malaysia and Singapore are the major contributors to IBF. The region hosts the fastest-growing economies, which are highly liberal, competitive and globally integrated. These three countries wish to use IBF as a powerful tool to attract business and investments from the Middle East and Muslim countries. They can perform an increasingly crucial role in promoting IBF in global financial markets.

Malaysia is the second biggest hub of IBF. In 1983, the Malaysian government established the first Islamic bank – Bank Islam Malaysia Berhad – and then introduced IBF in the country under a dual system by 1993. Presently there are 12 fully dedicated Islamic banks, 35 commercial banks, ten merchant banks and five development banks in Malaysia, offering IBF products and services. Existing IBF assets are worth RM117,393 million (US$32.06 million), representing 11.8 percent of total assets in the Malaysian banking sector with a growth rate over 27 percent in the last 10 years. The Malaysian government has devised a roadmap targeting a 20 percent share of the total banking industry for Islamic banking by 2010. A large number of key players from the domestic and international Islamic finance have commenced operations in Malaysia. Bank Negara issued licences to ten fully committed Islamic banks in 2006.[33] The country is the major contributor to recent developments and innovations in IBF products, systems and regulations. The Malaysian government has established separate legal, tax and regulatory frameworks for IFIs.

A *Takaful* industry began in Malaysia in 1989 and presently holds assets worth RM6.5 billion (US$1.77 billion). The country is the pioneer of Islamic capital markets and hosts the first international *Sukuk* centre. Islamic money instruments, mutual funds, unit trust funds, and managed funds are experiencing rapid growth in the Malaysian financial market. There are 886 *Shariah*-compliant Islamic securities representing 85 percent of the total Malaysian Stock market.[34] The Malaysian Islamic wealth management industry has also grown rapidly over the years. The Malaysian government staunchly believes that an efficient financial system is the key to stimulating savings, investments and economic growth in the country.

Indonesia, the most populous Muslim country in the world, embarked upon the IBF venture by establishing Bank *Muamalat* Indonesia in 1992. The bank achieved steady progress and at the present time it is one of the pioneer institutions of IBF worldwide. Two other fully dedicated Islamic banks, namely *Syariah* Mandiri and Bank *Syariah* Mega Indonesia, along with conventional banks, are offering IBF services in Indonesia. Presently IBF assets represent 1.8 percent of total Indonesian banking assets. Bank Indonesia has formulated a 10-year roadmap in which IBF operations will represent up to 6 percent of the total Indonesian banking industry by 2011 (Harisman 2006).[35] The *Takaful* industry has experienced inflated growth over recent years in the Indonesian insurance market. The Indonesia Stock Exchange offers 242 *Shariah*-compliant stocks and the Jakarta Islamic Index of 30 Islamic securities to Muslims and other investors. Jakarta Stock Exchange has experienced high growth in *Sukuks* trading over recent years. Indonesia has been working on improving the IBF regulatory framework, *Shariah* faculties and staff qualifications. This would ensure the worldwide competitiveness and exposure of the Indonesian IBF industry.

Singapore has been actively involved in promoting IBF operations in Southeast Asia since 2001. The country aims to become an international trading centre in Islamic property funds, hedge funds, *Sukuk*s and wealth management. Maybank Singapore and OCBC Bank are offering IBF products to Singaporean Muslims. Kuwait Finance House (KFH) and DBS Bank, CIMB's Singapore are also interested in offering IBF products to Singaporean Muslims. The *Takaful* industry in Singapore holds assets of worth more than US$500 million. HSBC Insurance and NTUC Income provide Islamic insurance services in Singapore. DBS Bank first introduced Singaporean *Ijarah Sukuk* worth US$38 million in 2001, and has since been working on developing *Sukuks* for *wakaf* assets and property management. The Singapore Stock Exchange has listed *Shariah*-compliant indexes, namely, Lion 30 and FTSE-SGX Asia *Shariah* 100 Index. The Monetary Authority of Singapore is committed to introducing changes to its tax and regulatory systems to facilitate the proper growth and development of IBF in the country (Venardos, 2006).

3.8.4 IBF in Africa: Sudan

The first Islamic bank in Africa – Faisal Islamic Bank Sudan – was established in Sudan in 1977 under the patronage of Saudi Prince Muhammad Bin Faisal Al Saud. In 1983, Tadamon Islamic Bank Sudan, Sudanese Islamic Bank and Islamic Co-operative Bank also came into being. The government of Sudan passed the Islamic *Shariah* Banking Act in 1984, which required the whole banking and finance sector of Sudan to be transformed on Islamic lines by 1 July 1984. However, prolonged political and economic turmoil in the country prevented IBF from growing and prospering. Since January 2005, IBF practice has been revived in Sudan under a dual banking system. There are four Islamic banks in northern Sudan, namely, Omdurman National Bank, Faisal Islamic Bank, Bank of Khartoum and an agricultural bank (Mudawi, 2005).[36] Sudan is known as a pioneer in *Takaful* products and services in the Islamic business and finance world. The country hosts six *Takaful* companies at the present time. It is to be hoped that the economy and political system of Sudan will become stable with the passage of time so as to allow the healthy growth and development of IBF in the region.

3.8.5 IBF in European and Western countries

IBF activities have been gradually gaining ground in Europe, North America and other Western countries. The United Kingdom (UK)'s Financial Services Authority (FSA) aims to develop London as a centre of Islamic finance and investment from the Middle East and other Muslim countries. The FSA removed double stamp duty provision on Islamic mortgage contracts from November 2006. Necessary changes to UK tax laws were introduced through the Finance Acts of 2003, 2005 and 2006, which removed hurdles in practising *Murabahah* and *Ijarah* mortgages, and diminishing *Musharakah*. The UK Treasury and the FSA have further regulatory and tax changes in the pipeline which would allow the issue of *Sukuks* in the UK's domestic market (Amin, M, 2007; Croft, 2007). Presently, Islamic Bank of Britain (established in 2004), European Islamic Investment Bank (established in 2006), Friends Provident International, HSBC *Amanah*, Lloyds TSB, Mortgage Insurance UK and United National Bank are offering a wide range of Islamic finance and insurance products and services such as fund management, retail and commercial property investment, consumer finance, saving products, credit cards and *Takaful* services to Muslims in the UK. There are over 2 million Muslims in the UK. The UK could act as a gateway to promoting IBF in other European countries.

IBF is gaining momentum in America and Canada, where the Muslim population is estimated to be 10 million. Presently IFB activities amount to US$1.5 billion and US$86.1 million in the USA and Canada respectively (Ranzini, 2007). An increasing number of Islamic and conventional institutions, including American Finance House LARIBA, University Bank of Michigan–University Islamic Financial, Devon Bank, Guidance Financial Group, Saturan Capital's *Aamaa* Mutual Fund Group, *Shariah* Capital and Anchor Finance Group have been offering *Shariah*-compliant products and services such as deposits, home finance and mutual funds project financing, real estate financing, venture capital, Islamic equity, hedge funds, *Sukuks*, and syndication to Muslims in the USA. Furthermore, IBF activities have recently emerged in Canada. United Muslims Financial Ontario now offers Islamic mortgage services to Canadian Muslims. It may offer other Islamic instruments in coming years.

The Muslim Community Co-operative Australia (MCCA) has been offering Islamic saving and investment opportunities in Australia since

1989. MCCA currently manages assets worth AUS$28.536 million (US$ 23.09 million) and it has over 8,000 members. It is actively involved in Islamic finance activities in the property and real estate sector. On average, MCCA annually transacts home mortgage contracts worth AUS$100 million (Sharif, 2006). Another conventional-based financial institution – APV Sydney Finance – also provides Islamic finance services to Australian Muslims. National Australia Bank is developing its own systems to introduce IBF products in Australia. Moreover, Oasis Group Holdings and AmInvestment Group are interested in offering IBF services in Australia

3.9 IBF: Challenges and prospects

The IBF industry is highly nascent in comparison with the conventional banking industry. It is striving to develop its own institutional, operational, regulatory infrastructures and Islamic-friendly socio-economic environments in which to grow and prosper. It has been facing a range of challenges and problems.

First and the foremost, IFIs are haunted by the chronic problem of excess liquidity. On average, IFIs carry 40 percent more liquidity than their conventional counterparts, because of a serious dearth of long-term *Shariah*-compliant investment tools and avenues (Hakim, 2002). Islamic banks commit 95 percent of their funds to short-term *Ijarah, Murabaha* and *Musharakah* instruments.[37] There are also *Shariah* requirements that further complicate the liquidity issue. IFIs cannot invest their funds in the conventional inter-bank market and other short-term instruments. They cannot accept interest accrued on the deposits they have in central banks under statutory requirements. The Islamic money market and capital market are highly nascent and do not offer a full spectrum of instruments to resolve the liquidity problem. In 2002, four major Islamic banks established LMC, which has been engaged in developing a secondary liquid market for Islamic bonds, government securities, equities, mutual funds and other instruments. Other institutions such as Bank of Malaysia, Islamic Chamber of Commerce and Industry (ICCI), IIFM, and DIFC have been working to develop liquidity risk management tools and structures for IFIs. Yet these ongoing efforts have so far proved insufficient to develop more effective and efficient solutions to liquidity issues at IFIs (Khan, M M and Bhatti, 2008a).

There is a serious shortage of competent *Shariah* experts in the IBF industry. It is a matter of serious concern that the small group of *Shariah* experts is serving on several *Shariah* boards of IFIs worldwide. These experts earn as much as US$88,500 per year per bank.[38] In some cases, they charge up to US$500,000 for advice on large capital market transactions (Tett, 2006). Most certainly, IFIs should establish the rule that a *Shariah* scholar can serve only one board or be an advisor to only one financial institution, as in Malaysia. Furthermore, *Shariah* scholars at small IFIs have little insight into the complexities of present-day financial markets. They always follow liberal interpretations of *Shariah* in complex financial matters. It is a really major challenge to establish the universal standardization of IBF terminologies and legal documents. This would remove much ambiguity about IBF from the minds of market players and the general public. IFIs should establish a Central *Shariah* Board and an external audit committee to secure a truly independent scrutiny of the Islamicity of their operations. They should also build a strong base of research and training to develop *Shariah* experts of high moral and professional integrity.

There is scope for improving the qualitative and quantitative aspects of accounting information and financial reporting in the IBF industry. IFIs follow many and varied accounting standards and practices. Some of them follow International Accounting Standards (IAS), others adhere to AAOIFI standards, and then small ones adopt the accounting standards prevalent in their local markets. Indeed, even financial mangers and researchers can be highly confused over the heterogeneity in accounting practices and disclosures at IFIs. In fact, accounting systems at IFIs should simply provide relevant and reliable information to stakeholders about their responsibilities in the financial, social, environmental and religious arenas (Sultan, 2006). It may be noted that AAOIFI and IFSB have been working over the years to develop universal accounting and auditing practices for IFIs. AAOIFI has developed more than 63 accounting standards for the guidance of and adoption by 130 member institutions, representing 30 countries of the globe.[39]

IFIs have a very unsatisfactory record in R&D and innovation. Some bottlenecks are holding them back from making much needed progress in R&D. The data and information on IFIs are neither easily available nor reliable. *Shariah* experts and financial experts lack a genuine aptitude for R&D, and there is not the desired level of mutual understanding and co-operation among their ranks. The majority of IFIs are small and cannot afford to develop their own or joint R&D facilities. Only big IFIs are engaged in some kind of serious R&D activity. Indeed, IFIs have been suffered huge losses due to their mediocre performance in R&D. There has been huge flight of indigenous oil wealth from the Gulf countries to Western financial markets. Sheikha Lubna Al Qasimi, Minister of Economy in UAE, pointed out that at present about 80 percent of the US$1.8 trillion of private wealth of the Gulf countries is invested abroad because there are insufficient Islamic-friendly investment opportunities in the region.[40] The IBF industry has made some progress in R&D and innovation over recent years, but it should take very, very seriously the challenge to come up with a full array of genuinely distinctive, innovative and competitive products.

IFIs have poor records in R&D as a matter of course, and so they rely heavily on conventional banking tools and systems to carry out their day-to-day operations. Haron and Ahmad (2000) have produced empirical evidence that IFIs use conventional profitability theories in determining the returns on their products. Kaleem and Isa (2003) have also empirically proved that IFIs take interest rates into account in adjusting returns on their deposits. It is no secret that IFIs always use the London Inter-bank Offered Rate (LIBOR), market interest rates, discounting tables and time value of money techniques to fix PLS ratios and returns on their *Murabaha* and other investments (Homoud, 1994; El-Ashker, 1995; El-Diwany, 2006). Moreover, *Sukuks* are always issued on the basis of LIBOR. For example, five-year *Al-Musharakaare Sukuks* issued by Investment Dar *Sukuk* Company in October 2005 and listed on the Bahrain Stock Exchange (BSE) bear the coupon rate of six-month LIBOR plus 2 percent per annum. The yield on Qatar Global *Sukuks* is calculated on the basis of LIBOR on dollar funds plus 0.4 percent per annum. Truly speaking, IBF practice has nothing as such to differentiate itself from conventional banking practice. One of the pioneers of IBF, Qureshi (2005), has described the whole IBF affair in the following words: 'Islamic banking, as it stands today, is with all due respect and humility, a labelling industry. Everything that is conventional is being labelled and you say it is Islamic.' In the given context it is easy to understand why the great majority of Muslims and market players have grave misgivings and doubts about the originality of IBF practice. There is a pressure on IFIs from their stakeholders to develop genuinely Islamic and innovative products and to stop copying conventional practice. Amongst others, Saleh Kamil, the president of Dallah Al Baraka Group Kuwait, reiterates, 'the strategy needs to discard imitation of Western banking tools and resort to developing initiatives based on original products that have an Islamic basis.'[41]

Another crucial challenge for IFIs is to improve their risk management strategies and corporate governance so as to successfully operate in the contemporary sophisticated, competitive and democratic business and finance environments. IFIs are exceedingly exposed to all sorts of risks in the market. They determine the prices of their products on the basis of LIBOR, which leaves them largely exposed to interest rate risk. They also bear high risks of non-payment or non-recovery on their contracts based on *Ijarah*, *Istisna*, *Murabaha* and PLS because they cannot claim or recover any penal interest or charges from defaulting customers due to *Shariah* bindings. *Sukuk* issues entail risks arising from interest rates, foreign exchange, credit and *Shariah*-compliance (Sundararajan and Errico, 2002; Hobson, 2006). IFIs also bear high risks of liquidity and mismatch of assets and liabilities due to a lack of medium and long-term investment tools. The majority of IFIs operate in developing markets where risk-management tools and systems are far from satisfactory. IBF cannot use conventional risk-management techniques and tools because these are based on interest, gambling and speculation, which are prohibited by *Shariah*. In the given context, good governance can greatly help to streamline the organizational structure of IBF on a more efficient and democratic basis. It can strengthen interactions between Islamic financial and *Shariah* experts for undertaking the R&D and innovation that is much needed at present (Archer, 2006; Claessens, 2006). Bank Negara Malaysia, IIRA, IFSB[42] and other supporting bodies have been pushing very hard for the development of prudential regulations and systems related to risk management, capital adequacy and corporate governance at IFIs.[43]

The IBF industry's legal and regulatory frameworks, systems, products, and terminologies are still very complex and unstandardized. The majority of IFIs are small in size and operate under the strong influence of domestic markets. They follow their own theory and practice, as warranted by indigenous market forces and conditions. The lack of standardization and harmonization in the IBF industry is the biggest obstacle to its growth and development worldwide. IFSB and other major players have been working hard to develop uniform regulations and systems for the IBF industry.

It is a good omen to see the increasing involvement of international rating agencies in providing information, assessment and opinions on the creditworthiness and overall risk profiles of IFIs and Islamic financial market instruments such as *Sukuks*. International rating agencies are playing a very crucial role in improving the credibility, transparency, and disclosures in the IBF industry (Obaidullah, 2005). More importantly, Islamic rating agencies such as Rating Agency Malaysia and IIRA are finding a growing scope for their operations in Islamic financial market. The Islamic rating agencies provide better and more comprehensive assessment of the financial competence and *Shariah*-compliance of client institutions. The prevailing culture of rating needs to be further encouraged to drive the IBF industry towards greater financial and *Shariah* discipline, sophistication and integration with international financial markets.

The majority of IFIs are operating in the fold of conventional environments. They are receiving due support from conventional banking and regulatory systems. For example, governments and monetary authorities in Bangladesh, Indonesia, Malaysia, the Middle East, Pakistan and Western countries such as the UK and Australia have become more receptive to changing their legal and tax systems so as to provide a level playing field for IFIs. Bahrain and Malaysia have excelled in establishing entirely independent nationwide legal, regulatory and financial frameworks for IBF operations, and other Muslim countries may follow suit. A number of supporting bodies, which include Dubai Financial Services Authority, IFSB and Malaysia's Securities, have been working with conventional banking authorities to sort out regulatory issues related to Islamic finance practice. There is a need for enhanced support and co-operation from regulators and market players in evolving a universal theory and practice of IBF.

Ironically, there is an acute shortage of human capital resources in the Islamic financial industry. The IBF leadership and financial managers have been drawn from the conventional banking world. They are neither properly trained nor devoted to learning and practising *Shariah*-compliant banking. They are interested in eliminating interest (*riba*) from IBF operations without realizing the real objective behind this exercise. On the other hand, *Shariah* scholars are also not capable of learning about and acquiring deeper insight into the modern financial world. Both *Shariah* and financial experts want to live in theirs comfort zones, which poses a serious threat to the IBF industry's growth and success (Usmani, 1996; Warde, 2000). Some major training institutions such as IRTI, Institute of Islamic Banking and Insurance, INCEIF and Islamic Finance Training organize numerous training sessions, conferences, colloquiums and workshops every year, but for all their efforts they are not taking up the real challenge of streamlining and developing IBF personnel with financial-cum-*Shariah* competence. It is high time for the IBF industry to make big investments in human resources development and training and research facilities. Internally groomed human resources and leadership can only add real value and solutions to the current issues and challenges facing IBF.

3.10 Summary and conclusions

IBF refers to *Shariah*-compliant tools and mechanisms to replace the interest-based financial intermediation with a risk-sharing paradigm. It primarily relies on equity modes to conduct business and finance operations. This ensures the most efficient, ethical and equitable use of economic resources in society. The IBF system uses PLS modes, namely *Mudarabah* and *Musharakah* as major, and *Murabaha, Ijarah, Bai Salam, Bai Istisna* as secondary, instruments to perform lending, borrowing and investment functions.

IBF emerged from Middle Eastern horizons after the mid-1970s and has flourished since then in Muslim countries, including Iran, Pakistan and Sudan, which made attempts in 1980s to adopt it economy-wide. Over recent years, it has made breakthrough developments and advances in 70 countries in Africa, Asia, Europe and North America. Not surprisingly, it has found fertile soil in the Middle East, Southeast Asia and South Asia. Among others, *Takaful, Sukuks* and Islamic equity funds and wealth management are the fastest-growing segments of Islamic finance. Factors such as spiralling oil prices worldwide, the prolonged boom in the Middle Eastern economies, product innovation and sophistication, an increasingly receptive attitude on the part of conventional regulators and advances in information technology have been acting as a catalyst allowing the IBF industry to go global. Increasing numbers of Western financial institutions are warmly embracing IBF to add innovation and diversity to their operations and to attract oil wealth and the Muslim clientele worldwide. Given all these growth patterns, IBF may be able to win over a majority of the 1.3 billion Muslims and other ethical groups across the global community in coming years.

Being a highly nascent industry as compared with its conventional counterpart, IBF has been facing a number of challenges in the contemporary financial world. Indeed, IFIs need to improve their liquidity, corporate governance and risk management techniques. There is an urgent need for IFIs to develop domestically compatible and internationally competitive Islamic accounting standards and practice. Additionally, they need to build up their *Shariah* departments and regulatory frameworks under common and universal principles. There are growing concerns in all Islamic quarters that IFIs should take R&D seriously so as to develop a wide spectrum of truly efficient and *Shariah*-compliant products. There is a desperate need for it to act on the growing crisis in human resource management. IFIs face the painfully serious challenge of proving that they are not only financially successful but also truly *Shariah*-compliant and value-based entities. Perhaps IFIs can succeed in international business and finance only if they adopt genuinely rigorous and professional ways to resolve the underlying challenges.

4
Conceptual Developments in Islamic Banking and Finance in Pakistan (1977–1980)

4.1 Introduction

The IBF movement had gathered significant momentum in the Muslim world by the late 1970s. An increasing number of Islamic banks had emerged in the private sectors of Muslim countries. However, no Muslim country had taken an initiative to establish its national economy and finance sector on Islamic lines. A major breakthrough in this regard occurred in September 1977 when the president of Pakistan General Mohammed, Ziaul Haq, expressed an interest in transforming the economy of Pakistan on Islamic lines. He directed the Council of Islamic Ideology (CII) to formulate a blueprint for an interest-free economy within 3 years.

The CII[1] is an expert body that assists the government over *Shariah* matters. The CII was created in 1957 under Articles 197 and 198 of the 1956 Constitution of Pakistan. It was established as a research-based Islamic institution to provide guidance to the government on transforming the personal and social institutions of the country so that they were in full conformity with Islamic precepts. Its status was also recognized in the 1962 and 1973 Constitutions of Pakistan. Article 230 of the 1973 Constitution of Pakistan fully explains the role and responsibilities of the CII. It is mandatory for the government to consider the recommendations of the CII in all matters pertaining to the law and practice of the country. It is the constitutional responsibility of the CII to safeguard the Islamic character of the polity of Pakistan.

The issue of interest-based transactions in the economy of Pakistan was first referred to the CII for advice in March 1963. The government requested the CII to give its expert view as to whether interest-based government borrowings fell under the definition of *riba* given in the holy

Quran. In January 1969, after examining the issue, the CII advised the government that its borrowings constituted *riba*, and therefore efforts in the direction of establishing an economy free of interest should not be unduly delayed.[2] The CII made further investigations into the matter, and in December 1969 it passed a resolution stating that interest was prohibited in all its forms under Islamic law and that the government should constitute a committee comprising economists, legal experts and Islamic jurists to assist the CII in reforming the prevailing interest-based economic and finance system in light of Islamic principles.[3]

The CII, comprising 12 members (see Appendix I-A), took some time to devise its strategy for preparing a blueprint of the interest-free economy. In November 1977 it appointed a panel of 15 economists, bankers and financial experts (see Appendix I-B) to examine the technical aspects of restructuring the existing economy and finance sector on Islamic lines. The panel took into account the existing theory and practice of IBF. In February 1980 the panel submitted its findings to the CII in a report form. The CII thoroughly examined the report and made some necessary changes to bring it into full conformity with *Shariah*. Afterwards the CII submitted the report to the government, titled, 'The Report on the Elimination of Interest from the Economy 1980'. In the forthcoming discussion this report is referred to as 'the 1980 CII Report'.

It should be noted that most members who were engaged in the preparation of the 1980 CII Report were experts in modern economics and finance. Others were knowledgeable in *Shariah*. This combination of two streams of expertise could be expected to produce a balanced set of recommendations from the CII. Moreover, the support and involvement of the head of the state provided much-needed political and economic support for this Islamic project. The CII had the opportunity to objectively explore the broader perspectives of Islamic financial ideology so as to explore its scope for application in the Muslim world and other societies inspired by it (The 1980 CII Report, p. xiv). The CII recognized its report as the first serious document for giving direction and shape to the efforts to establish an interest-free economic and financial system in the Muslim state (The 1980 CII Report, p. xiv). Thus, the primary aim of the CII was to lay a sound foundation for the development of IBF practice in Pakistan. Any study of the Islamic economic and finance system in Pakistan or indeed anywhere in the world would be incomplete if it did not contain a detailed analysis of the 1980 CII Report.

This chapter deals with the essential features, theoretical underpinnings and core recommendations of the 1980 CII Report in four inter-linked sections. The first section describes and evaluates theoretical and practical aspects of the policy instruments recommended by the CII for banishing interest from the financial system of Pakistan. The second section discusses the CII's strategies for performing commercial banking operations on the basis of its approved Islamic policy instruments. The third section deals with the guidelines provided by the CII for establishing an interest-free monetary and central banking system. The fourth section identifies some areas of the 1980 CII Report where there was scope for improvement and further research.

4.2 Policy instruments for eliminating interest

The CII explained the prohibition of interest in the light of the holy *Quran*. It argued that interest is prohibited in *Shariah* because of its exploitative nature (The 1980 CII Report, p. 5). Charging interest on commercial and consumption loans is the root cause of many socio-economic evils, and therefore such practice should be banished from the economy and financial sector of Pakistan. It recommended a number of primary and secondary Islamic policy instruments for eliminating interest. It classified an instrument as primary if it could eliminate interest and also contribute towards achieving an exploitation-free socio-economic order in the human polity. It categorized an instrument as secondary if it could help in eliminating interest but could not contribute anything towards achieving the real objectives of practising an Islamic economic system.

Figure 4.1 shows the policy instruments that the CII considered as suitable Islamic alternatives to conventional financing arrangements. The CII studied the basic characteristics of these instruments and divided them into three groups with respect to their suitability and scope for developing the IBF model. It approved profit and loss-sharing (PLS) instruments as a primary alternative to interest. In addition, it approved leasing, investment auctioning, *Bai Muajjal* (*Murabaha* or deferred payment sale), hire purchase, normal rate of return, time multiple counter-loans and special loan facilities as secondary alternatives to interest. However, it rejected the service charge and indexation systems, judging them to be unsuitable alternatives to interest (The 1980 CII Report, Chapter 1).

4.2.1 Primary and ideal instrument: The PLS system

Under the PLS system, instead of charging a fixed rate of interest on its lending, the bank enters into an equity-sharing relationship with the client and shares in the risk and return of a joint venture. Similarly,

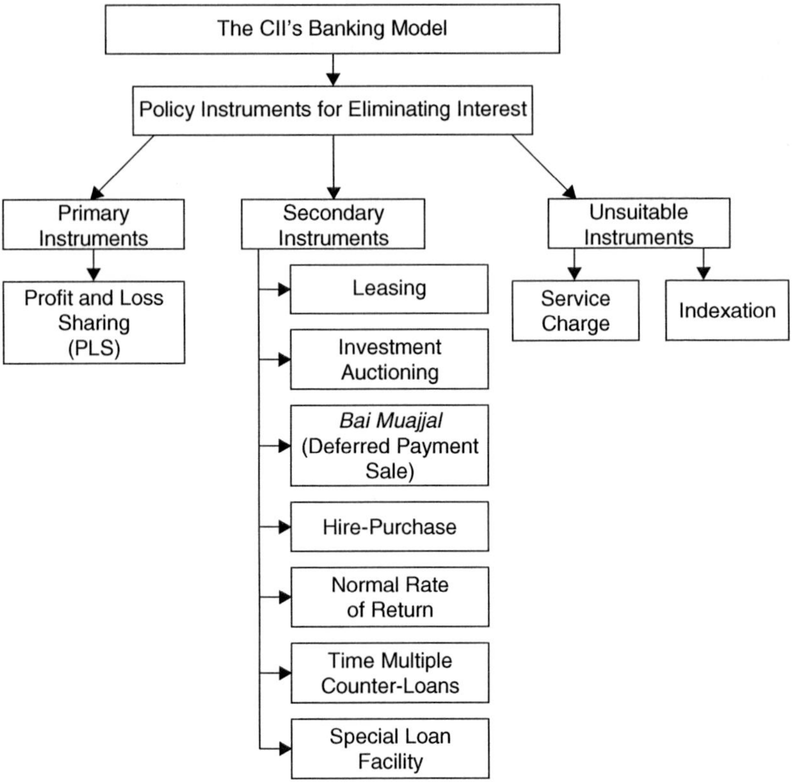

Figure 4.1 The CII's IBF model: main policy instruments
Source: Figure derived from the discussion on the 1980 CII Report.

instead of giving a fixed rate of interest to the depositor, the bank shares the profit or loss made on its investment with him. The rate of return in the PLS system is based on the actual productivity of capital. The PLS system stimulates demand for venture capital, innovation and investment. It ensures the fair and efficient utilization of economic resources to achieve the goal of broad-based economic development and growth with distributive justice. Thus, the PLS system is a central pillar of the IBF system by virtue of its ideal compatibility with the socio-economic objectives of Islam (see Chapter 3).

The CII argued that the PLS system could be the best alternative to an interest-based banking system. However, it maintained that the PLS system could not produce any desirable effects because if banks broadly practised it their cost of monitoring would be very high in view of the widespread prevalence of unethical practices among the tax-collecting machinery and business people of Pakistan (The 1980 CII Report, p. 9). It further stated that the likelihood of collusion between bank staff and clients should not be ruled out. It suggested that greater reliance on the PLS system may not benefit the economy of Pakistan. Therefore, in cases where the use of PLS system was not feasible or practicable, some secondary interest-free arrangements may be used for the time being. Meanwhile, the government should take serious steps to develop proper legal and institutional frameworks and a favourable socio-economic infrastructure in Pakistan for the adoption of the PLS system as a key alternative to interest-based banking in a long run (The 1980 CII Report, p. 10).

As explained in Chapter 3, the adoption of PLS banking could not succeed unless a supportive infrastructure is laid down and the moral standards of the Muslim polity are brought up to the *Shariah* mark. The CII may be justified in holding back the leading role for the PLS system at the very outset of its whole scheme. However, it did not devise a detailed roadmap to evolve PLS-friendly moral and socio-economic frameworks for eventually ensuring the productive and predominant use of the PLS system in the financial sector of Pakistan. The actual practice of IBF in Pakistan evolved on the basis of secondary interest-free instruments, with only a very meagre role for PLS instruments.

4.2.2 Secondary instruments: Interest-free modes

The CII recommended some secondary interest-free policy instruments as a temporary arrangement to deal with the problem of interest. The CII claimed that it secured necessary modifications in these policy instruments to rule out the possibility of any built-in element of interest in them, but their unrestricted use could open the back door to interest. Therefore, the application of these instruments should be restricted to exceptional cases where the use of the PLS system is not applicable or feasible (The 1980 CII Report, p. 5). These secondary interest-free policy instruments are described and evaluated in the discussion below.

4.2.2.1 Leasing

Under the leasing system, the owner retains ownership of an asset but allows its possession and usufruct to the lessee in return for rental payments made over the leasing contract period. The CII proposed two types of leasing system, namely finance leasing and operating leasing. The finance leasing system can be used to meet the long-term financing needs of the industrial sector. In this system, the lessor provides fixed assets, such as plant and machinery, for the use of the lessee over the period.

The operating leasing system may be used for meeting the short- and medium-term financing needs of business enterprises. In this system, the lessor provides business equipment, such as computers, motor cars, photocopiers and other similar items, to the lessee for the agreed period. The CII made it a condition of operating leasing that the lessor should bear the cost of insurance of the asset (The 1980 CII Report, p. 13).

The leasing system may be recognized as a viable alternative to interest provided certain vital preconditions of *Shariah* are met (see Chapter 3). First, the lessor should not enter into a contract of sale of the leased asset with the lessee before the expiry of the lease contract (see Chapter 8). Second, since the conventional insurance system involves interest, gambling and speculation, Islamic insurance institutions should be developed so as to comply with the requirement of insurance within *Shariah* bounds. Finally, leasing is a hybrid of equity and debt financing. In order to allow the leasing system to demonstrate its equity-based characteristics, lending and investment operations in Islamic economy should be largely based on risk-sharing mechanisms, and not on secondary instruments that almost yield fixed and risk-free rates of return on investment, since in this case the lease could become a debt contract, and the lease instalments could become as fixed as interest payments. In simple terms, the *Shariah*-based and efficient use of the leasing system is conditional upon the emergence of an economy and financial system based on the PLS principle. However, this was not the case with IBF practice in Pakistan. Indeed, lease financing appeared similar to conventional activity in IBF practice in Pakistan.

4.2.2.2 Investment auctioning

The system of investment auctioning is a form of credit sale for meeting the long-term financial needs of the corporate sector. According to the CII, under this method commercial banks form a consortium with other financial institutions to formulate detailed industrial projects. The consortium invites bids for the project, with a firm promise that the specified plant and machinery of the project will be provided at the time of its implementation. The consortium fixes a minimum price for the project, and accepts any bid exceeding the reserved price (The 1980 CII Report, p. 14). The successful bidder provides the plant and machinery to implement the project without any unnecessary delay. He pays the bid price in a number of instalments over the agreed period. He solely bears the profit or loss arising from the project. The CII proposed that long-term interest-based financing in the industrial sector could be replaced by financing through investment auctioning (The 1980 CII Report, p. 14).

Investment auctioning involves the sale of a project on a credit basis. Therefore, the consortium should invite bids for the project after obtaining the possession and ownership of its plant and machinery. Otherwise, this activity may become a speculative transaction or sale of the loan for a higher loan, that is, *riba* (see Chapter 2).[4] The CII claimed that the use of investment auctioning would significantly enhance the overall efficiency of the new financial system (The 1980 CII Report, p. 14). However, this might not be the case because the relationship between the consortium and the bidder would not be based on the principle of risk-sharing, which is the key prerequisite for ensuring fair and efficient use of resources in the Islamic economy. As under the conventional financing system, the bidder would be responsible only for bearing all losses and risks under the investment auctioning system (see Chapter 4). Some Western economists argue that bidding is a costly exercise for the winner, the loser, and the society as a whole (McAfee and McMillan, 1987). The developing market of Pakistan may not be able to make efficient use of the investment auctioning tool because of the high cost of its operations.

The investment auctioning system has an inherited tendency to allow a handful of business elites to emerge as big winners in most bidding cases (Laffont and Tirole 1993). This loophole of the system could be exploited by a small group of business people and industrialists in Pakistan who already have strong hold over bank credit (see Chapter 9). Furthermore, in view of low moral standards of the polity of Pakistan, there is a likelihood that the consortium may provide inside information about the projects to influential bidders, so undermining just and efficient use of the investment auctioning system. Given these factors and the market environments of Pakistan, investment auctioning cannot become an appropriate and efficient alternative to interest. Rather, in its real essence, it is like mark-up financing with added non-Islamic features of speculation, uncertainty and a tendency to be abused. Due to its complex nature and the cost involved, investment auctioning has remained only a theoretical option in actual IBF practice in Pakistan.

4.2.2.3 Bai Muajjal (Murabaha *or deferred payment sale)*

By nature and origin, the *Bai Muajjal* system is trade-based. The application of the *Bai Muajjal* system in IBF theory involves the sale of an item by the bank to the client on a deferred payment basis, payable either in a lump sum or by instalments. The CII stated that the *Bai Muajjal* system might be applied to financing the current input requirements of industry and agriculture as well as the domestic and import trade. According to the CII, under the *Bai Muajjal* system the bank could satisfy the *Shariah* requirement of obtaining possession of the item before its resale by authorizing the client to obtain that item from the supplier on the bank's behalf. Thus, *Bai Muajjal* is a quite simple financing mechanism that may yield almost a risk-free fixed rate of return on the bank's investment. However, the CII warned that this method bears an inherited tendency to degenerate into interest, and therefore it should be used for a temporary period and only in those rare cases where the PLS system cannot be used due to practical difficulties (The 1980 CII Report, p. 15).

Shariah recognizes the value of time only through pricing of goods. Therefore, the Islamic bank can charge a higher price for goods in the case of deferred payment. The trade-based origin of the *Bai Muajjal* system differentiates it from interest-based dealings. However, the trade-based nature of the system can be easily eliminated if the financier performs the trade-related functions on paper only. This misuse of the *Bai Muajjal* system could turn it into an interest-based activity (see Chapters 3 and 5). As explained in Chapter 3, the actual practice of *Bai Muajjal* in the IBF industry has largely failed to preserve its trade-based nature, and therefore remains highly controversial. Among others Islamic economists and *Shariah* scholars, M N Siddiqi (1983) warned that the CII's approval of the *Bai Muajjal* system could sabotage the whole process of financial Islamization in Pakistan.[5] The CII should have removed *Bai Muajjal* from its approved list of interest-free policy instruments in order to launch IBF practice in Pakistan on the right footing. Indeed, financial institutions in Pakistan found *Bai Muajjal* a perfect cover for continuing with their interest-based activities as usual.

4.2.2.4 Hire purchase

Under the hire-purchase system, the bank may provide the client with economic assets, such as machinery, equipment and consumer durable goods. The bank and the client become the joint owners of the asset. In order to acquire absolute ownership of the asset, the client pays the agreed number of instalments to the bank, which include repayment of the bank's principal and a share in the net rental value (after allowing for depreciation) of the asset in proportion to the bank's outstanding share of the investment. The bank and the client are jointly liable for the cost of the asset's repair and maintenance (The 1980 CII Report, p. 16).

The hire-purchase system has better prospects than the *Bai Muajjal* system of being an alternative to interest because it requires the bank to actually participate in mainstream economic activities and, therefore, to take risks. It could efficiently meet all the financing needs that could be satisfied under the *Bai Muajjal* system. Therefore, the CII should have relied on the hire-purchase system and dropped the *Bai Muajjal* system altogether. However, the CII did not do what was very much needed, and so the future of hire-purchase in IBF practice in Pakistan looked bleak. When *Bai Muajjal* was already on the cards, financial institutions in Pakistan grossly ignored hire-purchase in order to avoid the high risks and administrative costs involved in its practice (see Chapter 5).

4.2.2.5 Financing on the basis of normal rate of return

Under the normal rate of return system, the bank finances a business enterprise on PLS principles. However, the entrepreneur provides a guarantee that a minimum rate of return, known as normal rate of return, will be paid on the bank's investment. If the actual rate of profit on investment is higher than the agreed normal rate of return, the entrepreneur voluntarily pays the excess amount of profit to the bank. On the other hand, if the realized rate of profit is lower, or if there is a loss, the entrepreneur needs to provide solid proof to this effect to the bank. If the bank is fully satisfied with the given evidence, it accepts a lower rate of profit from the client. A specialized public agency would be constituted to determine the normal rate of return for different business sectors of the economy on the basis of their profitability data and other micro and macro economic factors (The 1980 CII Report, p. 16). The CII contended that this system could function as a risk-sharing instrument for financing small business enterprises and industries that do not maintain proper accounting records. The CII argued that the provision of minimum fixed rates of return is added to save the bank the time and money that would have been spent on monitoring and appraising the performance of business enterprises financed under this system. Conversely, if this provision were removed from the system, the bank's cost of monitoring would greatly increase, rendering financing under this system very expensive and untenable (The 1980 CII Report, p. 16).

In the given context, it appears that the proposed system could be used as a surrogate PLS system or interest-free system that may guarantee an almost fixed and risk-free rate of return on investment for the bank. The CII argued that institutional constraints and business ethics would limit the real scope and success of any system based on the risk-sharing mechanism (The 1980 CII Report, p. 5). Indeed, if entrepreneurs or borrowers under normal rate of return arrangements were not required to maintain systematic accounting records of their business operations, it would hardly be possible for banks to investigate cases of lower returns or losses. In actual practice, it may become a general rule that, if the realized profit on investment were greater than the agreed normal rate of return, the entrepreneur would not surrender it to the bank. On the other hand, if the actual profit turns out lower than the agreed normal rate of return, the bank would not accept it as a true outcome, and ask for the predetermined rate of return. Most certainly, the risk-sharing characteristics of this system would be defeated by their interest-like characteristics in practice.

As observed by the CII, a large number of business people in Pakistan are engaged in deflating profits or even showing losses to avoid tax payments (The 1980 CII Report, p. 5). It implies that the rate of return determined by an independent agency could not reflect a fair pricing mechanism for capital in a given industry as well as the market. Furthermore, the Pakistani economy and financial market have a track record of increasing inflationary pressures, higher volatility and uncertainty (Aleem, 1985, Hussain, 2007). The historical data on the market could be static and unreliable, and therefore provide little help in determining the rate of return on investment and in making informed decisions and economic policies. Apart from given market realities, the provision of a minimum rate of return also grossly conflicts with *Shariah*, which holds any fixed or guaranteed returns to be interest. In fact, if this controversial provision were eliminated, the normal rate of return system would turn into a PLS system, which has already been included on the CII's approved list. The inclusion of this system could not enhance the scope of PLS financing in the new financial system but instead provide a back door for the return of interest. Therefore, the CII should not have approved this system even as a temporary alternative to interest.[6] The system failed to win any representation in the actual practice of IBF in Pakistan.

4.2.2.6 Time multiple counter-loans

The system of time multiple counter-loans may be regarded as another alternative to interest. The CII described the functioning of this system with the help of an example. Suppose a small trader, A, wishes to borrow Rs 1,000 from B for 3 months free of interest. B may provide the required loan to A if the latter agrees to deposit a fraction of the loan (counter-loan) for a proportionately longer period, say Rs 100 for 30 months. After 3 months, A repays Rs 1,000 to B, but B repays Rs 100 to A after the expiry of 30 months. During this period B may use the deposit of A for making profit on his own account. The CII validated the system of 'time multiple counter-loans' as a temporary alternative to interest (The 1980 CII Report, p. 17).

A simple numerical exercise may show that the basic functioning of the time multiple counter-loans system has its roots in the conventional concept of time value of money and interest. For example, imagine there are two banks, one a conventional bank that lends Rs 1,000 for 3 months, the other an interest-free bank that makes interest-free loan of Rs 1,000 on the condition that the borrower lets the bank utilize his deposited Rs 100 against the bank's loan for 30 months. It can be assumed that the market interest rate is 10 percent per annum for the next 30 months.

In the first case, the conventional bank earn interest income of Rs 25 for investing Rs 1,000 for 3 months, which may be calculated as follows:

$$\text{Interest income} = \text{principal} \times \text{rate of interest} \times \text{duration}$$

$$\text{Interest income} = \frac{1,000 \times 10}{100} \times \frac{3}{12} = \text{Rs}\,25$$

Under the time multiple counter-loans system, the interest-free bank could easily manage to earn Rs 25 as a fixed and guaranteed return on Rs 1,000. The opportunity cost of Rs 100 for 30 months, that is, the income that the bank may earn by investing or utilizing the borrower's money (Rs 100) for the given period (30 months), may be computed as follows.

$$\text{The opportunity cost of capital or income} = \text{principal} \times \text{rate of interest} \times \text{duration}$$

$$\text{The opportunity cost of capital or income} = \frac{100 \times 10}{100} \times \frac{30}{12} = \text{Rs}\,25$$

The above-mentioned example is captured in Figure 4.2.

The underlying discussion indicates that the basic functioning of the time multiple counter-loans system is a crystal-clear case of a two-tier interest-based activity. The provision that the borrower should allow the bank to utilize his Rs 100 for 30 months for its own benefit is like an excess in terms of premium or favour or gift or service to the lender as a condition of the loan, which is an explicit case of *riba,* i.e., *riba al-nasi'h.*[7]

The CII also noted that the system of time multiple counter-loans does have little standing in the eyes of *Shariah,* and therefore it may be used only for the time being and in rare cases, and under the strict control of the central bank – State Bank of Pakistan (SPB). However, it can be argued that the use of this system should not be approved even for a short period because of its close similarity to interest-based dealings.[8] This system did not achieve any representation in actual IBF practice in Pakistan due to its complex and unrealistic nature.

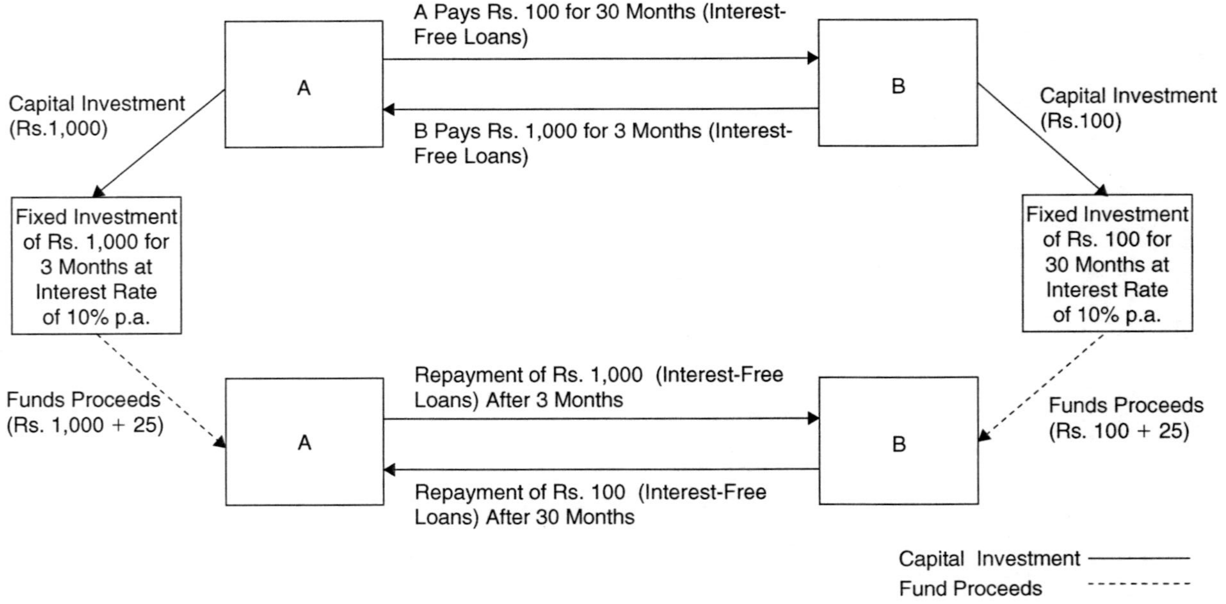

Figure 4.2 Time multiple counter-loans arrangement (hypothetical example)
Source: Figure captured from the discussion on the 1980 CII Report.

4.2.2.7 Special loan facility

Under the arrangement of the special loan facility, the bank provides an interest-free loan by imposing a fixed 'service charge' for meeting its administrative cost (The 1980 CII Report, p. 18). The CII stated that the special loan facility would be used to finance those social welfare projects which could not be financed under the PLS system or other interest-free policy instruments. It emphasized that banks charge a constant fee from all borrowers to avoid the reappearance of interest in different guise (CII Report, 18). It proposed that banks may provide such loans against deposits on which they pay no return and by seeking special financial assistance from the SBP under its subsidiary facility or refinancing schemes (The 1980 CII Report, p. 18).

The CII approved the special loan facility system with the intention of directing the flow of bank credit to under-served economic sectors to ensure a wider circulation of national resources and broad-based economic growth. However, collecting any fee or service charge from the borrower comes within the ambit of interest. The CII acknowledged this very fact by rejecting the service charge system of financing as an Islamic alternative to interest. Moreover, the SBP should have taken some precautionary measures to avoid the misuse of this scheme in Pakistan (Chapter 9).

4.2.3 Unsuitable instruments

The CII viewed a number of modes of financing as possible alternatives to interest. Service charges and indexation are two such proposed policy instruments of financing. The following section explores both alternatives, and deals with the CII's argument for rejecting them as Islamic instruments.

4.2.3.1 Service charge

Under the service charge system, the bank provides loans with a full guarantee of repayment of principal plus a service charge for covering its administrative cost only. The bank performs an intermediary role as a non-profitable institution, and therefore does not pay any return to its depositors or shareholders. The CII argued that interest could be replaced by the service charge system to meet the requirement of *Shariah* only in a literal sense. However, this solution may not accord with the true spirit of Islamic economic principles, which place a high value on the efficient and optimal utilization of economic resources (The 1980 CII Report, p. 11). The CII noted that the overwhelming majority of depositors would not commit their funds to banking institutions if they were not paid a competitive rate of return on their savings. If financial institutions failed to attract funds from the public, they would face serious difficulties in meeting the financial needs of different sectors of the economy. As a result, the economic growth and development of the country would be seriously handicapped. Therefore, the CII disallowed the service charge system as a viable alternative to interest (The 1980 CII Report, p. 11).

In the banking and finance sector of Pakistan in particular, the service charge system could not serve as a just and efficient alternative to interest. It is more likely that rich and powerful business people would exploit the service charge system to establish a monopoly over this cheap source of bank credit (see Chapter 9). They would make huge profits at the expense of depositors. Thus, the service charge system, if adopted, would further aggravate the problem of the gross distribution of wealth in the polity of Pakistan (see Chapter 9). The CII rightly concluded that the service charge system works against the socio-economic objectives of Islam and therefore should not be proposed as an alternative to interest.

4.2.3.2 Indexation of bank deposits and advances

Under the system of indexation, the borrower's debt to the banking system may be adjusted in money terms to reflect the change in the value of money, as measured by the Consume Price Index (CPI), during the outstanding period of borrowing. Lending under indexation may enable banks to compensate their depositors for the diminishing value of money during inflationary times. The CII pointed out that many macro economic and market factors, such as deficit financing, monetary expansion, devaluation of money, consumer behaviour, trade unions and natural constraints, have significant impacts upon inflation. Therefore, the borrower should not be held solely responsible for compensating the creditor for the erosion in the real value of the loan due to inflation (The 1980 CII Report, p. 12). The CII further added that, if the government was to compensate bank deposits and investments for inflation, workers would also put in demands for wage increases, resulting in a vicious wage–price spiral. As a result, the government would be likely to resort to public borrowings and deficit financing to meet its ever-increasing expenditures. This would further raise the prices of general commodities, including those used for indexing the bank's loans. In sum, the indexation of financial transactions would seriously jeopardize the economy of Pakistan. The CII resolved that the indexation system should not therefore be validated as an alternative to interest (The 1980 CII Report, p. 13).

Shariah recognizes money transactions as commodity-based transactions. Therefore, all loans should be repaid in the same kind and quantity, irrespective of any change in their real value or price at the time of return.

Furthermore, at the time of initiating a loan contract, the borrower should specifically know the liability in terms of monetary units, payable on the date of its maturity. In the indexation system, the borrower would most probably not know the exact amount of loan liability until its settlement date; this would add greater uncertainty and speculation to the loan contract, which could not be justified from the *Shariah* perspective (see Chapter 2). In sum, the indexation system is not a suitable alternative to interest from both the Islamic and economic perspectives (Hasanuz-Zaman, 1993).[9]

4.3 Elimination of interest from economy-wide operations

The CII laid down proper guidelines for performing commercial banking operations within the Islamic framework. The CII maintained that its recommended Islamic policy instruments could meet the financing needs of various sectors of the economy, i.e., industry, agriculture, commerce, construction, transport, etc. In all financing cases, the CII established the rule of thumb whereby, if the client maintains certified accounts, the bank may meet his financing needs under the PLS system, while if he does not maintain certified accounts, the bank may provide him with funds by using other approved interest-free policy instruments. At the same time, the CII strongly insisted that serious efforts should be made to ascertain a major role for PLS instruments in the new banking system (The 1980 CII Report, p. 34). It is notable that the CII recommended the system of *Qard-e-Hasanah* (loans free of cost) for meeting the financial needs of poor people and students on benevolent grounds. A summary in a tabular form of the CII's recommendations for financing different sectors of the Islamic economy is provided in Appendix II. The CII's main recommendations are explored in the forthcoming discussion. They include Participation Term Certificates, discounting of trading bills, the daily product method for the distribution of profit on bank deposits, and an action plan for gradually transforming the economy of Pakistan on Islamic lines.

4.3.1 Long-term financing: Participation Term Certificates (PTCs)

The CII proposed that Participation Terms Certificates (PTCs) may replace debentures for meeting the medium- and long-term finance needs of business and industry. A company may issue PTCs to procure funds from financial institutions on a risk-sharing basis. The holders of PTCs may receive a share in the profit of the issuing company instead of receiving a fixed rate of interest on their investments. The CII set out the following legal framework for PTCs to ensure their use as the PLS-based policy instrument (The 1980 CII Report, p. 36).

1. The company should utilize the proceeds from PTCs exclusively for implementing the project against which the PTCs are floated.
2. The issuance of PTCs beyond a certain limit should be subject to the approval of the Controller of Capital Issues, who would control and regulate the operations of PTCs.
3. Any change in the terms and conditions of PTCs should be subject to the mutual agreement of the issuers and the holders.
4. The welfare of the holders of PTCs would be safeguarded by giving them a right to appoint a trustee, who could inspect the records, call for any information and at any time visit the business premises of the companies.
5. The PTC financing would be secured by a mortgage on the fixed assets of the company.
6. The trading of PTCs would be encouraged in the secondary Islamic market.
7. The holders would be entitled to a tax exemption on the income from PTCs. The issuing company would be able to deduct the profit paid on PTCs as expenditure for income-tax purposes.
8. Losses would be borne by drawing on the profit and loss reserves or appropriating it to the holders in proportion to their share in the PTC investment. Any losses would be certified by chartered accountants, appointed with the consent of the trustees (The 1980 CII Report, p. 37).

The proposed PTCs may become a viable alternative to debenture financing. However, some observations in this respect may be noted. First, the provision of demanding collateral or mortgage on the fixed assets of the company is not in compliance with Islamic values such as mutual trust, free consent and benevolence (see Chapter 2). This provision could undermine the scope of PTCs for facilitating fairness and efficiency in Islamic business and economic dealings (see Chapter 3). Second, the real success of PTCs could not be ascertained without developing Islamic capital and secondary markets, which in turn envisages an overall reorientation of the economy and financial market of Pakistan on an Islamic basis, which has always remained a remote possibility (see Chapter 9). In the absence of a secondary Islamic market in Pakistan, trading in PTCs could not be encouraged at desirable levels, which would seriously undermine the real essence of this scheme. Third, the government of Pakistan has been engaged in heavy borrowings from national and international lenders for decades. The deficit-ridden economy of Pakistan, with its very weak tax base, could not afford to allow tax exemptions as a permanent feature of PTCs and other PLS-based instruments that may be introduced in future. Finally, there would be an indispensable need to launch a full array of PLS instruments to support PTCs, and thereby promote risk-sharing environments in the financial market of Pakistan. In the given risk-averse market environments, however, the predominant use of interest-free instruments would undermine any chance of success for PTCs (see Chapters 5 and 9).

4.3.2 Islamic discounting of trade bills

The CII proposed that the conventional technique of discounting trade bills may be replaced by the Islamic system, under which the bank would collect trade bills for its clients for the commission fee. The bank would charge a variable commission on the basis of the amount rather than the bill's maturity period. The client would enter into two separate agreements with the bank. In the first agreement, the client would appoint the bank as its agent for collecting the bill from the drawee. In the second agreement, the client would receive a cost-free loan from the bank, equal to the face value of the bill, for the duration of its maturity. The bank would charge a commission for the collection of the bill from the client in advance. It would use the proceeds from collecting the bill for settling the interest-free loan made to the client against the bill. If the bill were dishonoured, the client would be personally liable to repay the interest-free loan to the bank immediately (The 1980 CII Report, pp. 37–38).

In actual practice, the Islamic or un-Islamic use of this scheme would be conditional on charging a variable rate of commission. If the client finds that the bill's collection fee at the bank is lower than the market cost of the interest-free loan obtained against it, he would enter into collusion with another business friend to draw bills against one another (accommodation bills). Such fake bills would be used by the business community to exploit the relatively cheaper credit facility available from banks. Consequently, banks would be obliged to charge, under the cover of their collection services, the interest or market cost of the interest-free loans given against collection bills. In other words, this proposal would eventually precipitate interest in real terms (see Chapters 5 and 8). This would also unduly and unnecessarily expose banks to the higher risk of default and non-payment. It is notable that, in the case of the special loan facility, the CII maintained that the banks' service charges should not be linked to the amount of loans, because that might cause the reappearance of interest under the cover of the banks' fee and other such 'terms' (The 1980 CII Report, pp. 11, 18). Perhaps the CII should have followed its own established principle by advising banks to charge a fixed commission fee for the collection of bills. In actual practice, banking institutions found this recommendation too unrealistic and thereby continued to deal in trade bills under the old interest-based system (see Chapter 5).

4.3.3 Islamization of bank deposits

The CII advised that the elimination of interest from the deposit side of the banking sector of Pakistan should be treated with the utmost care so as to avoid any harm to depositors. The CII developed the daily product method to replace fixed returns on saving and time deposits with PLS returns (The 1980 CII Report, p. 48). The CII proposed that the banks' net profit would be distributed among saving and fixed deposits, capital and reserves. Current account deposits would not be given any share in the profits or losses made by banks. The profit or loss on deposits would be calculated on the basis of the daily products of their amounts. The SBP would assign different weights to daily products in order to ensure greater monetary rewards for longer-term deposits, capital and reserves. The duration of these fixed deposits would be 3 to 6 months, 1 year, 1 to 2 years, and so on. The loss would be distributed on deposits without taking into account their weights (The 1980 CII Report, p. 49). The CII described the daily product method by using the following hypothetical example.

Illustration

Case A

Bank's capital and reserves	Rs 200
Bank's total earnings	Rs 1,000
Administrative expenditure, reserve, tax etc	Rs 300
Distribution of profit	Rs 700

Case B

Bank's total earnings	Rs 100
Administrative expenditure	Rs 300
Total loss	Rs 200

Table 4.1 speaks of the CII's thoroughness in replicating and adopting the conventional method of distributing returns on deposits. The CII has

Table 4.1 Profit and loss distribution under the daily product system

Particulars	Amount	Period of Deployment	Product of I &II	Weights	Weighted Daily Product	Share in Profits (Amount)	Share in Loss
	(I)	(II)	(III)	(IV)	(V)	(VI)	(VII)
1.Capital and reserves	200	180 days	36,000	1.00	36,000	119.7	23.53
2.Savings deposits	200	90 days	18,000	0.30	5,400	17.9	11.76
3.Fixed deposits							
(i) 3–6 months	200	180 days	36,000	0.30	10,800	35.9	23.53
(ii) 6 months to 1 year	200	180 days	36,000	0.40	14,400	47.9	23.53
(iii) 1–2 years	200	180 days	36,000	0.60	21,600	71.8	23.53
(iv) 2–3 years	200	180 days	36,000	0.70	25,200	83.7	23.53
(v) 3–4 years	200	180 days	36,000	0.80	28,800	95.7	23.53
(vi) 4–5 years	200	180 days	36,000	0.90	32,400	107.7	23.53
(vii) 5 years and above	200	180 days	36,000	1.00	36,000	119.7	23.53
			Total		210,600	700.0	

Source: The 1980 CII Report, pp. 49–50.

explicitly based monetary rewards for different types of PLS deposits on the time value of money. In fact, *Shariah* does not recognize the time value of money in lending and borrowing operations (see Chapter 2). From the *Shariah* perspective, if Rs 2,000 each (same amounts) are taken from two different PLS term deposits for investing in a 6-month venture (same period), then both deposits should be assigned the same weight or monetary reward out of the profits. It may be permissible to determine different weights for different types of the PLS deposits based on their track record of productivity and demand in the Islamic market. However, the IBF practice has yet to develop its own independent pricing mechanism; moreover, there are insufficient data on PLS operations for doing so. The empirical findings suggest that IBF institutions rely on conventional theories of profitability for calculating returns on their products (El-Ashker, 1995; Bashir, 1999; Haron and Ahmad, 2000; Kaleem and Isa, 2003). In the given context, the assigned weights for PLS term deposits could be implicitly based on interest.

The CII argued that the proposed system would ascertain an average and uniform rate of return to depositors, so as to avoid any serious dislocation of national funds from inefficient financial institutions to efficient financial institutions, leading to serious financial turmoil and crisis in the country (The 1980 CII Report, p. 50). However, it implies that depositors would receive almost risk-free and predetermined rates of return on their investments after switching to the IBF system in Pakistan. It is sufficiently evident from the above discussion that the proposed daily product method is not truly based on the PLS system, but rather is based on the conventional concept of the time value of money.

4.3.4 The evolutionary plan to eliminate interest

The CII considered the following three action plans for eliminating interest from the economy of Pakistan.

1. The CII rejected the idea of establishing Islamic banking departments and models along with conventional banks on the ground that such arrangements would offer depositors an option that could prove counterproductive to the practice of IBF in Pakistan.
2. The CII rejected the idea of eliminating interest in one stroke. It argued that such approach might jeopardize the overall stability of the Pakistani economy.
3. The CII approved a stepwise transformation of the economy of Pakistan on Islamic lines (The 1980 CII Report, pp. 25–26).

The CII asserted that it preferred an evolutionary approach to implementing the IBF system in Pakistan so as to provide time to the government for bringing in the changes in regulatory, legal, tax, accounting and other systems of the country that are necessary for the success of new system (The 1980 CII Report, p. 31). The CII's phased approach includes the following three main stages.

1. In the first phase, starting from 1 January 1981, the CII described measures to transform government transactions and selected operations of banks and other financial institutions in full compliance with *Shariah*.
2. In the second phase, starting from 1 July 1981, the CII recommended the complete elimination of interest from the assets side of the banking sector of Pakistan. The CII demanded the abolition of interest-based government borrowings, such as Treasury bills, bonds and different saving certificates from 1 July 1981.
3. In the third and final phase, the CII stated that banks should cease to accept fresh deposits from the public on an interest basis, and accept them only on the basis of PLS, from 1 January 1982. The CII further added that inter-bank transactions should also be brought under the PLS system (The 1980 CII Report, p. 27)

4.4 Islamic framework for central banking operations

The CII set out a number of guidelines for evolving an interest-free monetary and central banking system. It argued that the SBP would continue to perform all functions as a central bank in an interest-free economy (The 1980 CII Report, p. 67).

Figure 4.3 shows the central banking mechanism in the Islamic framework. It explains that the existing conventional monetary management tools would be divided into two groups to restructure them on Islamic lines. The first group contains monetary tools that would remain almost unchanged or need minor changes. The second group includes the tools of bank rate and open market operations, which require overall remodelling to become operational under the Islamic monetary system. The discussion below evaluates the CII's recommendations on the conversion of these monetary instruments on Islamic lines.

4.4.1 Group one: Monetary policy tools requiring minor changes

Monetary tools such as the minimum cash reserve requirement, the liquidity ratio requirement, overall ceilings on lending and investment

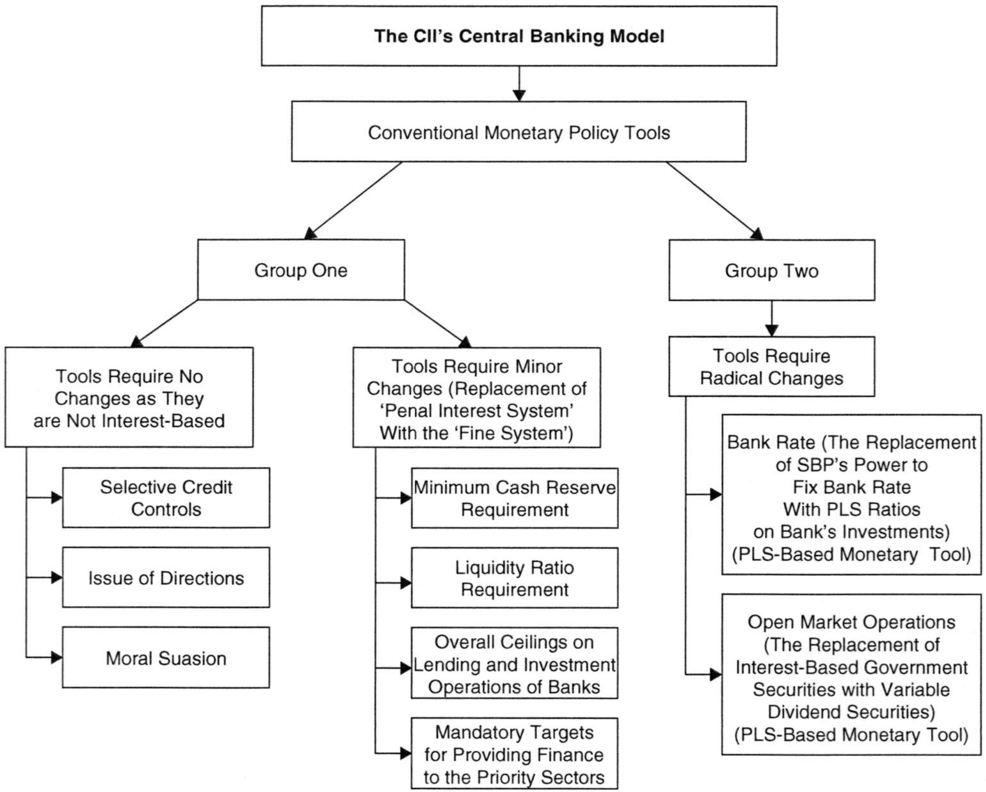

Figure 4.3 Policy instruments of the CII's central banking model
Source: Figure Compiled from the discussion on the 1980 CII Report.

operations of banks and mandatory targets for providing finance to priority sectors could become Islamic by replacing the system of penal interest in them with the fine system. If banks did not observe the regulatory limits ordained by these monetary instruments, the SBP would charge them fines instead of penal interest. Furthermore, the CII argued the SBP would use the tools of selective credit control measures, the issue of directions and moral suasion without bringing any structural changes as they contained no provision of interest (The 1980 CII Report, pp. 68–71). Theoretically speaking, the fine-based system offers a very simple solution to purging interest from these monetary tools. Therefore, the SBP might need to adopt highly precautionary measures to make sure that the fines collected on these monetary tools are not implicitly based on interest.

4.4.2 Group two: Monetary policy tools requiring radical changes

In the second group, the CII described monetary tools that might go through fundamental changes to become available in the Islamic monetary system. They include bank rate and open market operations.

4.4.2.1 Bank rate

Under the conventional baking system, the SBP was using the bank rate as a selective measure for regulating the supply of credit in the market. The CII proposed that the bank rate tool may be replaced by the SBP's power to fix the PLS ratios on its assistance to financial institutions. The CII further argued that the SBP may also be empowered to determine the maximum and minimum ranges of PLS ratios for banks in respect of their financing to clients. The SBP may manipulate these ratios from time to time to control and regulate bank finance in different sectors of the economy (The 1980 CII Report, p. 71).

The CII explained that the SBP would share with banks the profits on the financial assistance it provided to them. An increasing share of the SBP in the PLS ratios would ensure greater profit margins for the SBP. To control the over-expansion of credit supply, the SBP would increase its share in the PLS ratios in its financing to banks. Banks would follow suit by increasing their share in the PLS ratios in their financing to clients. This would squeeze the overall profit margins of clients across the board. Consequently, clients would decrease their bank borrowings for undertaking business enterprises. Thus, the overall demand for bank credit would fall to the desired level. The SBP would reverse the above steps in order to pursue an expansionary monetary policy. In other words, by increasing or decreasing the banks' share of profits, the SBP would be able to influence the demand for bank credit in a similar fashion to how it manipulated the bank rate under the conventional system (The 1980 CII Report, pp. 73–79).

Since the proposed monetary tool is based on the PLS system, its real success may be determined by the level of actual practice of the PLS system in the economy. In principle, the SBP may rely on active demand and supply for risk-sharing capital to fix the PLS ratios on banks' investments. As noted in Chapter 3, PLS operations have always comprised a very insignificant part of financings at IBF institutions due to business ethics and institutional constraints. The CII anticipated the same kind of bottlenecks reducing PLS financing operations in the economy of Pakistan to the lowest ebb (The 1980 CII Report, p. 5). In the given context, the proposed PLS-based monetary tools would remain only a theoretical option due to the limited use of the PLS system in the economy. When there was no significant or real use of the PLS system in the economy, the SBP would prescribe the PLS ratios for banks' investments as a proxy for market interest rate. Furthermore, *Shariah* recognizes the SBP as an outside party between the dealings of banks and their clients, and, therefore, any authority of the SBP for fixing the PLS ratios for banks' lending would be controversial from the Islamic viewpoint (see Chapter 7).

4.4.2.2 Open market operations

Under the conventional banking system, open market operations of the SBP were based on the sale and purchase of government securities, with the objective of increasing or decreasing the monetary supply in the economy. The CII proposed that the SBP might issue its own variable dividend securities by abandoning interest-bearing government securities for carrying out open market operations in the interest-free economy (The 1980 CII Report, p. 80). The CII argued that holders would share the profit or loss resulting from the actual performance of these securities. The share of profit for all types of stakeholders would be calculated under the daily product method that is explained in the case of bank deposits (The 1980 CII Report, p. 81).

The practical scope of this monetary tool may be evaluated in the light of a number of considerations and concerns regarding the economy of Pakistan. First, the SBP's dealings in the proposed securities would require it to undertake commercial activities in direct competition with financial institutions, which would be against its statutory role in the financial system of Pakistan (see Chapter 9). Second, the scope of open market operations for controlling the credit supply in developing markets has always fallen below the expectations of monetary authorities. The securities markets in developing countries are not efficient or broad-based enough to allow their central banks to undertake operations in government securities at a level that might affect the reserves and liquidity position of financial institutions in a desired way (Byrns and Stone, 1989; McConnell and Brue, 1996). The scope of open market operations on the basis of the proposed securities could be further undermined by the absence of well-established Islamic secondary and inter-bank money markets in Pakistan and worldwide (see Chapter 8).

Finally, open market operations on the basis of variable dividend securities may not be successfully conducted in the economy of Pakistan, which suffers from structural problems such as huge domestic and foreign debt, budgetary gaps, inflationary pressures, high volatility and an unfavourable balance of payments (see Chapter 9). The great majority of the holders of interest-based government securities are small savers who are strongly opposed to the idea of committing their funds to the proposed risk-based securities (see Chapter 8). In the given situation, it would be a highly complex and challenging task for the SBP to seek sufficient and constant interest-free sources of revenues for the government to pay off its interest-based loans and interest instalments (debt servicing) to domestic and international creditors (see Chapter 9). In sum, the successful adoption of this proposal would need the economy of Pakistan to be comprehensively remodelled on scientific and Islamic grounds.

4.5 The 1980 CII Report's scope and prospects

The CII engaged the best available team of economists and bankers in Pakistan to prepare a theoretical model for an interest-free economy that might be consistent and competitive with the modern financial world. However, some core prerequisites would need to have been satisfied in order to evolve a truly viable and efficient IBF practice on the basis of the CII's recommendations. The issues set out below may be taken into account to assess the real worth of the 1980 CII Report in providing the foundations of IBF practice in Pakistan.

4.5.1 Broader context of the interest problem

The CII argued that interest should be eliminated to establish a just and exploitation-free socio-economic order in the polity of Pakistan (The 1980 CII Report, p. 4). However, without abolishing other major sources of exploitation, such as the gross maldistribution of wealth and the monopoly of certain groups over the production and distribution hubs of Pakistan, the elimination of interest would not bring about any desirable change. The CII needed to devise a thorough strategy to eradicate exploitation in its all manifestations and from all arenas of the socio-economic life of Pakistan (see Chapter 9).[10]

4.5.2 The paradox of business ethics and moral hazard

The CII largely counted on a number of institutional and legal measures to resolve business ethics and moral hazard problems (The 1980 CII Report, pp. 22–27). However, the heavy reliance on strict institutional and legal measures could not solve the problem of morality at the grassroots level. The real solution to this problem requires the adoption of a moral and motivational approach – teaching the individual and society to adhere to Islamic moral codes in their all dealings. However, the CII did not strongly impress upon the government the need to adopt solid measures for enhancing the moral credentials of the polity of Pakistan. Thus, the CII left the problem of business ethics almost unresolved, which later undermined the real scope of IBF practice in Pakistan.

4.5.3 Fair and truthful accounts versus certified accounts

The CII advised financial institutions to provide finance on a PLS basis to those business people who maintain certified accounts. However, financial institutions could not rely simply on certified accounts to deal with the risks of misrepresentation and fraud. Indeed, auditors scrutinize and certify the fairness of accounting data based on claims that may not necessarily be true and fair. Furthermore, the possibility that auditors' judgements might be subordinated to the preferences of specific groups, including their clients, also exists in the real world.[11] The business community in Pakistan has serious reservations against the unfair tax system of the land. That is why the CII acknowledged that certified accounts may not necessarily be true in most of the business reporting cases of Pakistan. However, the CII's advice that financial institutions should demand certified accounts from the business community to avoid risk of fraud and corrupt practices has little significance or effect. Thus, it can be argued that a sole reliance on certified accounts could not combat the high risks of default and non-payment on banks' PLS investments in Pakistan. In the given set-up, financial institutions in Pakistan would arguably be highly reluctant to use PLS modes in their operations.

4.5.4 Uncertain future for the PLS system

The CII maintained that the core objective of its efforts is to ensure the greater use of PLS operations in the new IBF system in Pakistan. Therefore, secondary instruments should be used in exceptional cases only, and only until the development of a favourable legal and institutional framework for PLS banking practice (The 1980 CII Report, p. 5). However, a far better approach to the true promotion of PLS operations would have been for the CII to provide the most certain and clear-cut guidelines to banks about the exceptional cases where secondary interest-free policy instruments were to be used. Having done that, the CII could have declared the use of PLS instruments to be compulsory in all other cases. Appendix II, however, shows that in most of the cases the use of the PLS system is optional, along with other, secondary, interest-free policy instruments. In simple terms, the CII's recommendations contain the seed for the evolution of a dual banking system: (1) the banking system based on risk-sharing returns; (2) the interest-free banking system bearing a close resemblance to the conventional banking system.

In actual practice, however, secondary interest-free instruments may not allow the PLS system to succeed. Gresham's Law may dominate financial transactions, and therefore bad money may drive good money out of circulation.[12] Most likely, banks, due to the high level of risk, and business people, for privacy and tax reasons, would prefer to use secondary interest-free policy instruments such as *Bai Muajjal* over PLS instruments in each and every optional case (Khan, M A, 1989). Once the IBF practice was established on the basis of secondary interest-free modes of financing, it would be almost impossible to change its composition thereafter as argued by the CII. Indeed, the CII was utterly confused about the right time and ways to ensure the predominant use of the PLS system in IBF practice in Pakistan.

4.5.5 Islamic solutions to interest within conventional reach

As mentioned earlier, the CII is an expert body specializing in *Shariah* matters. Therefore, it entrusted the job of dealing with the technical aspects involved in transforming the existing interest-based financial system of Pakistan on Islamic lines to experts who were working in the top echelons of the Pakistani financial sector. These experts exercised a great deal of authority in conventional banking, although their Islamic knowledge was very limited (Rahman, 1997). Not surprisingly, they tried to resolve the problem of interest within conventional contexts. For example, they recommended financing on the basis of normal rate of return, time multiple counter-loans and discounting of trading bills, which were based simply on the time value of money and interest. Furthermore, they promoted the welfare of banks in several instances. For instance, they devised the system of daily product for distribution of profit among PLS depositors and the system of fixing PLS ratios between the bank and the client so as to ensure mostly risk-free and guaranteed returns for banking institutions.

4.5.6 The biggest obstacle to financial Islamization

The CII pointed out that it is a vast undertaking and beyond the capacity of any one Muslim country to suggest the means and measures for eliminating interest from foreign loans and international business transactions. Therefore, all Muslim countries should make joint efforts to abolish interest from their international commercial dealings (The 1980 CII Report, p. 31). Since the banking and finance sector is an integral part of the modern economy, the prevalence of interest in government borrowings, international trade and commerce might prove a formidable obstacle to adopting IBF practice in Pakistan.

4.6 Summary and conclusions

The efforts to Islamize the economy of Pakistan began in 1977 when the president of Pakistan, General Mohammad Ziaul Haq, advised the CII to prepare the blueprint for an interest-free economy and finance system. The CII took 3 years to develop the IBF model – The 1980 CII Report – by seeking help from the top economists and bankers of Pakistan. The 1980 CII Report was recognized in the Muslim world as the first comprehensive attempt to eliminate interest from the economy and financial sector of an Islamic state.

The CII observed that PLS and *Qard-e-Hasanah* instruments are the ideal alternatives to interest. However, the CII found that, due to inadequate institutional support and business ethics constraints, the widespread use of PLS instruments do cause serious harm to the economy of Pakistan. Therefore, the CII approved a number of secondary interest-free policy instruments as a temporary arrangement, so as to provide a reasonable time to the government to create the supportive regulatory and institutional set-up for practising PLS banking on a large scale. Some secondary instruments identified by the CII, such as leasing, hire purchase and special loan facility, could become viable alternatives to interest. However, other instruments, such as *Bai Muajjal*, time multiple counter-loans and normal rate of return could provide a cover for financial institutions in Pakistan to carry out interest-based operations as usual.

The CII provided guidelines for removing interest from the asset and liability sides of the banking and finance sector of Pakistan. The CII argued that banking and finance institutions can make all their financing and investments in industry, agriculture, commerce, construction, transport and other sectors of the Pakistani economy on the basis of its approved policy instruments. To eliminate interest from the liability side of financial institutions, the CII devised a daily product method for the distribution of profit among capital and reserves, saving and fixed PLS deposits. In the central banking mechanism, replacing the penal interest system with a fine system, as recommended by the CII, could not ensure that the use of the given monetary tools would be both efficient and Shariah-compliant. Similarly, the practical scope of the proposed PLS-based tools of bank rate and open market operations could not be ascertained due to practical difficulties. Moreover, the idea of replacing interest-bearing government securities with variable dividend securities could not be successfully applied without first rectifying the micro and macro mismanagement at the economy of Pakistan.

The CII suggested a gradual approach to phasing out interest from the economy of Pakistan within 3 years. There was too much to be done to provide a level playing field for IBF practice in Pakistan. Thus the CII advised the government to establish working committees of professionals to restructure the financial, fiscal, tax, legal and accounting systems in order to provide full support for the new system. It may be concluded that the CII's recommendations were meant to be a crude plan to provide a moderate but cautious start-up for IBF practice in Pakistan.

5
Islamic Banking and Finance Practice in Pakistan (1981–1991)

5.1 Introduction

In the early 1980s the government of Pakistan embarked upon the project of transforming the banking and finance sector on Islamic lines. It assigned this task to the Ministry of Finance. The Ministry then advised the State Bank of Pakistan (SBP) to take the necessary steps to evolve IBF practice on the basis of the 1980 CII Report. Another special organ of the Ministry of Finance, Pakistan Banking Council (PBC), took responsibility for formulating the legal and institutional frameworks for the IBF system in Pakistan.

This chapter evaluates the progress on the adoption and practice of IBF in Pakistan. Section 5.2 takes a brief account of the legal and institutional developments that took place to launch a full-fledged IBF system in Pakistan. Section 5.3 describes the main features of the IBF practice in Pakistan. Section 5.4 takes up the evaluation of the financial performance of the IBF system in Pakistan. Section 5.5 deals with some limitations and reservations about IBF practice in Pakistan from its inception in 1981 to the 1991 Federal *Shariat* Court (FSC) judgement on *riba* (interest).

5.2 Adoption and growth of IBF

The prevailing interest-based financial system of Pakistan was supported by the conventional framework and infrastructure. Banks played an intermediary role between the lender and the borrower on the basis of interest. In 1980, the PBC constituted a Superior Task Force[1] of experts and professionals to develop the legal and institutional framework for IBF practice. The Superior Task Force submitted its report in the same year, in which it suggested overhauling of the banking laws that provided for interest and promulgating some new laws to cover IBF practice. In the light of this report, the PBC made the major changes listed below to conventional banking laws and systems, in order to provide the required legal and regulatory framework for the IBF system. The SBP issued several directives from time to time to enforce these changes in the banking sector of Pakistan.[2]

5.2.1 Amendments to conventional banking laws

The 1962 Banking Companies Ordinance (BCO) largely covers banking practice in Pakistan. The 1962 BCO gives discretionary powers to the SBP to regulate the banking and finance sector of Pakistan. The 1962 BCO was amended to allow banks to perform manufacturing and trading activities under the systems of PLS, mark-up in price (*Bai Muajjal/Murabaha*), leasing and hire purchase.[3] The definitions of creditor and debtor were duly dealt with to cover the relationship between the financier and the borrower under the newly approved interest-free modes of financing.[4] The definition of finance was extended to include finance provided on the basis of PLS, mark-up in price, leasing and hire purchase.[5] The Negotiable Instruments Act was amended to allow dealings in trade bills on an interest-free basis.[6] A separate *Mudarabah* Companies and *Mudarabah* (Flotation and Control) Ordinance 1984 was promulgated to allow the operation of *Mudarabah* companies in the corporate sector. A number of other banking and corporate laws were also amended to provide operational grounds for the newly created interest-free instruments such as Participation Term Certificates (PTCs) and so on.[7] Some necessary amendments were made in the 1956 SBP Act to enable the SBP to regulate banking and finance institutions and provide them with financial assistance under the Islamic system.[8] Furthermore, the 1984 Banking Tribunal Ordinance was formulated to establish Banking Tribunals for expediting legal judgements on banking cases and thereby ensure a speedy recovery of banking funds from defaulting customers.[9]

5.2.2 Early breakthrough in IBF set-ups

The SBP took the first step towards Islamization by directing all banking institutions to open PLS counters in 7,000 domestic branches across the country from January 1981. The SBP instructed banks from time to time to invest their PLS funds in interest-free (cleaned-up) assets, such as commodity operations of the government, Participation Terms Certificates (PTCs), or National Investment Trust (NIT) units. The SBP advised banks to keep separate accounts of their PLS operations to ensure that returns on PLS deposits were free from interest.[10] The SBP allowed banks to invest PLS funds in interest-free trading operations of some major government business organizations, such as Rice Export Corporation of Pakistan, Cotton Export Corporation of Pakistan and Trading Corporation of Pakistan.[11] After some time the SBP advised banks to invest their PLS funds in the prescribed ten avenues of trade and investment, such as purchase and discount of trade bills, leasing and hire-purchase transactions, PLS securities, etc.[12]

5.2.3 Islamization of non-banking financial institutions

The process of Islamization of non-banking institutions had started earlier. On the basis of the 1978 CII's Interim Report, National Investment Trust (NIT), Investment Corporation of Pakistan (ICP) and House Building Finance Corporation (HBFC) transformed their operations on Islamic lines from 1 July 1979. The elimination of interest from NIT increased its business about Rs 151 million during 1979–80. NIT distributed profit of 12.40 percent to its PLS depositors in 1982 rates; these were very competitive rates. In 1980, ICP eliminated interest from its 12 closed-end mutual funds schemes. Under its new interest-free schemes, ICP accepted deposits from the general public and invested them in the stock market after adding 40 percent of its own share capital. ICP shared the profit from such investments with its depositors at a ratio of 60:40, but loss was to be shared at a ratio to the capital invested by both parties, i.e., 40:60. The elimination of interest from HBFC was largely covered by the rent-sharing mode of financing. During the first 9 months of 1982, HBFC approved 17,775 interest-free investment cases amounting to Rs 1,231 million (Faruqui and Habibullah, 1983; Qureshi, 1984).

5.2.4 Public response to PLS deposits

During the period January 1981 to June 1985, depositors were given a free choice to invest their funds either at the conventional banking counter or at the PLS counter at banking institutions in Pakistan. On the first day alone, i.e., 1 January 1981, banks mobilized Rs 92.6 million on a PLS basis (Faruqui and Habibullah, 1983). PLS deposits increased from Rs 6.5 billion at the end of 1981 to Rs 33.3 billion by March 1985 (Ahmed, 1987a). The rates of profit on PLS deposits were higher than the returns on interest-based deposits during January 1981 to July 1985 (Nomani and Rahnema, 1994). Foreign banks working in Pakistan also showed a keen interest in adopting the new system. They sent their top officials to overseas Islamic banks for training in, and to gain a better understanding of, IBF practice (Zaidi, 1987; Khan, A J, 1991).

5.2.5 IBF framework execution phase

The SBP concluded the task of implementing the Islamic system in the Pakistan banking and finance sector by issuing BCD Circular No. 13 on 20 June 1984. The circular prescribed 12 financing modes for practising full-fledged IBF at the domestic level. The approved 12 modes of financing were divided into three main categories. The first category contained service charges and *Qard-e-Hasanah* systems for financing by lending. The second category contained six trade-based modes, such as mark-up or mark-down financing under buy-back agreement (*Bai Muajjal/Murabaha*), leasing, hire-purchase and financing for property development on the basis of development charges. The third category contained investment-type modes of financing that include *Musharakah*, equity participation, *Mudarabah* and rent-sharing (see Chapter 3).[13]

The SBP directed banks to meet the finance needs of both the public and private sectors under the approved modes of financing. The SBP decided to abolish interest-bearing saving deposits from 1 July 1985. The holders of these deposits were given an option either to commit their funds under the PLS arrangement or to withdraw them before 1 July 1985. However, the holders of interest-bearing term deposits were allowed to complete the contractual period if they were not ready to convert their deposits to the PLS arrangement. The holders of current accounts were allowed to continue as usual because they were supposed to receive neither profit nor interest on their deposits.

The SBP established the following four committees to develop a legal and institutional framework for the practice of approved interest-free modes of financing.

1. Documentation Committee:[14] This committee was required to devise the detailed rules and regulations governing the contractual relationship between the bank and the customer under each approved mode of financing.
2. System and Auditing Committee:[15] This committee was assigned the task of developing a comprehensive accounting and auditing system for facilitating the practice of IBF.
3. Legal Committee:[16] This committee was entrusted with the responsibility to review and examine the documents prepared by the Documentation Committee and to offer its expert opinion in order to get them finalized.
4. Training Committee:[17] This committee was assigned the job of developing rigorous training programmes for educating and training

executive agencies, bankers, customers and business in IBF theory and practice.

The Documentation Committee prepared the draft documents for practising *Murabaha* (mark-up) financing on the patterns that were followed by most international Islamic banks under the guidance of their *Shariah* advisory boards. However, even though the CII approved these documents, PBC disapproved them without giving any plausible reason. Afterwards, PBC developed its own documents for practising mark-up financing with a buy-back agreement, without seeking any advice from the CII. The new documents defined mark-up financing with a buy-back agreement as follows:

> A client sells his goods to a bank for cash and simultaneously buys back the same goods from the bank at a higher price (marked-up price) payable at a future date, either in a lump sum or in instalments.[18]

The above definition is not in accordance with *Shariah* because it does not recognize the role of a third party or supplier of the goods. PBC adopted this definition to eliminate the risk factor for banks in performing mark-up financing operations (see Chapter 4). Furthermore, it devoted a great deal of effort to promoting only mark-up financing in the new set-up. It prepared 32 legal documents (1B-1 to 1B-32), and all except 1B-7 and IB-32 were related to mark-up financing with a buy-back agreement. On the other hand, it described other approved modes in general terms and advised financial institutions to develop their own model agreements and documents for practising them. However, it was beyond the capacity of financial institutions to develop documents on their own because they had no internally established R&D or *Shariah* advisory boards for doing so. Inevitably, financial institutions dropped their plans to finance on the basis of *Musharakah*, leasing and hire-purchase, and relied heavily on the mark-up mode to conduct their financing operations. Indeed, the BCD Circular No.13 of 20 June 1984 mostly reduced IBF practice in Pakistan to the mark-up banking practice (Zaidi, 1987; Khan, A J, 1991).

5.3 Critical features of IBF practice

Banking and finance institutions mostly relied on mark-up mode to manage their assets in the IBF era. Only minor representation was given to PLS modes in the new financial framework, which included the *Musharakah* investment scheme, *Mudarabah* companies and Participation Term Certificates (PTCs). The liabilities of banking and finance institutions were managed on a PLS basis and so rates of profit distributed among different types of deposits were based on the daily product method. The discussion below takes stock of the conceptual and practical significance of these policy instruments.

5.3.1 Mark-up (*Bai Muajjal/Murabaha*) financing

As stated previously, PBC developed documents for practising the mark-up mode of financing that were not *Shariah*-compliant. The actual practice on the basis of these documents was an artificial trade deal. The client approached the bank to secure a loan by selling his goods to the bank. At the same time, the client (seller) entered into a contract to buy his goods back from the bank at a marked-up or higher price payable in the future, in a lump sum payment or instalments. The transaction of sale and purchase of goods used to be fictitious because goods were used only as a reference point and were not present at the time of deal. There was no change in the possession and title of ownership of goods as strictly required by *Shariah*. Thus the bank performed its trade-related functions on paper only, without playing any active or real role in the commodity market (Ahmad, S M, 1992; Kadri, 1996).

In actual practice, clients were not given the right to refuse the goods after making a promise to purchase them from banks (see Chapter 3). The SBP allowed banks to include an additional mark-up for 210 days in the original price of the mark-up contract as a cushion against any likely delay or default in the repayment of the loan. If the client repaid the mark-up loan on time, banks returned the extra mark-up amount to him by calling it a 'rebate' for prompt or timely payment. If the client delayed the repayment of the mark-up loan but repaid it within 210 days, banks used to reduce the amount of rebate proportionately (Khan, M A, 1992).[19] These well-thought-through 'adjustments' made it possible for banks to earn almost fixed rates of return, similar to interest payments, on their mark-up contracts. The whole affair turned out to be a simple deal of borrowing on the basis of interest. The mark-up financing practice was not superior to the interest-based system; moreover, it was so complicated that the administrative cost to the bank as well as the client was significantly increased (Khan, F 1983).

The CII had recommended the use of mark-up financing under special circumstances and with strict precautionary measures so as to avoid its degeneration into an interest-based activity (see Chapter 4). However, the SBP allowed banks to heavily rely on mark-up financing. For example, banks' investment portfolios in mark-up financing amounted to 86.7 percent of total banking operations in 1984 (Ahmed, 1987a). The majority of Islamic scholars had serious reservations about the practice of mark-up financing in Pakistan. Lashkar (1991) critically remarked that the practice of mark-up financing in Pakistan amounted to hypocrisy. S M Ahmad (1992) pointed out that interest-based banking in Pakistan had not been eliminated but rather replaced by a higher interest-yielding system as the cost of borrowing rose from 14 percent to 17.15 percent after the introduction of Islamic banking. Kadri (1996) stated that mark-up financing was a concealed form of charging interest on banking transactions. Uzair (1997) showed his contempt for mark-up financing by saying, 'A new word came into use, i.e., "mark-up" which is just a "mark-up" for the word "interest" '.

The underlying discussion makes it crystal clear that the SBP took few pains to enforce the CII's recommendations in either the spirit or the letter. Rather it devised the most convenient way of eliminating interest from the finance sector of Pakistan by relying excessively on the controversial practice of mark-up financing.

5.3.2 *Musharakah* (equity participation) financing

Musharakah appeared as an optional mode of financing in the new banking and finance set-up in Pakistan. The SBP advised banking institutions to follow its prescribed terms and conditions for entering into *Musharakah* agreements with their clients.[20] Under a *musharkah* agreement, the client was required to submit its investment proposal along with profit projections. The client was allowed to have a certain percentage of profit as a 'good management fee' on achieving the projected rates of profit on the *Musharakah* investment. The bank enjoyed discretionary power to reduce or even forfeit a 'good management fee' in the event of the client's failure to achieve the predetermined rates of profit on *Musharakah* investment. The rates of profit on *Musharakah* investment were to be worked out on a daily product basis. Both the bank and the client were required to share the profit of *Musharakah* investment on the basis of an agreed ratio after making provision for a 'good management fee' and weightage,[21] if any. Any loss on a *Musharakah* investment was to be distributed between the bank and the client at the ratio of their capital investment (Khan, A J, 1991).[22]

In order to avoid the high cost of monitoring involved in managing the *Musharakah* investment, the bank advised the client to pay its provisional projected share of the profit in advance on a half-yearly basis, i.e., on

30 June and 31 December of each year. The client was required to compile final accounts for the year and to transfer any difference between the profit paid to the bank on provisional basis and the actual profit realized on the *Musharakah* investment for the year to a 'participation reserve account'.[23] The 'participation reserve account' was to be settled on the termination or expiry of the *Musharakah* agreement. Afterwards, the SBP adopted the policy of prescribing the minimum and maximum amounts of annual profit that banking institutions should earn on their *Musharakah* investments.[24]

The underlying characteristics of *Musharakah* investment are highly controversial from the *Shariah* perspective. The SBP's act of prescribing the terms of *Musharakah* agreements may be regarded as an interference with efficient market mechanisms and free consent of the bank as well as of the client. *Shariah* forbids partners from receiving a predetermined or provisional share of the profit on a partnership or *Musharakah* investment before its actual realization (see Chapter 3). Furthermore, *Shariah* ordains that the rewards for managerial efforts and time devoted by the partner or partners should be certain and covered by the PLS ratio sorted out at the time of entering into the partnership agreement (see Chapter 3). There is always a trade-off between risk and return, and depositors should therefore be entitled to get their share of the additional premium for bearing each additional unit of risk. Thus, the Islamic bank that acts as an agent of its shareholders and depositors has no right to arbitrarily decide in advance that it will take a certain rate of return for undertaking a certain level of risk on a given *Musharakah* investment or surrender the return over and above it to the client as a 'good management fee'. There is no avoiding the fact that the SBP unnecessarily complicated the simple contract of *Musharakah* to ensure almost fixed and guaranteed rates of return on the bank's investment.

While practising *Musharakah* financing, banks applied the prescribed maximum and minimum rates of profit to earn risk-free and predetermined returns on their investments. Non-banking financial institutions also set out the terms and conditions of *Musharakah* agreements that fully guaranteed the return on their capital investment along with fixed rates of return. For example, the documents of a *Musharakah* agreement of Small Business Finance Corporation of Pakistan (SBFC) contained a clause whereby, if the profit declared by the client exceeded the expected rate of profit (15 percent at that time), then SBFC would accept the client's accounts as true. But if the reported profit were below 15 percent, SBFC reserved the right to scrutinize the client's accounts unless the client paid 15 percent per annum (Akhtar, M R, 1996). Banks did not share in losses on the basis of their capital contribution in *Musharakah* investments. Clients were required to contribute their total capital towards losses before asking banks to make any contribution towards them (Khan, M A, 1985; Ingram, 1986). Despite this, banks showed a great reluctance to practice *Musharakah* financing. The overall representation of *Musharakah* financing was as negligible as 3.1 percent of the total financing operations of Pakistani banks in 1984 (Ahmed, 1987a). Some critics contended that banks did not practise *Musharakah* and other PLS modes of financing in reality but on paper only (Akhtar, M R, 1996). The underlying discussion reveals that *Musharakah* financing practice was not based on risk-sharing principles as envisaged by *Shariah*.

5.3.3 *Mudarabah* (joint venture) financing (companies)

The government of Pakistan promulgated the *Mudarabah* Ordinance in 1980 to promote the PLS system in the corporate sector. In 1981 it set out a regulatory and institutional framework for *Mudarabah* companies. A separate registrar of *Mudarabah* office was established along with the tribunal and religious board to look after the affairs of the *Mudarabah* sector. *Mudarabah* companies were required to have a minimum paid-up capital of Rs. 2.5 million for the flotation of *Mudarabah* business, which included a 20 percent contribution of their own capital. They were allowed to receive 10 percent of a net profit of a *Mudarabah* business as a management fee along with a profit share on 20 percent of the capital investment in a *Mudarabah* business. The government imposed some restrictions on the dealings, margin requirements and maintenance of liquidity of *Mudarabah* companies to safeguard the interest of investors. At the beginning, banks were allowed to register themselves as *Mudarabah* companies but after some time they were forbidden to enter *Mudarabah* businesses (Hussain, H, 1994).

The government granted tax exemptions and other incentives to encourage local and foreign investors to enter the *Mudarabah* industry. In spite of these incentives, *Mudarabah* companies took some time to get going in Pakistan. There were only seven *Mudarabah* companies in Pakistan by 1989. However, the growth of the *Mudarabah* sector was greatly boosted during the period 1990–91 when 23 new *Mudarabah* companies started operations in Pakistan (Siddiqui, 1994). Yet the majority of investors remained reluctant to enter the *Mudarabah* sector. *Mudarabah* companies therefore faced serious problems in mobilizing funds on a risk-sharing basis. Depositors and financial institutions regarded *Mudarabah* companies as highly risky (Khan, S R, 1987; Khan, T,

1996). Due to lack of access to equity-sharing capital, *Mudarabah* companies failed to undertake PLS ventures in industrial and non-financial sectors. Instead, they engaged in activities wherein they bought equipment and machinery from banks on a mark-up basis and either leased them or sold them to their clients with added mark-ups. Consequently, *Mudarabah* companies ended up offering products and services that were already available from financial institutions, such as leasing firms, commercial banks, mutual funds and brokerage houses (Abbasi, 1994; Haqqani, 1994). For example, on average 70 percent of *Mudarabah* operations were concentrated in leasing. *Mudarabah* companies experienced high cost of operations and so they unnecessarily added to the cost of borrowing for their clients (Siddiqui, 1997a). They appeared to be an unwanted middleman, without any genuine or productive role in the business and economy of Pakistan.

One of the main problems with the *Mudarabah* sector was that a large number of genuinely interested unemployed professionals failed to meet the requirement to contribute 20 percent, i.e., Rs 0.5 million, of the total paid up capital of Rs 2.5 million from their own pocket to initiate the *Mudarabah* business. On the other hand, many rich borrowers with good creditworthiness entered the *Mudarabah* sector only for the sake of taking advantage of its tax exemption and low tax rates.[25] As a result, *Mudarabah* companies largely remained incapable of encouraging broad-based entrepreneurship and sustainable economic growth in Pakistan. Some *Mudarabah* companies were found guilty of violating the prescribed regulations and avoiding the cash dividend payments to their shareholders.[26] These malpractices seriously tarnished the image of the *Mudarabah* sector in the eyes of the general public. In 1993, the government withdrew tax concessions from the *Mudarabah* sector and consequently its inflated growth came to a halt. The share prices of many *Mudarabah* companies fell below their face value, and many potential subscribers and investors scrapped their plans to enter the *Mudarabah* business.[27] In a nutshell, *Mudarabah* companies largely failed to promote the PLS system in the financial sector of Pakistan.

5.3.4 Participation Term Certificates (PTCs)

The CII recommended that Participation Term Certificates (PTCs), based on the equity-sharing principle, be used to replace debentures in the corporate sector of Pakistan (see Chapter 4). In June 1980 the SBP made the necessary amendments to the corporate and financial structure in order to provide an appropriate institutional and regulatory framework for PTCs. Under the new arrangement, borrowing firms were required to issue PTCs to obtain finance from financial institutions on a risk-sharing basis. In actual practice, however, financial institutions asked the borrowing firms to pay a pre-production discount rate (i.e., 12 percent per annum) during the gestation period of a project so as to cover the opportunity cost of their funds. The borrowing firms were required to pay the fixed rate of projected profit (i.e., 15 percent per annum) to financial institutions after going into production. If the actual rate of profit was less than the projected rate, the borrowing firms were required to pay the difference by issuing additional PTCs to financial institutions (Khan, M A, 1994). The borrowing firms were required to appropriate losses against their past reserves or future profits (Ahmed, 1987a). As a matter of fact, PTCs operations were not truly based either on *Shariah* or on the CII's recommendations (see Chapter 4).

In 1989 the SBP abandoned the PTC financing scheme due to its unpopularity among financial institutions, and instead introduced Term Finance Certificates (TFCs), which carried a mark-up rate calculated on the basis of a compound interest formula (Chishty, 1994). The replacement of PTCs by TFCs seriously handicapped the practical scope of PLS instruments in the financial sector of Pakistan. This was quite contrary to the CII's recommendations, which had urged the government to adopt measures for gradually phasing out secondary interest-free modes of financing and replace them with PLS modes of financing (Khan, M A, 1992; see Chapter 4).

5.3.5 PLS deposits

The SBP had completely shut down interest-based counters at banking institutions in Pakistan by July 1985 in order to fully transform the deposit-taking function on Islamic lines. The SBP categorized PLS deposits on the basis of their duration. The profit distribution mechanism on PLS deposits is set out in Table 5.1.

The profit distribution procedure presented in Table 5.1 is based on the daily product system, which was thoroughly discussed in Chapter 4. This table shows that PLS deposits with a longer maturity period were assigned higher premiums or greater monetary rewards. For example, five-year saving deposits were given a 40 percent higher share in profit than one-year saving deposits for the same investment period, i.e., six months. It implies that the given policy of profit distribution on PLS deposits was explicitly based on the conventional concept of time value of money, which is strictly prohibited by *Shariah* (see Chapter 2). The basic rate reflected a risk-free rate of return on interest-based government securities. Therefore, it was absolutely out of the question to apply

Table 5.1 Profit rates on PLS deposits on the basis of the daily product method

PLS Saving Deposits	Rate of profit (percentage per annum)
Basic Deposits	Basic rate
6-month Deposits	Basic rate + 5 percent premium
1-year Deposits	Basic rate + 10 percent premium
2-year Deposits	Basic rate + 20 percent premium
3-year Deposits	Basic rate + 30 percent premium
4-year Deposits	Basic rate + 40 percent premium
5-year Deposits	Basic rate + 50 percent premium

Original Source: Economic Advisor's Wing, Finance Department of Pakistan.
Secondary Source: Zaidi (1991).

the base rate for calculating returns on PLS deposits. More interestingly, the SBP simply relied on market interest rates to prescribe rates of profit on PLS deposits in banks. In practical terms, the underlying profit distribution mechanism was not at any point distinct from the conventional profit distribution system.

5.4 Financial performance evaluation of IBF

This section evaluates the financial performance of the banking sector under the IBF system during the period 1981–90, so as to respond to the question whether the adoption of Islamic system brought any improvement in the business efficiency of financial institutions of Pakistan. Due to lack of data and proper documentation of the economy, a detailed analysis of the IBF system in Pakistan could not be carried out. Therefore, data on the rates of return (ROR) on PLS deposits and rates of return on equity (ROE) of the banking sector of Pakistan during the course of 1981–90 have been examined to appraise the performance of the banking sector after Islamization (Zaidi, 1991). It may be noted that until the early 1990s the banking industry of Pakistan mainly comprised five major nationalized banks enjoying a market share in the country in excess of 92 percent.[28] However, this situation gradually changed after rigorous moves to privatise and deregulate the financial market undertaken by the government of Pakistan in the early 1990s.

5.4.1 Rate of Return (ROR) on PLS deposits

The rates of profit on PLS deposits during the period 1981–90 are given in Table 5.3, which shows rates of profit on PLS deposits that were declared by the nationalized banks of Pakistan for the period June 1981 to December 1990. As mentioned previously, from January 1981 to June

Table 5.2 Rate of Return (ROR) on PLS deposits in the nationalized commercial banks of Pakistan for the period 1981–1990 (percentage per annum)

Period	**Allied Bank**	**Habib Bank**	**Muslim Bank**	**National Bank**	**United**
December 1981	8.50	9.00	9.00	8.50	8.50
December 1982	8.00	8.50	8.50	8.00	8.00
December 1983	7.00	8.50	7.25	7.25	8.25
December 1984	8.55	7.25	8.15	9.00	7.10
December 1985	7.00	7.80	7.70	7.80	7.00
December 1986	7.10	7.30	7.10	7.30	6.50
December 1987	6.70	6.80	6.70	6.80	6.00
December 1988	6.50	6.00	6.70	6.00	6.00
December 1989	7.00	7.10	7.00	7.10	6.30
December 1990	7.00	7.10	7.00	7.10	6.30
Average	7.34	7.36	6.81	7.49	6.99

Original Source: Economic Advisor's Wing, Finance Department of Pakistan.
Secondary Source: Zaidi (1991).

Table 5.3 Return on Equity (ROE) of nationalized banks of Pakistan for the period 1981–1989 (percentage per annum)

Nationalized Bank	**1981**	**1982**	**1983**	**1984**	**1985**	**1986**	**1989**
Allied Bank	10.40	12.92	14.75	14.79	15.34	17.86	13.64
Habib Bank	43.79	44.80	39.60	37.79	30.01	26.71	16.06
Muslim Bank	26.46	32.29	28.13	24.95	19.82	18.27	17.32
National Bank	14.23	17.75	19.18	20.14	20.51	18.43	11.92
United Bank	15.90	17.82	19.14	28.95	15.54	14.13	8.69
Average	22.16	25.12	24.16	25.32	20.24	19.09	13.53

Original Source: Economic Advisor's Wing, Finance Department of Pakistan.
Secondary Source: Zaidi (1991).

1985 depositors were given the right to commit their funds at either the interest-based counter or the PLS counter. Therefore, the aggregate profit trend may be divided into two phases: the first phase from 1981 to June 1985, and the second from December 1985 to December 1990. In the first phase, rates of profit were almost flat, but they declined in the second phase.

The question arises whether the comparatively higher rates of profit in the first phase reflected allocative improvements in the financial sector of Pakistan under the Islamic system. Among others Islamic scholars, S R Khan (1987) argued that the SBP deliberately declared rates of return on

PLS deposits that were greater than market interest rates so as to attract a large number of depositors at the PLS counter. In fact, no discernible growth was observed in demand deposits and term deposits after the introduction of IBF in Pakistan. The CII also registered that there was no noticeable increase in the total volume of deposits after the changeover to the IBF system.[29] This implies that economic considerations played a significant role in attracting deposits from the interest-based pool to the PLS pool. This point may be further strengthened by reference to the constant assurance by the governor of the SBP to the general public that rates of profit on PLS deposits would be higher than market interest rates.[30] The same assurance was frequently repeated by banks to their PLS depositors. Under the government's directives, banks invested PLS funds in the most lucrative government schemes. The government exempted from tax on annual earnings of PLS deposits up to Rs 5,000 (Nomani and Rahnema, 1994). Thus, it may be argued that comparatively higher rates of profit in the first phase did not reflect better management techniques or higher growth in savings and investments under the IBF system (Khan, S R, 1987).

After the absolute ban was imposed on interest-based deposits, rates of profit on PLS deposits declined. The governor of the SBP argued that the banking sector of Pakistan was experiencing low rates of profit because it needed to invest in certain less profitable but socially desirable sectors.[31] In contrast, some Islamic scholars contended that lack of Islamic investment experience, the high cost of transactions and surplus liquidity due to the ban on investment in interest-based avenues adversely affected revenues and the profit-earning capacity of banking institutions, leading to diminishing rates of return on PLS deposits (Nomani and Rahnema, 1994). However, it may be noted that the cost of borrowing significantly increased after IBF practice was introduced in Pakistan. The underlying facts reveal that the SBP firstly tried to popularise the PLS system by giving the people greater financial incentives. However, the SBP could no longer afford such high costs of establishing artificial efficiency in the IBF system, and it therefore distributed lower rates of profit on PLS deposits after completely banning interest-based deposits. This may imply that there was no real improvement in the profitability of the banking sector of Pakistan and that the general public did not receive any true benefit from doing banking under the Islamic system.

5.4.2 Return on Equity (ROE)

ROE is the most popular yardstick for evaluating the operational performance of banking and other sectors of the modern economy (Higgins,

1997). Table 5.4 illustrates the ROE of five nationalized banks of Pakistan for the period 1981–89.

Table 5.3 reveals that, on average, the ROE of the banking sector of Pakistan dropped from 22.16 percent to 13.53 percent during the course of 1981–89. The most significant decline was observed in ROE of Habib Bank, which decreased by 63.32 percent. However, the ROE of Allied Bank increased by 23.75 percent for the given period. Since all banks functioned in similar economic and regulatory environments in Pakistan, the sign of improvement in the Allied Bank's ROE may imply that there was scope for banks to improve their financial performance. In the light of the given data, it could not be contended that the IBF system brings improvements in allocative efficiency, offers better risk management techniques or ensures broad-based economic growth.

5.4.3 Strictly regulated market environments

The banking sector's assets and liabilities largely reflect real rates of return in various sectors of the advanced economies. However, the SBP denied the banks' right to make their saving and investment decisions on their own account, on the basis of market forces (Mirakhor, 1988). Generally, banks and other business enterprises distribute profit to their depositors and shareholders on the basis of their ROE (Helfert, 1997; Higgins, 1997). However, features of Table 5.3 and Table 5.4 show that Pakistani banks did not follow this market-based policy to distribute profit to their depositors. For example, from 1981 to 1989 the ROE of Allied Bank increased by 23.75 percent but its overall rates of profit distributed to depositors decreased by 17.65 percent for the same period. Similarly, the differences in the banks' rates of profit distributed to depositors did not correspond to the differences between the rates of profit they earned for the given period. For example, the ROE of Habib Bank was about 4.21 times greater than the ROE of Allied Bank in 1981, but rates of profit of both banks were almost same (difference: 0.05 percent). In 1989, the ROE of Commercial Bank was about twice the ROE of United Bank, but the difference between their rates of profit was extremely insignificant (difference: 0.70 percent). The SBP strictly regulated the profit distribution policy of the banks to ensure uniform rates of return to all depositors across the board. The SBP took such measures so as to discourage the movement of funds from inefficient banks to efficient banks, which would have caused serious financial disruption in the country (Mirakhor, 1988).

The SBP advised banks to observe a 'credit ceiling' in financing different sectors of the economy. Banks were required to meet mandatory financing targets, such as 30 percent credit for the public sector and

35 percent credit for the private sector. Furthermore, they were under regulatory compulsion to maintain 'statutory reserves' equal to 35 percent of their deposits in the form of cash and low-yield fixed interest-based government securities such as Treasury bills, which could yield interest of a maximum of 6 percent per annum. Perhaps the very conservative and highly regulated finance sector of Pakistan did not enjoy any of the benefits of diversification and innovation. Due to business ethics problems and a high level of market uncertainty, banks largely promoted short-term mark-up investments. Perhaps the financial sector's performance in Pakistan further deteriorated after the introduction of the IBF system (Khan, S R, 1987, Mirakhor, 1988; Khan, A J, 1991).

5.5 Some reservations about IBF practice

It was the prime responsibility of the SBP to transform the economy and financial sector of Pakistan on Islamic lines in the light of the CII's recommendations. The task of eliminating interest from the economy of Pakistan was highly complex and required radical changes in the financial and administrative set-up of the country. A number of deficiencies and concerns were observed in the adoption and practice of IBF in Pakistan.

5.5.1 Gross deviations from the CII's recommendations

The CII had emphasized the need to design a well-integrated plan to evolve full-fledged IBF practice in Pakistan. It recommended that the task of phasing out interest from the financial sector of Pakistan should be started on its assets side and completed on its liabilities side. The CII informed the government that the transformation of the assets side of the banking sector on a PLS basis could not be guaranteed without the introduction of rigorous reforms in the regulatory, legal, tax and accounting systems of the country. The CII advised the government that these preconditions should be satisfied in order to develop a conducive socio-economic infrastructure for ensuring the smooth adoption and functioning of the PLS system. In addition, the CII strongly rejected the proposal to start the task of transforming the banking and financial sector on Islamic lines by opening and running interest-free counters alongside interest-bearing counters at the banking and financial institutions of Pakistan (Rahman, 1997).

The SBP, however, simply ignored all the crucial recommendations made by the CII. On the contrary, it started with eliminating interest from the liabilities side of banking sector, which promoted a parallel IBF system within the conventional banking framwork.[32] The SBP advised banks to open PLS counters from January 1981. Since a total of five government-run banks mainly constituted the banking sector of Pakistan, they enjoyed a kind of monopoly over public funds and did not face any problem in transforming their deposit-taking functions on a PLS basis. However, the regulatory, tax, legal and socio-economic frameworks of the country remained seriously at odds with the IBF system. Due to institutional constraints and high risk exposures, banks did not utilize their funds under the PLS system, and mostly invested them on a mark-up basis.

The CII had strongly recommended that interest should be eliminated first of all from government borrowings because this was the most serious obstacle to enforcing Islamic economy and finance in Pakistan. However, policymakers totally ignored the task of eliminating interest from government borrowings, and that eventually led to the failure of IBF in Pakistan. The banking sector remained a captive source for financing the government's budget deficit (see Chapter 9). In August 1985 the SBP allowed the banking sector to invest their PLS funds in interest-based government securities. In addition, the government introduced many interest-based schemes such as *Khas* (special) deposits, national certificates, monthly income schemes and NDFC certificates, which were yielding predetermined and risk-free rates of return that were higher than rates of profits from Islamic investment avenues (Rahman, 1997; Siddiqui, 1997b).[33]

The SBP did not offer any advisory role to the CII in the process of transforming the countrywide banking and financial system on Islamic lines. The CII, on the other hand, continually warned the SBP about substantive procedural shortcomings in adopting IBF practice. The Ministry of Finance always dealt with such objections by reassuring the CII that it was only for a transitory period that banks would be largely relying on mark-up financing; the ministry was working on devising concrete plans that would ensure a greater application of the PLS system and only rare use of the mark-up system in the long run.[34] After some time, however, PBC argued that it was an absolutely utopian idea for over 7,000 branches of commercial banks countrywide in Pakistan to use PLS financing and to sort out the terms and conditions of loan applications on a case-by-case basis (Rahman, 1997).[35]

It is evident from the above discussion that neither the government of Pakistan nor the SBP was serious about implementing the CII's recommendations in either the spirit or the letter. They adopted delaying tactics and gradually deviated from the prescribed evolutionary steps for adopting the IBF system in Pakistan. The government did not follow Islamic discipline in its expenditures and borrowings, and largely relied on the banking sector to meet its finance needs. The banking sector of Pakistan remained deeply involved in interest-based government and foreign transactions, which left hardly any scope for it to truly adopt Islamic operations. The SBP successfully managed the status quo in the banking sector of Pakistan by riding on the mark-up mode of financing.

5.5.2 Lack of proper Islamic training for bankers

The SBP did not establish an internal *Shariah* advisory board to seek technical guidance and feedback on its Islamization policies. It did not advise individual banks to establish their own *Shariah* boards to ensure Islamic guidance and surveillance over their operations. Therefore, bankers in a position to institute the new system did not fully understand its real essence and spirit. They were not qualified to interpret or apply *Shariah* rules in the banking sphere. They were educated and trained in a Western environment and were unsympathetic to the cause of Islamic banking. The CII was fully aware of this problem and had repeatedly argued for devising rigorous training programmes for officers of the Economic and Finance Ministries and financial institutions to build up their understanding of money and banking on Islamic lines.[36] However, no one paid much attention to the CII' warnings over the issue. Thus, bankers never made a wholehearted attempt to successfully adopt the IBF system in Pakistan (Rahman, 1997).

5.5.3 Public concerns and doubts

As explained in Section 5.3, PLS banking in the new financial framework was highly controversial. The SBP largely reduced all *Musharakah* instruments to conventional-based tools with fixed and risk-free rates of return. There were no fluctuations in rates of profit on PLS deposits. The SBP tried to remove *Shariah* objections by adding a clause that the 'rate of profit is expected to be [x] percentage per annum', or that the rate announced is the 'incentive rate' (Siddiqui, 1997b). However, the economic survey published by the Economic Adviser's Wing of the Ministry of Finance of the government of Pakistan in June 1985 acknowledged:

> According to the *ulema* [religious scholars] the form in which PTCs have so far been used, buy-back arrangements and mark-down do not conform to the Islamic *Shariah*. Influenced by the position of the *ulema*, a number of doubts remained in the minds of the common public about the Islamic modes of saving and financing.[37]

5.5.4 The cover of Islamic nomenclatures

The SBP did not ensure the transformation of certain conventional banking activities on Islamic lines and simply directed banks to replace the word 'advances' with 'financing', and 'interest' with 'returns' in their documents and reports. However, in the published annual reports of Pakistani financial institutions such words as 'loans, credit and advances', bearing the hallmark of interest-based banking, were not replaced with the word 'financing'. The inter-bank transactions and the SBP's transactions with commercial banks were based on predetermined fixed rates of return (ibid). Most of the banks' assets, such as money at call and short-term notice, investment in federal and provisional government securities, legal reserve requirements of the SBP, purchase of farm inputs and their sale to clients on mark-ups on a deferred payments basis, and purchase of trade bills, were still managed on the basis of interest (Khan, M A, 1992).

The underlying facts imply that the SBP ceased its half-hearted effort to implement the IBF system before it could reach a meaningful end. Regarding the achievements of IBF in Pakistan, Zaidi (1991), a senior banker of Pakistan, observed that the present form of the banking and financial system was based on simple interest and that the government had eliminated only compound interest from the economy of Pakistan. In November 1991 the Federal *Shariat* Court (FSC) confirmed in its judgement on *riba* that the conversion of the interest-based system to the Islamic system had not taken effect in the banking and financial sector of Pakistan.

5.6 Summary and conclusions

This chapter looks into means and measures adopted by the leading policymakers of Pakistan to enforce an Islamic order in the banking and financial sector of the country. The Ministry of Finance of Pakistan advised the SBP and PBC to implement the CII's recommendations in the economy of Pakistan. The SBP amended the conventional banking laws and drafted a number of new laws to provide a proper legal and institutional framework for IBF practice. However, the SBP did not feel any need to seek religious and technical scrutiny of and guidance for its policies of Islamization. It did not develop a proper infrastructure to ensure the smooth adoption and practice of the Islamic system in the financial sector of Pakistan. It likewise did not provide proper guidance and help to financial institutions to enable them to evolve an IBF practice in the light of CII's recommendations.

The CII had clearly warned of serious repercussions from using the mark-up (*Bai Muajjal*) system on a large scale; yet the SBP encouraged and obliged financial institutions of Pakistan to practise mark-up financing in bulk. The SBP show no enthusiasm for promoting PLS modes of financing in the new system. Due to the lack of a proper Islamic framework and infrastructure, banking operations based on PLS principles did not achieve any real success. Banks largely invested their PLS deposits in interest-based venues and other fixed mark-up investments, and paid almost risk-free and predetermined rates of return to PLS depositors. The government as well as the SPB made frequent moves to impair the growth and development of IBF in Pakistan. In November 1991 the FSC judgement on *riba* confirmed that the IBF system had yet to be adopted in Pakistan.

6
The 1991 Federal Shariat Court (FSC) Judgement on *Riba* (Interest) and Islamic Banking and Finance Practice in Pakistan

6.1 Introduction

In the late 1980s there were growing concerns and complaints over the practice of IBF in Pakistan, from various quarters. On 14 November 1991 the Federal *Shariat* Court (FSC) gave the verdict that the existing banking and finance practice and a number of fiscal laws in Pakistan were based on interest. The FSC ordered the government to take legislative measures to eliminate interest from the economy and financial sector of Pakistan by 30 June 1992. The FSC judgement on *riba* revived the IBF movement in Pakistan, which had lost momentum over the years. This chapter highlights the main features of the FSC judgement and other related developments that had a profound impact on the IBF movement in Pakistan in the early 1990s.

6.2 Judicial status of the FSC in Pakistan

The FSC of Pakistan is a constitutionally recognized authority in *Shariah* matters. It was created in 1980 under a Presidential Order by the insertion of a new Chapter 3A in Part VII of the 1973 Constitution of Pakistan. Under Article 203D, the FSC is empowered to examine and decide on the question whether any law or provision of law is repugnant to *Shariah* as enunciated in the holy *Quran* and *Sunnah*. If any law or provision of the country is found repugnant to *Shariah*, the FSC may call upon the government to defend its position before the court. Having taken into account all relevant facts, if the FSC decides that the law or provision in question is repugnant to *Shariah* due to certain reasons and to certain extent, then it is binding upon the government to bring such law or provision into full conformity with *Shariah*; otherwise it would become ineffective after the expiry of given time. However, no verdict of the FSC can take effect before the expiry of the time allowed for making an appeal to the Supreme Court (SC) of Pakistan, or, where the appeal has been so made, before the ruling on that appeal. Any citizen of Pakistan has the right to appeal against the FSC judgement in the SC within 60 days. The government, however, has the right to appeal within 6 months of the decision.[1]

6.3 The FSC's questionnaire

The FSC realized that interest is deeply rooted in the entire economic and financial system of Pakistan. Therefore, the FSC decided to take up the issue of interest and other related issues simultaneously in order to seek a comprehensive solution to the problem of interest. The FSC prepared a questionnaire covering the issues of the impugned fiscal laws, definition of *riba*, banking system, paper currency, indexation and inflation, and sent it to the most accomplished Islamic jurists, scholars, economists and bankers of the contemporary Muslim world to seek their opinion.[2] The FSC also requested a number of renowned IBF theoreticians and practitioners to present their viewpoints on the subject before the court.[3] The FSC made the final verdict on *riba* and related issues in the light of the holy *Quran* and *Sunnah* and opinions of experts in *Shariah* and Islamic Economics.

6.4 The FSC judgement

The FSC remained incapable of dealing with the case of interest in the early years of its foundation (1980), because its jurisdiction of entertaining petitions over fiscal laws and banking matters was banned through special Presidential Orders.[4] On 25 June 1990, when the constitutional power of the FSC was restored, 115 *Shariat* petitions and three *suo moto Shariat* notice cases[5] were filed with the court between 30 June and 24 October 1991, challenging a host of banking and fiscal laws in Pakistan on account of interest provision in them.[6] A full bench of the FSC, comprising three judges, namely, Chief Justice Tanzil-ur-Rahman, Justice Fida Mohammad Khan and Justice Abaid Ullah Khan, thoroughly considered the views of all parties to the *riba* case. After lengthy deliberations, the FSC concluded its hearing on *riba* on 14 November 1991. The FSC announced the following verdict on *riba*:

> A transaction which contains excess or additional over and above the principal amount of loan, which is predetermined in relation to time

> or period to be conditional on the payment to predetermined excess or addition, payable to the creditor (such a transaction containing the said elements) constitutes *riba* and any sale, transaction or credit facility, in money or in kind, has been considered to be a transaction of *riba*, which is unlawful (harm) in the territory of Islam and in Muslim society. There is a consensus (*Ijma*) of the Muslim jurists on it.[7]

The FSC further added that any stipulated increase on capital, whether high or low, simple or compound, taken for personal or private or productive or consumption purposes, for short- or long-term, between two Muslims or between a Muslim and non-Muslim or between a citizen and state or between two states, comes under the ambit of *riba*.[8] The FSC decreed that bank interest falls under the definition of *riba*.[9] The FSC resolved that the practice of mark-up (*Bai Muajjal/Murabaha*) with a buy-back arrangement in the banking and financial sector of Pakistan involves excess on the amount of principal and thereby constitutes interest.[10] The FSC adjudged 20 banking and fiscal laws[11] that contained provisions of interest and mark-up as repugnant to the injunctions of Islam. The FSC ordered the government to bring these laws into full conformity with *Shariah* by 30 June 1992; otherwise they would cease to be effective on and from 1 July 1992.

6.5 The un-Islamic features of the Pakistani finance sector

The FSC judgement on *riba* proved to be a significant contribution to the literature on Islamic Economics and Finance. This scholarly document entails a thorough discussion on interest and related issues, and reflects upon the views and arguments propounded by the related parties. The FSC judgement also provided sufficient guidelines for establishing an interest-free economic and financial system in the country. The FSC repudiated the government's claims that interest in financial transactions was not *riba*, which is prohibited by the holy *Quran*, because it did not involve any exploitation and was, rather, the backbone of modern economy. It also dismissed the contention that the global economy is based on interest, so that any departure from it would cause the economic collapse of Pakistan.[12] The FSC held that, if absolute prohibition of *riba* or interest is proved from the holy *Quran* and *Sunnah*, then the doctrine of *Ijma* or *Ijtehad* could not be applied for considering or justifying its permissibility in the banking and financial sector under the Islamic jurisprudence doctrines of '*Maslahah*' and '*Mutashbaha*' (see Chapter 2).[13]

The FSC resolved that an interest-free economic and financial system could be established by using PLS instruments as the chief modes of financing and other interest-free instruments, such as leasing, *Bai Muajjal*, *Bai Salam* and hire-purchase as supplementary modes of financing. The FSC pointed out that the 1980 CII Report provided sufficient guidelines for establishing an interest-free economy in Pakistan (see Chapter 3). The FSC urged that the existing banking system and market environments should be reoriented on the basis of the objectives, principles and priorities of Islamic Economics, and, moreover, the banks should directly participate in commerce, industry and developmental schemes.[14]

The FSC resolved that the government should abandon interest-based instruments to finance its expenditures because interest was absolutely prohibited in Islam for the individual Muslim as well as the Islamic state.[15] The FSC held that *Shariah* does not recognize capital as an independent factor of production, and therefore it may be committed to productive use through the efforts of the entrepreneur, but not by letting it for a given time on the basis of a pre-agreed fixed sum (see Chapter 2).[16] The FSC concluded that prize bonds, bearer certificates and other similar instruments involved gambling in addition to interest.[17] The FSC further resolved that the existing insurance system was strictly un-Islamic because it involves interest, gambling and speculation (see Chapter 2).[18] The FSC concluded that inflation indexation was an interest-based idea and its adoption should not be allowed in the Islamic economy.[19]

It may be noted, however, that the FSC judgement did not satisfactorily cover certain core issues, such as protecting the value of money in the Islamic economy, differences between cash and credit prices, Islamic alternatives to existing interest-bearing loans, saving schemes and provident fund schemes.[20]

6.6 Public response to the FSC judgement

The announcement of the FSC verdict stirred up intense debate over interest and IBF in all walks of life in Pakistan. The views and responses of people were highly mixed, and varied in intensity, depending on the socio-political or economic group to which they belonged. Borrowers from, and defaulters on debts to, financial institutions hailed the FSC judgement because its enforcement would render their liabilities and dues to the banks null and void. Financial institutions strongly opposed the FSC verdict because it threatened their profitability due to the remission of interest on their investments, so placing their future in jeopardy.[21] Depositors were also against the FSC decision as they were of the view that it would be a gross injustice if interest on loans owed mostly by a small group of influential business people and industrialists to banking institutions were to be remitted under the FSC judgement.[22]

Some people argued that the *riba* case had not been conducted impartially in the court because the Chief Justice of the FSC, Tanzil-ur-Rahman, was himself a party in the case. He decided the case by relying heavily on the 1980 CII Report, which was produced under his own supervision and chairmanship at the Council of Islamic Ideology (CII) of Pakistan (see Chapter 4). While serving as the CII's chairman, he constantly criticized the SBP and the government for their ineptness and mishandling of the project of transforming the economy of Pakistan on Islamic lines. Therefore, when he acted as the Chief Justice of the FSC, government officials showed reluctance to present their viewpoints before the court because they were certain that Tanzil-ur-Rahman would not be convinced by arguments that he had already rejected as a chairman of the CII. Then the CII's chairman also complained about the lack of political will over the Islamization of the economy in the court, which made things harder for the government.[23] Different quarters of society strongly criticized the government for the casual stand and tentative manner in which the case was argued by its counsel at the FSC court.[24]

6.7 Government reaction to the FSC judgement

Responsibility for implementing the FSC judgement fell upon the Islamic *Jamhori Itehad* (IJI) government, which had come to power in the name of Islam. The government had sponsored the Enforcement of *Shariat* Act, 1991, which contained a national commitment to bring Islamic order to the personal and social lives of the citizens of Pakistan. It had already established the Commission for Islamization of Economy in July 1991 to take up the matter of eliminating interest from the economy and financial sector of Pakistan (see Chapter 8).

The government faced tremendous pressure from different sections of society to implement the FSC judgement. Its own camp was divided over the issue. The government's right wing, representing the politico-religious parties, argued that the leadership should comply with the FSC judgement and meet its promise of enforcing *Shariah* in the economic sphere of the country.[25] The government's left wing, comprising the so-called modernists, argued that the FSC existed as a super-legislative body. It was a non-democratic act of President General Mohammad Ziaul Haq to empower the FSC to dictate terms to the elected government for amending the national laws. It was unnecessary because the Islamization provisions of Article 226 of the 1973 Constitution of Pakistan had already conferred upon the elected parliament the power to take appropriate measures for the Islamization of laws under the non-binding guidance of the CII.[26] This group added that the implementation of the FSC judgement would isolate the economy of Pakistan from the international economy. It would deprive Pakistan of its share of foreign trade and numerous benefits that came from being connected with global business and financial markets. The economy of Pakistan has been relying heavily on interest-based domestic and foreign loans, and if the FSC judgement were to be implemented it would make the payment of interest and debt void. Consequently, there would be a massive flight of foreign investments and capital from the financial market of Pakistan, triggering a financial emergency in the country.[27] Therefore, the government should plead with the Supreme Court (SC) of Pakistan to set aside the FSC verdict; and if the SC would not act as desired then the government should amend the constitution to deprive the FSC judgement of binding force. However, the government's top leadership remained undecided for some months on whether to appeal against the FSC judgement or to take measures to enforce it.[28]

6.8 The FSC judgement on foreign investments

Before the announcement of the FSC judgement, the government had organized many investment conferences in Washington, London, Tokyo and Los Angles for providing first-hand information to foreign governments and investors on investment opportunities in Pakistan following the privatization and deregulation of its economy and financial market. The controversy surrounding the FSC judgement grossly undermined the government's efforts and its incentives for attracting foreign business parties and investors into the country. There were serious doubts in the minds of foreign governments, investors and donating agencies. They were concerned about the structure of the Pakistani economy and banking sector and the status of interest after implementation of the FSC judgement.[29] There was a sharp decline in the flow of foreign investment, aid and loans into Pakistan, and progress on more than 204 major debt projects was stalled due to the FSC judgement.[30] Having realized the sensitivity of the situation, the government made a promise to foreign parties that international financial dealings and contracts would not be affected by implementation of the FSC decision, but it was too late to repair the damage done to the climate that had attracted foreign capital, technology and entrepreneurship into the market of Pakistan.

6.9 Appeals against the FSC judgement

First, the government made a firm promise to religious parties in the country that it would not appeal against the FSC verdict. However, all financial institutions in Pakistan, including those fully controlled by the government, opted to appeal against the FSC judgement in the SC.[31] Just two days before the deadline (26 May 1992) for challenging the FSC judgement, the government also lodged an appeal against it at the SC. The government reiterated its principled position that the FSC judgement should be set aside because there was no proper definition of *riba* in the holy *Quran* and *Sunnah*. *Shariah* prohibits only the exorbitant rate of interest on consumption loans, and the government had already eliminated that sort of *riba* from the banking and financial sector of Pakistan. Productive loans were the backbone of the Pakistani economy, and they did not involve any exploitation or *riba*. Therefore, the existing interest-based economy and financial system should be allowed to function in the country.[32]

6.10 Lessons learned from the FSC judgement

The FSC judgement emerged as a landmark in the history of IBF in Pakistan, on many accounts. It brought some core factors to light that could be helpful in assessing the future of IBF in Pakistan. The decision revived the issue of transforming the economy of Pakistan on Islamic lines, which had lost its impetus and direction due to lack of political will. It resolved the old controversy over the legal definition of interest that should be observed in the economic and financial affairs of the country. Moreover, it left no room for the government to strengthen its support for interest by excluding fiscal laws and banking matters from the jurisdiction of the FSC (Siddiqui, 1997b).

The FSC judgement revealed the government's double standards over the matter of implementing the IBF system in the country. It became obvious that the government had made no progress in the previous 10 years towards transforming the economy and financial sector of Pakistan on Islamic lines. Rather, it had successfully maintained the status quo under the cover of 'evolutionary process'. Furthermore, the lack of public commitment and consensus over the issue of *riba* implied that the people of Pakistan had become more materialistic and liberal. The 'clash of interests' among different groups in society implied that the prevalent interest-bearing socio-economic set-up of the country was exploitative and not based on *Shariah* principles, which cater for the welfare of each group and develop an altruistic and mutually beneficial atmosphere in the polity (see Chapter 2). The FSC judgement brought to the surface the central fact that the Pakistani polity was not ready to make any real sacrifice to establish the Islamic economic and financial system in the country. The matter of abolishing interest from the economy of Pakistan had been delayed for the previous 45 years (1946–92), and by lodging an appeal with the SC the polity of Pakistan further deferred it for the time being (Khan M M, 2003; 2008c).

6.11 Summary and conclusions

On 14 November 1991 the Federal *Shariat* Court gave its judgement that interest in all its forms is *riba* and strictly prohibited by the holy *Quran* and *Sunnah*. It resolved that the existing banking and financial system and a host of fiscal laws in Pakistan were based on interest. It repudiated the government's claim that the elimination of interest from the economy of Pakistan would isolate it from the world economy and trigger a serious economic and financial crisis in the country. It resolved that government securities, prize bonds, and bearer certificates were interest-based instruments and that the government should cease its reliance on interest-based borrowings from public and foreign lenders. The FSC ordered the government to take firm and immediate action to transform the economy and financial sector of Pakistan on Islamic lines by 30 June 1992.

The FSC judgement proved to be a wake-up call to the government that it should meet its constitutional responsibility of eliminating interest from the economy and financial sector of Pakistan. It evoked mixed reactions in the polity of Pakistan. Financial institutions and depositors were against the FSC judgement because its implementation was harming their interests. Rich borrowers hailed the judgement because its enforcement was supposed to bring an automatic cancellation of accrued interest on their liabilities towards banks. Foreign parties were nervous over the FSC judgement, and consequently a sharp decline in the flow of foreign investment, aid and loans was experienced in Pakistan. The religio-political parties pressed the government to enforce the FSC judgement. The so-called modernists urged the government to challenge the FSC judgement in the SC of Pakistan. Eventually, the government and the financial institutions of Pakistan lodged appeals against the FSC judgement at the SC. The controversies over the FSC judgement revealed that the polity of Pakistan had no unified commitment or will to abolish interest from its economic and business life.

7

Efforts to Revive Islamic Banking and Finance in Pakistan (1992–1998)

7.1 Introduction

The Federal *Shariat* Court resolved in November 1991 that the prevalent interest-based banking and finance system has not been replaced by the IBF system and that the government should take immediate steps to transform the economy of Pakistan on Islamic lines. Earlier in July 1991 the government had constituted a Commission for Islamization of Economy (CIE) with the main objective of adopting measures for restructuring the economic and financial sector of Pakistan on Islamic lines. The CIE had been working on the same assignment when the FSC judgement on *riba* was announced. The government put pressure on the CIE to finalize its recommendations for eliminating interest from the banking and financial sector of Pakistan. In June 1992 the CIE submitted the *Report on Banks and Financial Institutions* for abolishing interest from the existing financial set-up of Pakistan.

The government took no interest in implementing the report of the CIE. It had already challenged the FSC orders in the Supreme Court of Pakistan. Due to the incomplete quorum, the SC remained unable for some years to deal with interest petitions. This gave full freedom to the government and financial institutions to continue with their interest-bearing dealings as usual. Even though the CIE was created as a permanent institution to guard banking practices in Pakistan against un-Islamic features, it was not properly equipped with material and intellectual resources to accomplish the gigantic task of eliminating interest from the economy. In May 1998, the CIE sought help from the International Institute of Islamic Economics (IIIE) at International Islamic University Islamabad, Pakistan, on the Islamization issue. In response, the IIIE submitted its findings on transforming the economy and financial sector of Pakistan on Islamic lines to the CIE in July 1998.

This chapter captures the crucial developments of IBF in Pakistan during the period 1992 to 1998. The CIE's first attempt, *The 1992 Report on Banks and Financial Institutions,* is evaluated in the first part of this chapter, while the second attempt of the CIE, which covers the 1998 IIIE's recommendations for evolving an Islamic financial system, is appraised in the remaining part.

7.2 The CIE's role and responsibilities

The Commission for Islamization of Economy (CIE) was established in July 1991 under Section 7 of Enforcement of *Shariat* Act of 18 June 1991. The government appointed 12 members, including the governor of the State Bank of Pakistan (SBP) as chairman, to the CIE (see Annexure I-D). The CIE was established as a permanent national institution to make consistent efforts to ensure the true and absolute elimination of interest from the economy of Pakistan. The main objective of the CIE was to examine all fiscal, banking and insurance laws, identify their shortcomings and thereby suggest appropriate remedies and alternatives for bringing them into full conformity with *Shariah.* The CIE constituted three working groups, on banking, on finance and on socio-economic problems respectively, to develop a comprehensive strategy for eliminating interest from the economy of Pakistan. The CIE was required to submit regular reports to the government, to be placed before the National Parliament of Pakistan for discussion and final approval (The 1992 CIE Report, p. 3).

7.3 The CIE's first initiative: *The 1992 Report on Banks and Financial Institutions*

The FSC verdict of November 1991 exerted tremendous pressure on the government to do something urgently to eliminate interest from the economy of Pakistan. The government urged the CIE to give top priority to proposing an Islamic system for the financial sector in Pakistan. Therefore, the CIE devoted all its efforts to recommending measures for eliminating interest from the financial sector as a matter of urgency (The 1992 CIE Report, p. 4). On 6 June 1992 the CIE submitted its recommendations, titled *Report on Banks and Financial Institutions,* to the government of Pakistan. (This report will henceforth be called 'the 1992

CIE Report', in which terms it has been cited throughout this study.) The main features of the 1992 CIE Report are outlined below.

7.3.1 Gross irregularities in IBF practice

The CIE observed serious irregularities and un-Islamic features in banking practice in Pakistan. It registered that banks' investments in money at call and short notice, trade bills and all types of government securities were based on fixed rates of interest (The 1992 CIE Report, p. 6). The practice of mark-up (*Bai Muajjal/Murabaha*) financing with a buy-back agreement was very common and almost an interest-based activity. The use of the PLS system was negligible, and contained a number of un-Islamic elements (The 1992 CIE Report, pp. 13, 35). Financial institutions had abandoned the application of rent-sharing for mark-up financing with a buy-back agreement (The 1992 CIE Report, p. 15). The major part of banks' investments and PLS deposits was invested in interest-based government securities and other un-Islamic investment avenues (The 1992 CIE Report, p. 32). The return bearing deposits and foreign currency deposits were paid interest-based returns under the SBP's directives. The banks' borrowings mainly comprised borrowings from the SBP, other banks and foreign lending agencies on the basis of interest (The 1992 CIE Report, pp. 16, 34).

The CIE identified the main obstacles to adopting IBF concepts in Pakistan. It argued that the 1980 CII Report was implemented without adequate preparation. The SBP allowed the banks to choose any of the 12 approved Islamic modes of financing to conduct their operations (The 1992 CIE Report, p. 35). Consequently, banks relied heavily on mark-up financing with a buy-back agreement because of its close resemblance to the existing conventional banking system. They shunned other modes of financing, such as PLS, leasing, hire purchase and rent sharing (The 1992 CIE Report, pp. 13, 17). Banks did not adopt the PLS system due to business ethics problems, and business people avoided it for tax and privacy reasons. Business people found *Musharakah* financing schemes very complex and a source of interference by banks in their business management and privacy. Business people also complained that banks did not share losses under *Musharakah* arrangements, especially in the case of Participation Term Certificates (PTCs), despite the risk-sharing relationship. The CIE concluded that the increasing scope of interest-based borrowings and deposit mobilization schemes, sponsored by the government and financial institutions, left hardly any chance to promote IBF practice in Pakistan (The 1992 CIE Report, pp. 32–36).

7.3.2 Main recommendations

The CIE made a number of major recommendations for restructuring the banking and finance system of Pakistan on Islamic lines. It concluded that the legal framework for *Musharakah* financing might include certain features to enhance its practical scope. The bank and the client should be given full freedom to determine the PLS ratio and other relevant matters of the *Musharakah* contract. The SBP should not fix the minimum and maximum rates of profit on PLS schemes because this was against the spirit of *Shariah* (The 1992 CIE Report, p. 32). The client should submit regular progress and annual reports to the bank on *Musharakah* investments. A provisional share of the profit on *Musharakah* investments should be paid to the bank at regular intervals. The client should pay the bank's share of the profit before distributing any dividend among shareholders. All losses incurred on account of poor management and misappropriation should be borne solely by the client. The bank should enjoy a right to convert its outstanding long-term investments into ordinary shares of the client's company if the client failed to achieve the projected rates of profit on *Musharakah* investments (The 1992 CIE Report, pp. 19–21).

The CIE asserted that banks were not permitted under *Shariah* to charge 210 days additional mark-up to cover the risk of delay or default in the repayment of mark-up loans. It demanded that this un-Islamic practice should be abandoned and banks should straightforwardly recover fines from loan defaulters for the period of delay. It further advised that the amount of fine so collected would not count as legitimate income for banks, and it therefore should be spent on the welfare of poor people (The CIE Report, pp. 28–29).

The CIE urged the government to replace its interest-based borrowings with interest-free borrowings. It suggested a temporary arrangement whereby the government would replace its interest-based securities with interest-free securities based on an income-tax rebate (instead of a fixed rate). Banks and financial institutions may buy the proposed securities to meet their liquidity requirements and also for investment of their surplus funds. However, the CIE acknowledged that this was not a viable solution because it would have a negative impact on banks' profitability and returns to depositors, leading to low levels of investment, saving and economic growth (The 1992 CIE Report, p. 32).

The CIE argued that mark-up financing under a buy-back arrangement was an interest-based activity; it should therefore be abandoned at once and the true form of *Bai Muajjal* should be adopted in the financial sector of Pakistan (The 1992 CIE Report, p. 33). It demanded that trade bills should be transacted on a collection basis as prescribed in the 1980 CII Report (The 1992 CIE Report, pp. 9–10). It further argued that financial institutions should abandon all interest-based investment schemes (The 1992 CIE Report, p. 36). Furthermore, it emphasized the need to establish a permanent advisory board of *Shariah* and financial experts to assist the CIE and the government in dealing with various aspects of the Islamization of the banking and finance sector of Pakistan (The 1992 CIE Report, p. 37).

7.3.3 Critical assessment of the CIE's recommendations

The CIE presented its review of the contemporary banking system in Pakistan and made some suggestions for transforming its interest-based mechanisms and tools on Islamic lines. The discussion below appraises the 1992 CIE Report and envisages its impacts on the IBF movement in Pakistan.

7.3.3.1 Narrow vision on interest problem

The CIE was required to devise a multidimensional strategy for eliminating interest from the economy of Pakistan. It took the first step in the right direction by formulating three working groups to identify and evaluate the main obstacles within banking industry and on the socio-economic fronts to transforming the economy of Pakistan on Islamic lines. However, due to increasing pressure from the government, it confined itself to resolving the problem of interest without addressing its root causes. Therefore, it did not deal with the interlinked socio-economic factors that worked against the practice of IBF and prevented it from taking root in Pakistan. Consequently, the possibility that the 1992 CIE Report would eliminate interest from the economy of Pakistan was remote (see Chapter 9).

7.3.3.2 The pro-banking mentality

The CIE was required to sort out mutually beneficial relationships between financial institutions and their clients within the Islamic framework. However, most of the CIE's recommendations aimed at promoting the welfare of financial institutions. For example, the CIE's recommendations for *Musharakah* investment did not deal with tax and privacy issues from the client's perspective, even though such issues constitute the main reasons why business people are reluctant to enter *Musharakah* relationships with banks (see Chapter 3). The adoption of the CIE's recommendations would make the *Musharakah* agreement a very strict legal deal between the bank and the client, which could further undermine the scope of *Musharakah* in actual IBF practice in Pakistan (see Chapter 8).

The CIE seemed to rely mainly on the system of *Bai Muajjal* and so recommended it for meeting the short- and long-term financing needs of different sectors of the economy, such as farms inputs, imported merchandise, and finance for agricultural development, house building, plant construction and acquisition of machinery (The 1992 CIE Report, pp. 24–27). However, it ignored the CII's warning that the *Bai Muajjal* system should be used only in exceptional cases, since its indiscriminate use would degenerate into interest (see Chapter 4).

7.3.3.3 Lack of creativity and practicability

The CIE did not provide a detailed framework for successfully adopting its recommendations. For example, it recommended *Musharakah* for meeting all types of business finance, such as an export refinance, import bills drawn under import, Letter of Credit (LC) and bills drawn under inland LCs. Furthermore, it advised that the SBP's financial assistance to banks in the shape of counter-finance, refinance or as lender of last resort should be based on risk-sharing arrangements (The 1992 CIE Report, pp. 24, 34). However, it did not set out a detailed procedure for the successful adoption of PLS techniques in these cases.

The 1992 CIE Report was devoid of any creativity. Its subject matter comprised 40 pages only, which were repetitive and largely reiterated the basic ideas of the 1980 CII Report with some additions and modifications. Like the 1980 CII Report, the CIE prescribed that business people should keep certified accounts; defaulters of bank loans should be blacklisted; tax and legal systems should be restructured on a more just and efficient basis; bankers should be given rigorous training in Islamic banking; banks should rely on foolproof accounting and audit systems to deal with malpractices in the business community; the government should undertake reforms in the financial sector and take serious steps to eradicate false values and improve the moral standards of the people. The CIE contended that these measures should be adopted to restructure the overall system of the country on *Shariah* principles (The 1992 CIE Report, pp. 35–37). However, it did not provide a more detailed roadmap or definite strategies for implementing its recommendations, and, most importantly, it did not explain why the government had failed to adopt them in the first place when they were made in the 1980 CII Report.

7.3.3.4 Time constraints and absence of devotion

Most members of the CIE were preoccupied with their primary duties in different official capacities. They were unable to devote sufficient time and effort to meeting their responsibilities to the CIE. The CIE concluded its work after a total of seven meetings. As revealed in the CIE's annexure of attendance, only once, in the second meeting, did the full bench of 12 members attend; otherwise on average only eight members attended.

7.3.3.5 Political considerations

The scholarship of the CIE's work was overshadowed by political considerations. The 1992 CIE Report was supposed to serve the political interests of the government. The ruling party had constituted a coalition government with the support of religio-political parties that were demanding for the Islamization of economy as a first step towards implementing the overall Islamic order in the polity of Pakistan (see Chapter 6). The real essence of the 1992 CIE Report can be best ascertained by reference to the fact that it was submitted to the government in June 1992 and contained the testimony that the prevailing banking system of Pakistan was based on interest. In contrast, the government challenged the 1991 FSC judgement on *riba* in the Supreme Court (SC) in May 1992 by arguing that the banking system of Pakistan is free from interest: banking transactions are so important and helpful to individuals and society that they should not be regarded as being based on *riba* (interest), which is prohibited in the holy *Quran* and *Sunnah* because of its exploitation of weak economic groups (see Chapter 6).

The government did not submit the 1992 CIE Report to the National Parliament of Pakistan for discussion. It did not take any practical measures to implement the CIE's recommendations. On the other hand, the SC remained impotent for some years in the face of petitions against the 1991 FSC judgement on *riba* due to lack of a full quorum of judges necessary to hear them. The government and financial institutions continued to busy themselves as usual with their interest-based dealings. The IBF movement in effect turned into a legal issue whose fate was to be determined by the SC. During the period from mid-June 1992 to early 1997, there was no political, legal or intellectual progress worth mentioning on the issue of IBF in Pakistan.

7.4 The CIE's second initiative: The 1998 IIIE Report

The CIE was constituted as a permanent institution for promoting the overhaul of the economy of Pakistan on Islamic lines. However, members of the CIE had neither sufficient expertise nor time to deal with the task of Islamization, which had become more complex due to the market reforms introduced by the government of Pakistan in the early 1990s under its liberalization policy and the effects of globalization. In May 1997 the CIE invited the International Institute of Islamic Economics (IIIE) of International Islamic University Islamabad, Pakistan, to make suggestions for the adoption of the IBF system in Pakistan. The IIIE is a well-known research-based institution in the Islamic economic and finance world. The IIIE's members have been involved in basic and applied research over the years to establish the means and measures for resolving the economic and financial issues of contemporary Muslim society on the basis of *Shariah*. The IIIE formulated a team of 14 members (see Appendix I-E) to devise a viable strategy for banishing interest from the financial system of Pakistan.

The IIIE asserted that many radical changes in the financial sector of Pakistan had been occurred over the previous few years which undermined the scope of the 1980 CII Report to deal successfully with the problem of interest (*riba*). In addition, the IIIE pointed out certain deficiencies in the 1980 CII Report as well as in the 1992 CIE Report (The 1998 IIIE Report, Chapter 2). For example, it observed that both reports adopted a partial view of both the problem of interest and its solution. The reports ignored a number of *Shariah*-compliant alternatives to interest such as *Bai Salam*. The experts who worked on the reports did not undertake thorough research to resolve the problem of interest in government borrowings. They did not have a clear vision of the practical issues involved in phasing out interest from the economy of Pakistan. More importantly, they concentrated their efforts on rectifying the existing banking and finance system of Pakistan rather than suggesting a new course of action for developing the IBF system. The IIIE contended that the overall recommendations of these reports could not help to establish a full-fledged and sustainable IBF system, and therefore a renewed and more comprehensive attempt might be made to eliminate interest from the financial sector of Pakistan (The 1998 IIIE Report, pp. 25–27).

In July 1998 the IIIE submitted its findings to the CIE, titled, *The International Institute of Islamic Economics (IIIE)'s Blueprint of Islamic Financial System, including Strategy for Elimination of Riba* (referred to hereinafter as 'the 1998 IIIE Report'). The IIIE claimed that its report contained a refined model for the Islamization of the financial system of Pakistan (The 1998 IIIE Report, pp. 25–26). The IIIE Report was composed of nine chapters, covering the areas of modern commercial banking, government transactions, international transactions, central banking, a detailed strategy of phasing out interest from the economy of Pakistan and legal cover for the Islamic financial system. The discussion below evaluates the main recommendations of the 1998 IIIE Report for establishing an Islamic financial system in Pakistan.

7.4.1 The IIIE's banking model

The IIIE established that an Islamic bank may act as an intermediary between the fund provider and the fund seeker. The bank may rely on some Islamic modes for creating debt but without engaging itself in the conventional lending mechanism (The 1998 IIIE Report, p. 50). It argued that Islamic modes may be applied in such a way that the bank may experience a minimum departure from the existing conventions. The IIIE discussed the following Islamic modes to derive its basic model.

Trading-based modes:	*Bai Muajjal and Bai Salam*
Leasing-based modes:	*Ijarah* (operating lease)
Partnership-based modes:	*Mudarabah and Musharakah*
Lending-based modes:	*Qard-e-Hasanah* and service charge (non-approved)

These four modes have already been explored in Chapters 3 and 4. Therefore, the discussion here briefly describes these modes and mainly evaluates what was new in the IIIE's recommendations for adopting them.

7.4.1.1 Bai Muajjal *(deferred payment sale)*

Under the *Bai Muajjal* system, the bank sells goods to the client on a deferred-payment basis payable in a lump sum or in instalments (see Chapter 4). The IIIE described almost the same characteristics of the *Bai Muajjal* mode as those mentioned in the 1980 CII Report and the 1992 CIE Report. However, the IIIE argued that, since the bank entered into a contract to buy goods from the supplier on the basis of the client's promise to buy them from the bank, if the client changed his mind and refused to buy these goods then he should pay off the bank's liabilities to the supplier resulting from this breach of promise (The 1998 IIIE Report, p. 50). This suggestion is quite contrary to the views of Islamic economists and scholars on the issue. The majority of Islamic scholars hold that the Islamic bank could not transfer to the client any losses and liabilities that may arise during the course of acquiring a legitimate title and possession of goods before their resale to the client under the *Bai Muajjal* agreement (see Chapter 4). *Shariah* clearly demands that the bank bear all risks and losses that may arise in satisfying the requirement of acting as a trader under the *Bai Muajjal* system (see Chapter 3).

7.4.1.2 Bai Salam *(advance payment)*

Under the *Bai Salam* system, the client receives advance payment from the bank for selling his farm's output or manufactured goods at an agreed price, to be delivered to the bank on a specified future date (see Chapter 3). The IIIE proposed that the bank may use the *Bai Salam* mode of financing for meeting the working capital needs of farmers, manufacturers and other business people (The 1998 IIIE Report, p. 52). However, the 1980 CII Report and the 1992 CIE Report did not consider this Islamic mode to be an alternative to interest. It may be noted that *Shariah* does not allow the bank to offer *Bai Salam* goods for sale before acquiring their actual possession on the specified date (see Chapters 2 and 3). Furthermore, the Islamic bank is not allowed to apply conventional techniques for hedging the risk involved in its *Bai Salam* contracts against price fluctuations (see Chapter 2). It implies that the actual practice of *Bai Salam* may place an avoidable demand on the bank to allow radical changes in its conventional structure and thereby take an active part in the commodity market as a trader and stockist.

7.4.1.3 Ijarah *(operating lease)*

Under the operating lease system, the bank meets the short- and medium-term financing needs of business people by providing them business equipment on a rental basis for an agreed period (see Chapters 3 and 4). The IIIE described the same characteristics of leasing that had already been captured by the 1980 CII Report and the 1992 CIE Report (The 1998 IIIE Report, p. 53; see Chapters 3 and 4). However, the IIIE's contention that the bank may sell the leased asset to lessee before the expiry of the lease contract was not validated by the 1980 CII Report or the 1999 Supreme Court Judgement on *riba* (The 1980 CII Report, p. 13; The 1999 SC Judgement on *Riba*, p. 478). *Shariah* clearly holds that the lessor and the lessee should not enter into a contract of sale of the leased asset before the expiry of a lease contract, because to do so would most likely affect the Islamic credibility of the original lease contract and precipitate interest (The 1999 SC Judgement on *Riba*, p. 478; see Chapter 8).

7.4.1.4 Mudarabah *(joint venture) and* Musharakah *(equity participation)*

Under the system of *Mudarabah*, the bank acts as a fund manager (*Mudarib*) for depositors to undertake productive business activity for mutual benefits. Similarly, under the system of *Musharakah*, the bank pools its own funds and depositors' funds to manage a joint business venture to make profits. The banking operations on the basis of *Mudarabah* and *Musharakah* have been elaborately discussed in Chapter 3.

The IIIE maintained that the bank might mobilize funds on the basis of *Mudarabah* and *Musharakah*. However, it did not recognize the right of depositors to play an active part in managing *Musharakah* investments. On the fund application side, the IIIE allowed the client to manage *Musharakah* investments on the condition that the bank would deal with all accounting, auditing and tax matters, and with the payment and collection of *Musharakah* investments. The bank would charge the client for the actual cost incurred in performing these operations (The 1998 IIIE Report, pp. 54–56).

It may be noted that *Shariah* recognizes equal rights of the bank and depositors to manage *Musharakah* businesses. However, depositors can allow the bank to act as an agent on their behalf for managing the affairs of *Musharakah* businesses (see Chapter 3). Therefore, the bank may either give depositors the genuine option of playing an active part in managing *Musharakah* enterprises or drop the idea of accepting deposits on the basis of *Musharakah* altogether.

7.4.1.5 Qard-e-Hasanah *and service charge (non-recommended modes)*

Under the *Qard-e-Hasanah* system, the bank grants interest-free loans to destitute people on benevolent grounds. Under the service charge system, the bank plays an intermediary role as a non-profitable institution. The bank recovers only service charges from all types of borrowers to meet its operating costs. As a result, the bank pays no return to its shareholders and depositors.

The IIIE recommended that the bank should not provide *Qard-e-Hasanah* to destitute people on the grounds that Islamic banks are not charity houses. Moreover, providing *Qard-e-Hasanah* to needy people was the Islamic state's responsibility. In the context of the service charge system, the IIIE remarked that any addition to the original loan, including the amount of service charge, would be interest. Therefore, the bank should not use the service charge system in its financing operations (The 1998 IIIE Report, p. 57).

The literature on Islamic Economics and Finance recognizes Islamic banking institutions as value-based entities. They should actively contribute to the socio-economic relief of poor and weak members of the polity (see Chapters 4 and 6). The IIIE's viewpoint is materialistic and contrary to the Islamic spirit of benevolence and universal brotherhood.

Although the 1980 CII Report rejected the service charge system, it approved the special loan facility system to ensure disadvantaged people easy and cheap access to bank credit (see Chapter 4). However, the IIIE did not greatly care about ensuring a flow of bank funds to weak economic groups and underserved sectors of Pakistani economy on soft terms so as to ensure economic growth with social justice in Pakistan (see Chapter 2).

7.4.2 IBF practice within *Shariah* framework

The IIIE contended that full-fledged IBF operations could be performed on the basis of its recommended policy instruments. The IIIE laid down the scheme set out below to transform interest-based banking and finance operations along Islamic lines in Pakistan.

7.4.2.1 Mobilization of funds (deposits)

The IIIE contended that most types of interest-based deposits could be replaced by the PLS system. However, some other secondary arrangements such as *Ijarah* may be used for mobilizing funds in special cases. The bank may accept current account deposits as usual (The 1998 IIIE Report, p. 62). The IIIE's recommendations for the mobilization of deposits under the PLS system are explored in the following discussion.

The IIIE argued that the bank would act as a fund manager (*Mudarib*), accepting deposits on a *Mudarabah* basis and managing them in risk-sharing investments. The bank would maintain *Mudarabah* deposits in different pools, classified on the basis of time and purpose. It would debit direct expenses, such as cost of stationery and telephone charges, to each type of *Mudarabah* account incurred and paid to a third party for carrying out its operations. It would not charge management fees, staff salaries or other overhead expenses against *Mudarabah* investments, because the bank's share in them would cover the cost and profit margins. It would also accept deposits on a *Musharakah* basis and invest part of its own capital along with them. The adoption of proper accounting and other relevant procedures would enable the bank to calculate the profit on premature withdrawals of PLS deposits (The 1998 IIIE Report, pp. 60–61).

The IIIE maintained that the banking sector of Pakistan should mobilize funds from depositors under the risk-sharing system. However, the 1980 CII Report asserted that, without radical changes in its existing institutional framework, Pakistan was unlikely to adopt the PLS system in banking operations (The 1980 CII Report, p. 5). The IIIE itself acknowledged that no discernible change had occurred in the given socio-economic order of Pakistan since 1980 (The 1998 IIIE Report,

p. 128). Thus, it was hardly possible to foresee any real scope for implementing the above recommendations unless the preconditions mentioned in the 1980 CII Report were duly satisfied. Furthermore, the prevailing market realities in Pakistan did not allow this proposal to succeed.

Investment in the equity market of Pakistan has declined in recent years. The general level of public confidence has been eroded by unsatisfactory systems of corporate governance, business ethics problem and a high level of risk. For some years a handful of companies have opted for public floating. National saving rates have averaged around 11–13 percent of Gross Domestic Product (GDP) for a number of years. The number of public issues of shares declined from 85 percent in 1992 to less than 3 percent in 1997 (*Business Recorder*, 11 June 2002). During the hearing of *riba* case review at the Supreme Court (SC) of Pakistan in June 2002, the SBP and the Task Force of the Ministry of Finance submitted their research findings that interest-based deposits and other investment schemes could not be replaced by risk-sharing instruments because a large majority of depositors were risk-averse and preferred to commit their funds only to those investment avenues where capital preservation and a fixed return on capital were almost guaranteed (The 2002 Task Force Report in Ministry of Finance, Chapter 6).

It may be noted that IBF institutions have yet to develop their own project-evaluation systems and tools or accounting models that might enable them to efficiently work out the expected rates of return and time schedules on their PLS investments. Deposit-taking on the PLS basis may present several accounting complexities and puzzles. The withdrawals of bank deposits may take place on a daily basis, creating serious complications for banks in determining their share of profit on short-term deposits and withdrawals of deposits after short periods. Most importantly, it would be hardly possible for banking institutions to make provision for losses or to determine losses on short-term deposits (Ibid). In the present situation, arguably there is very little chance to mobilize funds on the PLS basis because of the absence of proper accounting systems and a lack of willingness and support from financial institutions and depositors in Pakistan.

7.4.2.2 Funding different sectors of the economy

The IIIE claimed that its recommended modes of financing could be successfully applied to meeting the finance needs of all sectors of the economy of Pakistan. It argued that the *Bai Muajjal* and leasing modes might be applied to financing the customers' needs for non-income generating assets. Banks may use PLS and *Bai Muajjal* modes for financing micro-enterprises, such as retail stores, cottage industries, etc. (The 1998 IIIE Report, pp. 65–66). They may meet the financial needs of farmers for inputs such as seeds, fertilizers and implements under the *Bai Muajjal* system. The financing needs of farmers for durable goods, such as tractors and heavy machinery, may be fulfilled under leasing and *Bai Muajjal* arrangements. Banks may finance projects under the PLS system. They may provide machinery and equipment to different business enterprises under the *Bai Muajjal* arrangement. The working capital needs of clients may be met under the PLS system. Banks may provide finance to property developers under the *Bai Salam* system and to the buyers of homes under the *Bai Muajjal* arrangement. Banks may modify the standard *Musharakah* system to develop the Islamic technique of *Shirakah al-Matanaqish* (redeemable or decreasing-participation arrangement) for purchasing houses in joint ownership with clients (The 1998 IIIE Report, p. 68).

The recommendations presented above have already been tried in contemporary IBF practice but failed due to certain real-life difficulties. For example, financing the working capital requirements of business people under the PLS system was found infeasible, because in most of the cases business people need such funds for non-productive purposes and for investments whose short-term profit could not be calculated in practice (see Chapter 3). Furthermore, the 1992 CIE Report observed that financial institutions in Pakistan had to drop the technique of *Shirakha al-Matanaqish* for financing house-building because of the practical difficulties involved in determining the actual cost of a house and estimating its rental value (The 1992 CIE Report, p. 16).

7.4.3 Central banking and monetary management

The IIIE entrusted the responsibility of managing the money supply and the liquidity of the banking sector to the SBP. It divided monetary tools into two sets, i.e., regulatory measures and control measures. Regulatory measures included the bank rate and open market operations. The IIIE treated all other monetary tools, such as the minimum cash reserve requirement and the liquidity ratio requirement, as control measures. It asserted that it would be mandatory for banks to comply with control measures; however, banks would be affected by regulatory measures when they approached the SBP for seeking financial support or productive use of their idle short-term funds (The 1998 IIIE Report, pp. 113–114).

The IIIE disapproved of the prevailing practice whereby the SBP prescribed minimum and maximum PLS ratios on banks' investments. It claimed that this practice amounted to interference with the contracting parties' free and mutual consent, which might harm the market mechanism. The SBP might use any combination of these instruments to efficiently regulate the credit supply in financial markets. The monetary authority might work in collaboration with the fiscal authority. In order to pursue their objectives, the fiscal and monetary authorities may trade widely in interest-free government securities on the Islamic inter-bank money market (The 1998 IIIE Report, p. 118).

7.4.3.1 Islamic inter-bank money market

The proposal to set up an Islamic inter-bank money market holds a central position in the IIIE's proposed financial system. The IIIE developed a wide range of interest-free securities for trading in the Islamic money market. It stated that these securities would form the greater part of banks' portfolios and serve both the short- and the long-term financing needs of business people. These securities would also facilitate inter-bank transactions. Furthermore, the fiscal and monetary authorities would largely rely on trading in these securities to control the volume of liquidity in the money market. These securities included *Bai Muajjal*-based tradable securities, *Salam* certificates, asset *Ijarah* securities, transferable *Ijarah* warrants, general *Musharakah* certificates, special *Musharakah* certificates and decreasing-participation/redeemable *Musharakah* certificates (The 1998 IIIE Report, Chapter 5).

The scope for an Islamic money market may be evaluated in light of the existing features of the Pakistani financial market. It is likely that the exposure of an Islamic money market to globalization and foreign investment would remain very limited and that financial managers would face practical difficulties in managing investment portfolios efficiently for their customers. Due to the lack of economy of scales and volumes, there would probably be considerable transaction costs in the Islamic money market, which consequently may not be able to offer quick paybacks, short-term cash, market diversity, timing flexibility and other options that are available in contemporary conventional markets. The market players would largely remain exposed to risk due to the non-availability of *Shariah*-compliant risk-hedging techniques in the Islamic money market. Lack of knowledge and understanding on the part of the players about the Islamic market could further add to its inefficiency and instability. The given issues could lead to a situation in which the Islamic money market may fail to co-ordinate choices to ensure the efficient utilization of resources (Foley, 1971; Fry, 1997).

The government of Pakistan has always relied on interest-based securities to attract public funds for paying off interest instalments and loans to its domestic and international creditors (see Chapter 9). As noted in Chapter 4, the 1980 CII Report demanded the elimination of interest from government borrowings as a core precondition for establishing an interest-free economy and financial system in Pakistan. However, the government did not take any practical steps to conduct its borrowing operations on an interest-free basis. On the contrary, the SBP directed banks (in August 1985) to invest their PLS funds in interest-based government securities under IBF practice (see Chapter 5). In sum, it may be argued that prevalent socio-economic factors, such as structural imbalances, budget deficits and political influence on the banking sector, may eventually discourage the establishment and efficient functioning of the proposed Islamic money market in Pakistan (see Chapters 8 and 9). The IIIE's proposal has yet to encounter circumstances favouring its successful implementation in the contemporary IBF world. The IBF industry has been trying over the decades to develop a wide range of short-term instruments, liquidity investments tools and government securities for deepening Islamic money and capital markets, but it has had little success so far.

7.4.3.2 Monetary control measures

The IIIE contended that most of types of conventional deposits may be replaced under the PLS system. Accordingly, the CIE's recommendations on monetary control measures for deposits collected on a PLS basis, i.e., *Mudarabah* and *Musharakah*, are evaluated in the discussion below.

The IIIE asserted that the SBP might not impose regulatory measures on PLS deposits because banks would accept them on the basis of risk-sharing, which means that holders are totally willing to be exposed to business risks. Thus, the SBP may not adopt the safety measure of requiring banks to observe the minimum cash reserve requirement and liquidity ratio requirement on these deposits (The 1998 IIIE Report, pp. 117–118).

The above proposal may offer an opportunity for banks to dispense with cash and liquidity reserves against PLS deposits and to utilize their full capacity to earn good profit margins. However, some serious repercussions from granting greater credit capacity to banks may be taken into account. The adoption of this monetary proposal could increase the credit overflow in the Islamic market, which could generate inflationary pressures and unsustainable economic growth patterns. Furthermore, depositors do not like to take any risks with their funds. For example, in 1997 some employees of the Dubai Islamic Bank (DIB) recklessly approved loans to certain clients and consequently the bank sustained a loss of $US50 million. This news caused a run on deposits. The bank's depositors made withdrawals of $US137 million in a single day, comprising seven per cent of its total deposits. The bank was able to bring things back to normal by asking the Dubai Central Bank and the United Arab Emirates authorities to fully guarantee depositors' capital (Warde, 2000).

The financial sector of Pakistan has experienced a number of scandals in the recent past that deprived thousands of depositors of their savings. These incidents have caused an erosion of confidence on the part of depositors in the banking and finance sector of Pakistan (see Chapter 9). Under the above proposal, if the SBP did not provide any real backup, such as acting as lender of last resort for banks' PLS funds, depositors would become more reluctant to invest their funds in banks under the PLS system. Moreover, if the PLS banking system were hit by a scandal, it would trigger a run on deposits in banks (see Chapter 9). It may be argued that the practice of the proposed monetary policy may not only undermine the PLS system but also exacerbate the liquidly risk, market risk and non-payment risk for the banking and finance sector of Pakistan (The 2002 Task Force Report of Ministry of Finance Pakistan, Chapter 6).

7.4.3.3 Monetary regulatory measures

The IIIE suggested that the SBP might apply the monetary tools of bank rate and open market operations by trading widely in interest-free government securities. Under the new arrangement, the SBP would purchase interest-free government securities from banks at the time of pursuing the expansionary policy on the one hand, and providing budgetary help to the government on the other. The SBP would follow the reverse process to pursue a contractionary monetary policy. The SBP would also increase margins on securities to control credit expansion. The IIIE further asserted that as a regulatory measure the SBP might collect trade bills on behalf of banks and recover from them only the actual cost incurred on such operations (The 1998 IIIE Report, p. 119).

It is worth repeating that the effective use of aforementioned regulatory tools may be conditional upon ascertaining the greater use of Islamic securities and developing the Islamic inter-bank money market, which appears too hard a task to be accomplished for the reasons explained in the previous section. In the context of using trade bills as a monetary tool, it may be noted that if the SBP charges banks strictly for the actual cost incurred on the collection of bills, it cannot adjust such a cost upward or downward to discourage or encourage the banks' dealings in bills so as to affect their liquidity position. Thus, the cost of collection of bills should neither affect nor be affected by the credit supply in the Islamic market. It implies that the use of bills as a monetary tool may turn the discounting mechanism into an interest-based activity or a selling of a debt for a higher debt, which is un-Islamic.

7.4.3.4 Co-ordination in fiscal and monetary management

The IIIE argued that fiscal measures should support and reinforce monetary policy in the Islamic economy. It placed heavy reliance on tax measures to assist monetary policy. It asserted that the levers of income tax and commodity tax would be applied to drive the volume-based purchasing power and economic activities in the direction desired by the monetary management. It further contended that different taxation rates for different economic sectors would facilitate the regulation of credit flows into special or preferred sectors of the economy of Pakistan (The 1998 IIIE Report, p. 120).

This idea may be evaluated in the context of existing market conditions in Pakistan. It is generally argued that monetary and fiscal policies are closely interlinked. For example, economists in the classical tradition argue that monetary policy is effective in influencing aggregate demand, output, prices, market rates of interest and employment in most cases (Amacher and Ulbrich, 1995). Economists in the Keynesian tradition believe the opposite, namely, that monetary policy occupies a subordinate position to fiscal policy (Friedman, 1969; Persson and Tabellini, 1994). However, there is a lack of co-ordination between monetary and fiscal policies in Pakistan due to weak monetary management, macroeconomic instability, structural imbalances and budget deficits (see Chapter 9).

The IIIE's proposal to use the tax lever for reinforcing monetary policy may find strong support from modern theories of monetary and fiscal management. In the advanced economies, a reduction in personal income tax shifts the consumption schedule upward. Cuts in corporation tax or other business tax improve profit expectations, shift the investment-demand curve to the right and stimulate investment. An increase in tax weakens profit expectations and reduces willingness to invest (Tansi, 1990; Kearl, 1993; Bowden and Bowden, 1995). However, these mechanisms may lose much of their relevance and effectiveness if applied in the developing market of Pakistan. The tax collection machinery of Pakistan is inefficient, and tax laws lack width and elasticity. A large number of business people report low profitability in order to avoid tax. In addition, the economy of Pakistan is not sufficiently or systematically documented (see Chapter 9). In such circumstances, the tax lever would have little to work on to ascertain the volume of economic activities in the market or to regulate them in specific directions, so as to help monetary policy achieve its objectives.

The inefficiency of Pakistan's tax system has seriously aggravated the problem of the budget deficit, which inevitably has adverse effects on the country's monetary policy (see Chapter 9). These fatal and inherited flaws in the fiscal and tax frameworks of Pakistan have seriously hampered the adoption of the IBF system in the country (see Chapter 9). To sum up, without addressing these microeconomic and macroeconomic constraints, fiscal and monetary managements could not work in harmony, and so fiscal policies may not reinforce monetary policies in achieving financial stability and economic growth in Pakistan.

7.4.4 Critique of the IIIE's overall themes

It may be worthwhile to explore the IIIE's mindset, spirit and generic strategies for transforming the economy and financial sector of Pakistan on Islamic lines. The discussion below explores some core aspects of the IIIE's approach to eliminating interest from the financial sphere of Pakistan.

7.4.4.1 Tentative premises to eliminate interest

The IIIE's basic approach to eliminating interest from the financial system differs significantly from the conceptual foundation laid by the worldwide literature on IBF. The IIIE developed its financial model on the following basic assumptions.

1. By experiencing a minimum departure from the existing conventional banking framework, the Islamic bank could act as an intermediary between the fund depositor and the investor.
2. The Islamic financial system could function without requiring the absolute elimination of interest from the economy and moral elevation of the society of Pakistan.
3. The problem of the low moral standards of business people could be resolved by making the demand for collateral compulsory, and by the adoption of foolproof accounting and auditing systems on the part of IFIs.

7.4.4.2 *Islamic financial system versus conventional financial system*

These assumptions of the IIIE may be evaluated in the light of basic principles of Islamic Economics (see Chapter 2). It is highly debatable that the Islamic financial system could be developed by making only minimal changes to the existing conventional financial system. The Islamic financial system is an integral part of Islamic philosophy of life, which is enlightened by divine guidance and gives proper foundation and shape to every institution in the Islamic polity (see Chapter 2). The Islamic financial system caters for the spiritual and physical welfare of human beings. It is based on the moral values of Islamic Economics, such as equity-based financing, innovation, risk-sharing and fairness in business dealings (see Chapter 2). From the Islamic perspective, economic activity is not an end in itself but a means to achieve the supreme goal of real success in this life and the life hereafter – eternal salvation or *falah* (see Chapter 2). The conventional financial system, on the other hand, is a product of capitalism, which is secular in nature and regards economic activity as an end in itself. The materialistic parameters, such as efficiency, the market mechanism and self-interest, are the very foundations of the capitalist system. The differences between the Islamic ideology of life and the capitalist ideology of life are very great, which necessitates radically different institutional frameworks for the Islamic financial system and the conventional financial system. There is neither any reason nor any space to develop the Islamic financial system within the conventional financial system.

7.4.4.3 *Moral and motivational reinforcements*

Only ethically based confidence-building measures can ensure the wholehearted compliance of the people with the Islamic financial system. Thus precautionary measures, such as demanding collateral, adopting foolproof accounting and auditing systems and setting up a stringent legal system, could achieve only limited success in dealing with the problem of poor business ethics. Even modern accounting and auditing systems suffer from inherited flaws and could not eliminate the chances of fraud beyond a certain level. Similarly, the act of procuring third-party guarantees and collateral could not render financial institutions fully immune from losses arising from fraud, default and other malpractices.

It may be noted that, due to the weak judicial framework of Pakistan, the cost of default may be very detrimental to the finance sector of Pakistan. Financial institutions may sustain a great deal of loss of time and money in realizing their funds through enforcing contracts and executing collateral (see Chapter 9). After adopting strict measures, financial institutions may yet find that the risk of non-payment on PLS investments remains at an alarming level. As a result, financial institutions may avoid giving any respectable presentation of the PLS system in their financing operations. Like conventional financial institutions, they may become very conservative and biased in favour of rich and creditworthy borrowers in loaning out funds. It may be further noted that the demand for collateral violates Islamic values, such as free will, universal brotherhood, mutual trust and co-operation. In fact, the IIIE simply failed to appreciate the real significance of moral reinforcements in the successful adoption of the Islamic financial system (see Chapter 3).

7.4.4.4 Passive approach towards practical difficulties

The IIIE sought the practical success of its financial model on the basis of two key assumptions that are not supported by the principles of Islamic Economics and prevailing market realities in Pakistan. First, the IIIE contended that reliance on strict legal measures could enable its proposed banking and finance model to be successfully adopted without seeking any active support from other socio-economic institutions in the country. However, this premise is strongly opposed to the views of various Islamic quarters. For example, the 1980 CII Report, the 1992 CIE Report and the 1991 Federal *Shariat* Court (FSC) judgement on *riba* maintained that, without radical changes in the financial and socio-political and economic institutions of Pakistan, the adoption of the IBF system is simply out of the question (see Chapters 4, 5 and 6). In 1992, the CIE formulated a separate working group to deal with socio-economic problems that could hinder the smooth adoption and practice of IBF in Pakistan. In 1999, the CII remarked that a lack of proper institutional support led to the failure of IBF practice in Pakistan (see Chapter 9). However, the IIIE tried to eliminate interest from finance institutions without realizing that all institutions of Islamic society are closely interlinked and reinforce each other to work for the welfare of the people under *Shariah* guidance (see Chapter 2).

Second, the IIIE held that interest-bearing securities could be easily replaced by interest-free securities, so that central banking operations could be conducted under the *Shariah* framework. However, the proposed changeover would be largely conditional upon resolving fiscal and other micro and macro problems of the economy and financial market of Pakistan. These problems are highly complex and demand the complete reorientation of the economy and market of Pakistan on scientific and Islamic lines (see Chapters 8 and 9).

The IIIE tried to cover most aspects of the Islamic economy and financial system in the space of 142 pages. In doing so, it lost any deep insight into the practical and technical aspects of the problem to hand and turned out more general and theoretical. Furthermore, it did not establish an advisory panel, comprising *Shariah* experts, bankers, lawyers, businessmen and public representatives to develop a truly workable plan with due support from the polity of Pakistan. The IIIE recognized financial institutions as profit-making entities, and as such without ethical and social responsibilities towards poor and other weak groups of the polity. In order to obtain more flexible and practical solutions, it tried to shift the paradigm of Islamic Economics and Finance closer to the paradigm of conventional economics and finance.

7.5 Summary and conclusions

The CIE was constituted in 1991 to make recommendations for improving the credibility of IBF practice in Pakistan. It submitted its *Report on Banks and Financial Institutions* in June 1992. It observed that the prevalent banking and financial system of Pakistan was based on interest in the garb of mark-up financing. The use of the PLS system was insignificant and not in compliance with *Shariah*. Banks were investing PLS deposits in interest-based and mark-up investment avenues. All dealings of financial institutions with the public and the SBP were based on interest. Fixed and predetermined rates of profit were paid to PLS depositors. Having diagnosed the problem of interest in the financial sector of Pakistan, the CIE failed to seek its solution in the socio-economic context of Pakistan. Consequently, its recommendations did not bring any improvements in IBF practice in Pakistan.

In May 1997 the CIE invited the IIIE to offer recommendations to revamp the financial sector of Pakistan on Islamic lines. In July 1998 the IIIE submitted its findings on the subject. The IIIE's IBF model was primarily based on *Mudarabah, Musharakah, Bai Muajjal, Bai Salam* and *Ijarah*. In the system of *Bai Muajjal*, the IIIE made a controversial recommendation that clients should bear all losses arising from their refusal to buy *Bai Muajjal* goods. The IIIE contended that *Bai Salam* may be used in Islamic financial institutions without bringing any radical changes to the existing conventional infrastructure. However, the true adoption of this system may require banks to become active players in the commodity market. The IIIE suggested that Islamic banks were not charity houses, and therefore should not provide *Qard-e-Hasanah* (goodly loans) to destitute members of society. Furthermore, it disallowed the service charge system by calling it an interest-based activity. It strongly argued that financial institutions of Pakistan may accept deposits on a PLS basis.

The IIIE contended that the SBP should control the activities of the Islamic financial market by creating a regulatory environment but not by dictating terms to financial institutions in their dealings with clients. It strongly advocated establishing an Islamic inter-bank money market. It came up with a large number of interest-free securities that may be traded in the Islamic money market, to serve the short- and long-term financing needs of economic agents. Furthermore, it suggested that the SBP may trade in these securities to regulate the money supply and provide financial assistance to the government. However, problems of the budget deficit, foreign debt and other inherited structural imbalances of the economy of Pakistan may leave little scope for replacing interest-based government securities with interest-free securities.

The approach of the IIIE to eliminating interest from the financial system of Pakistan was narrow because it aimed at replacing interest-based instruments with interest-free instruments by requiring a minimal departure from the existing conventional framework. It relied little on moral and motivational reinforcements, and more on strict legal and regulatory measures to ensure the compliance of market players, investors and business people with the proposed Islamic financial system. The IIIE prepared its report without properly consulting *Shariah* and financial experts, stakeholders and other groups in society. In sum, there was a great need to develop a comprehensive Islamic financial system for replacing the complex and globally integrated interest-based financial system of Pakistan, but the substance of the 1998 IIIE Report was not enough to successfully meet this serious challenge.

8

The Impact of the Supreme Court Judgements of 1999 and 2002 on *Riba* (Interest) on the IBF Movement in Pakistan (1999–2007)

8.1 Introduction

As described in Chapter 6, the Federal *Shariat* Court (FSC) gave its verdict on *riba* in November 1991 and ordered the government to adopt the necessary measures for eliminating interest from the economy of Pakistan by 30 June 1992. In response, the government and financial institutions lodged appeals against the FSC judgement at the Supreme Court (SC) of Pakistan. The appeals against the FSC judgement remained pending at the SC for some years due to the lack of a full quorum of judges to conduct hearings. After achieving its quorum in February 1999, the SC commenced hearing the appeals, and declared its verdict on 23 December 1999. The SC unanimously affirmed the FSC's declaration that *riba* violated *Shariah* principles. The SC prescribed parameters that the government should observe in abolishing the interest-based economic and financial system of Pakistan by 30 June 2001.

The government took some steps to implement the SC orders but failed to do so within the prescribed time limit. Therefore, it sought from the SC an extension to 30 June 2002 to complete the transformation. Previously, United Bank Limited (UBL), a government-run bank, had moved a review petition, requesting the SC to suspend its judgement on *riba* because bank interest did not fall into the category of *riba* prohibited in the holy *Quran*. The SC deferred its hearing on the UBL's petition for the time being.

On 6 June 2002, the government submitted to the SC that its prescribed parameters for enforcing an Islamic economy were infeasible, and therefore any attempt to implement them may cause permanent damage to the economy of Pakistan. The UBL fully supported the government's petition. On 24 June 2002, the SC decided to send back the *riba* case to the FSC for re-examination in the light of points raised by the concerned parties during the hearing.

This chapter takes stock of developments in the judicial and financial spheres of Pakistan from 1999 to 2007. It reviews the main observations of the 1999 SC judgement on the existing banking practice in Pakistan. It describes the parameters suggested by the SC for transforming the economic and financial system of Pakistan on Islamic lines. It highlights the steps taken by the government for enforcing an Islamic economy. It takes account of the points raised by the concerned parties at the SC during the *riba* case review of June 2002. It assesses the credibility of this judgement and the government's sincerity in implementing the SC orders of 1999 on *riba*. Finally, it explores the impacts and implications of the SC judgements on contemporary IBF practice in Pakistan.

8.2 The SC's stature in the judicial system of Pakistan

The SC is a forum at the apex of the judicial system of Pakistan. Article 203F of the 1973 Constitution of Pakistan recognizes the right of any citizen of Pakistan to lodge an appeal against a judgement made by the FSC at the SC within 60 days of its announcement. The government of Pakistan has a right to appeal against the decision within 6 months. No judgement of the FSC may take effect before the expiry of the time allowed for making appeals to the SC, or, where an appeal has been so made, before the disposal of such appeal. Moreover, Article 188 of the 1973 Constitution of Pakistan allows any citizen of Pakistan to seek a review of the verdict made by the SC. The SC contains a special bench – the *Shariah* Appellate Bench – which deals with appeals against any judgement made by the FSC. According to Article 203F (3a) of the 1973 Constitution of Pakistan, the *Shariah* Appellate Bench of the Supreme Court should comprise five judges. Three of them should be regular judges of the SC and the other two should be religious scholars, to be appointed by the president of Pakistan.

8.3 Main observations on the 1999 SC judgement

On 22 February 1999, the SC started hearings on the appeals against the 1991 FSC judgement on *riba*, and it declared its verdict on 23 December 1999.[1] The SC unanimously confirmed the order of the FSC declaring *riba* to be repugnant to the injunctions of the holy *Quran*. The SC ordered that all existing laws and rules (see Appendix IV-C) containing the provision of interest would cease to be effective as on and from 30 June 2001, and therefore the government should transform the economy of Pakistan on Islamic line by this time.

The judgement contained a comprehensive discussion on *riba* and the other main issues involved in the abolition of *riba* in the economy of Pakistan. Like the FSC, the SC circulated a questionnaire among *Shariah* experts and practitioners of IBF to seek their opinions on the *riba* case (see Appendix VI). After taking into account all such available sources of knowledge on the subject, the SC made the following observations on the prevalent economic and financial system of Pakistan.

8.3.1 The SC's definition of *riba* (interest)

The SC observed the following definition of *riba*:

> Any amount, big or small, in excess of the principal, in a contract of loan or debt, is '*riba*', prohibited by the holy *Quran*, regardless of whether the loan is taken for the purpose of consumption or for some production activity.[2]

The SC further resolved that there was no difference between usury and interest, simple and compound interest, interest at a nominal rate and at an exorbitant rate. All these types of interest fell within the category of *riba*, which is absolutely prohibited by *Shariah* (see Chapter 2).[3] The SC observed that bank interest was unambiguously covered by the prohibition of *riba* in the holy *Quran* and *Sunnah*, because when the revelation about the prohibition of *riba* was proclaimed, all types of consumption, commercial, industrial and agricultural loans were widely practised in Arabia and neighbouring countries (see Chapter 2).[4]

8.3.2 The *Bai Muajjal* (deferred payment sale) practice

The SC observed that in its real essence, *Bai Muajjal* was a trade-based activity.[5] Therefore, the relationship between the bank and the client under *Bai Muajjal* should originate in a genuine sale of a commodity with all its substantive consequences.[6] The SC held that, when the bank and the client concluded the price of a *Bai Muajjal* contract, it became a form of debt payable by the client to the bank either in a lump sum or in instalments. Therefore, the bank could not unilaterally change the original price of a *Bai Muajjal* contract for any reason.[7]

The SC resolved that subclause (i) of Section 79 of the 1881 Negotiable Instrument Act, which allowed the bank to recover from the client an additional amount at the rate of the original *Bai Muajjal* contract for any period of delay in the repayment of debt, was against the injunctions of Islam.[8] The SC further resolved that a penalty in the case of default may be recovered from the client but the amount so collected should not become a permissible source of income for the bank, as mentioned in Section 79 of the 1881 Negotiable Instrument Act.[9] The SC observed that subsections 114 and 117(c) of Section 79 of the 1881 Negotiable Instrument Act, which allowed banks to charge a 'mark-up on a mark-up', were repugnant to the injunctions of Islam.[10] The SC registered that the existing practice of banks in adding default fines to the original value of a *Bai Muajjal* contract was an interest-based activity.[11] The SC resolved that the prevalent *Bai Muajjal* (mark-up) practice under a buy-back agreement was an interest-based activity, because it involved pure lending on the basis of a mark-up or fixed rent on the loaned capital.[12] The SC resolved that Section 9 of the 1962 Banking Companies Ordinance was repugnant to the injunctions of Islam in so far as it prohibited banks from purchasing and selling goods, and from undertaking trading activities under Islamic modes of financing such as *Bai Muajjal* or *Murabaha* on a mark-up basis, *Ijarah* or leasing, hire purchase and *Musharakah*.[13]

8.3.3 The *Ijarah* (leasing) practice

The SC observed that banks and the leasing companies were practising the finance lease, which was another form of interest.[14] The SC held that clause (i) of Section 79 of the 1881 Negotiable Instrument Act, which entitled leasing institutions to recover an amount of penalty from the lessee in the event of delay was interest, for the reasons given in the case of *Bai Muajjal*. The SC further observed that the lessor could sell the leased asset to the lessee only after the expiry of the lease contract.[15]

8.3.4 The service charge practice

The SC observed that Section 79 of the 1881 Contract Act allowing interest on the 'service charge' contract in the event of default was repugnant to the injunctions of Islam.[16] The SC asserted that under the service charge system the lender was entitled to recover a service charge based on the actual expense incurred and not on the basis of market rates of interest or at a certain fixed rate.[17]

8.3.5 The PLS practice

The SC determined that subclause (ii) of Section 79 of the 1881 Contract Act, which dealt with the return on the basis of PLS, gave the misleading impression that finance extended by the financier under the PLS arrangement was a form of debt.[18] Furthermore, the relevant clause did not mention that the financier and the client should share the profit on the PLS investment on the basis of a mutually agreed ratio.[19] If the PLS business were liquidated and any amount left as a part of the financier's investment, then no return over and above it should be permissible, because it would become interest on the debt.[20] The SC resolved that Section 79 of the 1881 Contract Act contains the stipulation that any further return that the financier was entitled to receive over and above the debt created through PLS modes and other interest-free modes of financing was nothing but interest.[21] The SC resolved that Section 79 of the 1881 Contract Act was against *Shariah* in its entirety.[22]

8.3.6 The indexation system

The SC upheld the decision made by the FSC to the effect that the indexation system could not become a *Shariah*-compliant alternative to interest in an Islamic economy for dealing with inflationary environments.[23] The SC resolved that prohibition of *riba* essentially requires that all types of loans should be settled on an equal basis in terms of the unit of loan or object.[24] *Shariah* recognizes the time value of money only through the pricing of goods in trading operations (see Chapter 3).[25]

8.3.7 Negotiable instruments and debt-based securities

The SC affirmed the view of the FSC that the purchase of bills, debentures, bonds and other commercial instruments on the basis of interest was contradictory to the injunctions of Islam.[26] The SC explained that a 'bill of exchange' was a debt agreement payable by the debtor to the holder in a future date. The bill's endorsement to a third party should be based on its face value. Therefore, the SC resolved that the prevalent practice of discounting bills or promissory notes or cheques was an interest-based activity.[27] The SC held that paper representing money or debt could not be traded in the Islamic financial market. However, paper representing the holder's ownership of some tangible assets, like shares or other interest-free securities, could function as a valid instrument in the Islamic financial market.[28] The SC stated that the FSC had rightly declared that Sections 114 and 117(c) of the 1881 Negotiable Instrument Act were un-Islamic.[29]

8.3.8 Government borrowings

The SC held that defence saving certificates, treasury bills, federal investment bonds, foreign exchange bearer certificates and prize bonds were interest-based securities. Therefore, any return over them in the name of a mark-up or profit was nothing but interest.[30] The SC observed that internal and external debt amounting to 96.7 percent of the GDP of Pakistan, along with government borrowings, were so great that the underlying real assets were barely sufficient to accommodate them.[31] The SC resolved that domestic and foreign loans were the most formidable obstacle to transforming the economy of Pakistan on Islamic lines (see Chapter 9).[32]

8.3.9 Need for a sound IBF infrastructure

The SC resolved that the culture of wilful bank loan defaults had developed due to inadequate prudential regulation and the country's weak legal system (see Chapter 9).[33] The SC took close notice of the scandals in the financial sector of Pakistan during the period 1986–94, which deprived a large number of depositors of their hard-earned money (see Chapter 9).[34] The SC emphasized that present financial, legal, tax and administrative structures of Pakistan should be radically reoriented on a scientific basis in order to provide much-needed support for IBF practice in Pakistan.[35] The SC urged the SBP to ensure vigilant and prudent governance of the financial system, so as to restore public confidence in the deposit-taking institutions of Pakistan (see Chapter 9).[36]

8.4 The SC's parameters for the Islamization of the economy

The SC advised that the economy of Pakistan could be transformed on Islamic lines without being harmed.[37] It recommended that the government adopt certain measures for the successful enforcement of the Islamic economic system in Pakistan. It advised the government to efficiently manage its expenditures to combat the growing budget deficit (see Chapter 9).[38] It advised the government to establish institutions like a Serious Fraud Office to control white-collar crimes, such as wilful bank defaults and indulgence of bank staff in financial irregularities. It advised the government to establish independent institutions for credit rating and analysing the feasibility reports of projects in different sectors of the economy.[39] It further advised the government to establish the following three important departments at the SBP:

- an Islamic *Shariah* board for the scrutiny of the standard procedures and products developed for practising the Islamic financial system;
- a board for providing special assistance to financial institutions in obtaining information about projects, market, credit rating agencies, etc.; and

- a board for providing technical assistance to financial institutions for dealing with practical difficulties and other anomalies that may arise in practising the Islamic financial system.

8.5 The process of Islamic transformation

The SC outlined a framework within which the government could abolish interest from the existing economic system of Pakistan. The SC ordered the government to devote its efforts to working out a viable infrastructure and conceptual model for the Islamic financial system.[40] It advised the government to set up a number of working groups to accomplish the task of transforming the economy of Pakistan on Islamic lines.

8.5.1 Commission for transformation in the SBP

The SC ordered the government to set up a Commission for Transformation in the SBP within 1 month of the announcement of this decision. The Commission could comprise Islamic scholars, bankers, economists and chartered accountants. The Commission was assigned the job of devising measures and directives for completing the task of transforming the existing conventional economic system on Islamic lines.[41] Within 2 months of its constitution, the Commission was supposed to take on the job of evaluating two main reports, namely, the 1992 CIE Report and the 1998 IIIE Report (see Chapter 7). The Commission was required to circulate these reports among the Ministry of Finance, the SBP, leading banks, Islamic scholars and economists and to solicit their comments. The Commission was expected to develop a practicable Islamic financial model in the light of feedback on these reports received from the concerned parties. This model was to be sent to the Ministries of Law, Finance and Commerce for approval and afterward adoption by banks and financial institutions in Pakistan.[42]

8.5.2 Task force in the Ministry of Law and Parliamentary Affairs

The SC advised the government to constitute a Task Force in the Ministry of Law and Parliamentary Affairs within one month of the announcement of this judgement. The Task Force could comprise officials of the Ministry and two *Shariah* scholars from the Council of Islamic Ideology (CII) or Commission for Islamization of Economy (CIE).[43] The Task Force was required to accomplish three important tasks: (a) to draft a new ordinance for the prohibition of *riba* and other un-Islamic laws; (b) to review and amend the existing financial and fiscal laws in the light of Islamic economic principles; and (c) to draft new laws to provide a proper legal framework for practising the IBFsystem.[44]

According to the SC order, the Commission for Transformation was required to examine the final recommendations of the Task Force before putting them through the constitution-making process. Within 6 months of the announcement of the SC judgement, banks and financial institutions needed to prepare their model agreements and documents for all their major operations, and thereafter submit them to the Commission for Transformation in the SBP for examination and final approval.[45] Afterwards, banks and financial institutions were required to conduct educational and training programmes and seminars on Islamic Economics and Finance for their staff, business people and the general public.[46]

8.5.3 Task force in the Ministry of Finance

The SC advised the government to constitute a Task Force of experts in the Ministry of Finance within 1 month of the announcement of its judgement. The Task Force was given the primarily task of suggesting means and measures to convert domestic borrowing into project-related financing, and to establish a Mutual Fund (MF) based on the risk-sharing principle for government borrowings.[47] The MF units were supposed to replace the existing interest-based government securities. They were to be tradable in the secondary Islamic market on the basis of their net asset value.[47]

The SC emphasized that domestic inter-government and federal government borrowings should be conducted on an interest-free basis.[48] It urged the government to make serious efforts to relieve the nation of the burden of domestic and foreign debt as soon as possible. It further demanded from the government that existing foreign loans should be renegotiated in the *Shariah* context and thenceforth should be taken out on an interest-free basis and only in unavoidable circumstances.[49]

8.6 The start-up process of Islamization

In the pursuance of the SC orders, the government set up working groups to devise a strategy for replacing the existing interest-based financial system with the Islamic one. In February 2000, the government established a 12-member Commission for Transformation under the chairmanship of I A Hanfi, a former governor of the SBP (see Appendix I-F). In January 2000, the government set up a task force in the Ministry of Law and Parliamentary Affairs under the chairmanship of Dr. Mahmood

Ahmad Ghazi to develop a legal framework for the Islamic economic and financial system in Pakistan (see Appendix I-G). In January 2000, the government also constituted a six-member task force under the chairmanship of Javed Ahmad Noel in the Ministry of Finance to devise a plan for the transformation of government finances on Islamic lines (see Appendix I-H).

At the beginning of June 2001, these special working groups held a total of 22 meetings to devise a framework for establishing an Islamic economic and financial system in Pakistan. At the same time, major amendments to Section 9 of the 1962 Banking Companies Ordinance were in progress, and the Commission for Transformation had completed its work in this regard. The Money Lenders Ordinances in all provinces were repealed by June 2001.[50]

8.7 The government's appeal for an extension

On 14 June 2001, the government petitioned to the SC for a time extension for transforming the economy on Islamic lines. The government registered its reservations and contended that the given deadline was not feasible as neither the task forces nor the Commission for Transformation had yet developed a 'comprehensive alternative' in terms of financial instruments, an accounting system, a legal system, and inter-bank and inter-government transactions within the *Shariah* framework. The government requested permission to accomplish the transformation task by 31 December 2005.[51] The SC evaluated the government's progress on the issue, and thereafter granted an extension up to 30 June 2002.[52] Furthermore, the SC deferred the hearing on the UBL's petition for the review of the *riba* case of 1999 for the time being. The religious parties and other groups expressed their displeasure over the extension. They blamed the government for unnecessarily delaying the issue of abolishing interest from the economy and financial sector of Pakistan.[53]

8.8 Dramatic U-turn on Islamization

After being granted a 1-year extension, the government continued to evince a positive intention to abolish the interest-based economic system of Pakistan. The governor of the SBP, Dr. Ishrat Hussain, mentioned on different occasions that he was a staunch supporter of the move to introduce the Islamic economic system because it is best suited to the needs of Pakistan.[54] However, as the date for completing the transformation drew near, the government started to set its face against the SC orders.

The governor of the SBP and the Finance Minister started to argue that, despite all their serious efforts, no perfect plan had yet been developed to replace the existing interest-driven financial system, and any premature termination of the present system could cause permanent damage to the economy of Pakistan.[55]

In an Inter-Ministerial meeting chaired by Pervez Musharraf, the president of Pakistan, in early September 2001, a detailed presentation on the issue of enforcing the Islamic financial system in the country was made by the Minster of Religious Affairs. After a thorough discussion, it was agreed that the government could not meet the SC prescribed deadline of 30 June 2002 for transforming the economy on Islamic lines. Therefore, the government should follow a 'gradual and evolutionary' process to eliminate interest from the economy of Pakistan. This would avoid any possibility of disrupting the international dealings and financial stability of the country. However, the resolution of this meeting was kept secret for the time being.[56]

On 1 December 2001 the SBP issued detailed criteria for setting up an Islamic commercial bank in the private sector of Pakistan.[57] The government contended that the establishment of the first Islamic bank in the country would amount to a partial implementation of the SC orders, and other plans in the pipeline would shortly be implemented to fully comply with the SC orders.[58] On the other hand, the government reassured international parties that it would be able to seek the approval of the SC for adopting a dual system wherein conventional and Islamic financial institutions would co-exist. There would be no serious implications in adopting *Shariah* principles for the financial sector of Pakistan. Therefore, IBF should be regarded as a useful tool to diversify financial instruments and broaden financial intermediation in Pakistan.[59]

Explaining the government's strategy, the World Bank in its *Pakistan Development Policy Review* of March 2002 observed: 'The government's vision for a market-based financial system proposes the approach to provide choice to people and let the market work, so that those who want Islamic instruments can easily get them while those who are more risk-averse and want to assure capital preservation can likewise have access to such instruments.'

8.9 The SC bench manoeuvring

In early June 2002, the government filed a review petition at the SC on its earlier judgement on *riba* of 1999. By this time, three of the judges who had previously dealt with this case had left the bench for one reason or another. The government did not fill the position vacated by a religious scholar, Justice Mahmood Ghazi, in March 2000. The government released the second religious scholar, Justice Muhammad Taqi Usmani, in May 2002 by requiring him to retire early.[60] At the end of May 2002, the government reconstituted the bench, which comprised Chief Justice Sheikh Riaz Ahmed, Justice Munir, Justice Qazi Muhammad Farooq, and two newly appointed ad hoc judges, namely, Dr Allama Khalid Mahmood and Dr Rashid Ahmed Jullundhari, in the seats reserved for the religious scholars.[61]

8.10 The 2002 *riba* (interest) case review

The newly reconstituted bench of the SC held its first session on 6 June 2002 to deal with petitions from the government and the UBL, seeking the suspension of its *riba* judgement of 1999. Two major religious parties, namely, *Jamaat-e-Islami* and *Jamiat-e-Ulema-e-Pakistan*, were the main opponents of the review of the *riba* case.[62] The petitioners in this case put the arguments set out below before the SC.

8.10.1 The government's arguments before the SC

The government presented the following main arguments before the SC in seeking suspension of its *riba* judgement of 1999. First, the government made the point that judgements of the FSC and the SC on *riba* were both unconstitutional. Under Articles 203B (c) and 38(f) of the 1973 Constitution of Pakistan, it fell outside the jurisdiction of the judiciary to order the government to enact laws for the elimination of interest from the economy. Under Article 37 of the 1973 Constitution of Pakistan, it was the exclusive responsibility and privilege of the government to adopt legislative measures to eliminate interest from the economy as early as possible.[63]

Second, the government contended that the *riba* judgement of the FSC was biased. The Chief Justice of the FSC, Justice Dr. Tanzil-ur-Rahman, had delivered the judgement with a predetermined mind. He decided the *riba* case by relying heavily on the 1980 CII Report, which was produced under his own leadership when he was serving as chairman of the CII.[64] Similarly, at the time of reviewing the appeal against the FSC *riba* judgement, the SC largely confined itself to the opinions of a 'particular group of scholars' having a 'particular viewpoint'. As a result, the SC judgement on *riba* also lacked objectivity and the support of the majority of Islamic scholars and groups in the country. Moreover, both judgements failed to take into account the indispensable role of *riba* in the modern global economic and financial system.[65]

Third, the government claimed that it made the utmost efforts to implement the SC orders of 1999 for abolishing interest from the economy of Pakistan.[66] Amongst many documents, the government submitted a 74-page report of the Ministry of Finance and a 98-page report of the SBP to the SC. The research findings of the Ministry of Finance observed that the government's external borrowings could not be renegotiated on the terms suggested by the SC, since Pakistan had a weak bargaining position and could not prevail upon foreign lenders to amend their policy framework and standard charters to accommodate the request of Pakistan alone.[67] Regarding the government's domestic borrowings, the research held that interest-based government securities could not be converted into a Mutual Fund, because the great majority of the holders were small-time savers who were strongly averse to the idea of restructuring their fixed interest-generating investments on a risk-sharing basis. The research referred to certain other institutional constraints, such as the absence of specialized firms of sufficient size and a lack of financial capabilities and technical expertise, which seriously undermined the practical scope of this proposal.[68]

Then SBP's research findings also referred to the same kind of risks, problems and obstacles in the transformation of the interest-based fixed deposits of the banking sector under the PLS system.[69] Both research studies contended that any attempt to switch to the PLS-based fund mobilization schemes could result in a drastic reduction in savings, undue risk on capital, a mushrooming of unofficial and unregulated banking houses, speculative trading and flight of capital from the country, leading to a serious destabilization of economic growth and development in Pakistan.[70]

Finally, the government contended that the underlying facts and figures on transformation provided strong evidence that the parameters defined by the SC for establishing the Islamic financial system were neither practical nor feasible, and any attempt to enforce them may pose a high degree risk of permanent damage to the existing fragile economy of the country.[71] Therefore, it was in the interest of the national economy and the people of Pakistan to promote the Islamic financial system on a parallel basis and not to the exclusion of the existing interest-based financial system.[72] The government informed the SC that the SBP has already adopted serious measures for the regulation and promotion of IBF under a dual system. The first Islamic bank, Meezan Bank Limited, had successfully opened for business in May 2002. In the given context, the government petitioned the SC to suspend its earlier *riba* judgement of 1999, and instead affirm the idea of adopting a dual banking system in Pakistan.[73]

8.10.2 UBL's arguments before the SC

UBL strongly argued that the judgements on *riba* given by the FSC and the SC were based on an incorrect interpretation of the *holy Quranic* verses on *riba*. These judgements did not properly distinguish the terms 'usury', '*riba*' and 'interest.'[74] UBL cited the works of a few commentators of the holy *Quran* to contend that the holy *Quran* does not prohibit what were 'reasonable and fair rates of interest' and all that it prohibits was 'doubled' and 'multiplied', that is, compound and exorbitant rates of interest.[75] The holy *Quran* allows sale, business, trade and investment, and therefore the existing banking business could be classified under such permissible activities. Moreover, UBL fully supported the government's petition in the court.[76]

8.10.3 The religious parties' arguments before the SC

The religious parties opposed the petitions of the government and UBL at the SC. They contended that the vast majority of Muslims strongly supported the FSC *riba* judgement of 1991 and the SC *riba* judgement of 1999. Rational arguments and practical difficulties could not override the absolute prohibition of *riba* in the holy *Quran* and *Sunnah*.[77] The religious parties asserted that the issues raised by the government and UBL had already been addressed by the 1999 SC judgement on *riba*, and therefore the same case could not be reopened under the 'garb of review'. They charged the government and UBL of misrepresenting the Islamic injunctions on *riba* in order to mislead the judiciary and public.[78] They presented arguments that were advanced by Islamic scholars against the interest-based economy. They blamed the government for delaying the matter of abolishing interest from the economy of Pakistan over the previous 54 years. They petitioned the SC to order the government to take immediate action to complete the transformation of the economy on Islamic lines.[79]

8.11 The SC judgement on the 2002 *riba* (interest) case review

The SC delivered its verdict on *riba* on 24 June 2002.[80] The SC set aside the judgement of its predecessor handed down in December 1999, and the FSC *riba* judgement handed down in November 1991. The SC returned the *riba* case to the FSC for re-examination in the light of points raised during the hearing of the review petitions. The SC resolved as follows:

> Since the FSC did not give a definite finding on all the issues involved, the determination whereof was essential to the resolution of controversy involved in these cases, it would be in the fitness of things if the matter is remanded to the FSC which under the constitution is enjoined upon to give a definite finding on all the issues falling within its jurisdiction.[81]

The SC further observed that the FSC and the concerned parties would be at liberty to raise any other issue relevant to the *riba* case.[82]

8.12 Anomalies in the 2002 SC judgement

The SC judgement on the *riba* case review evoked strong reactions in the polity of Pakistan. Any court's judgement may not please all the concerned parties, but some contentious issues related to this judgement may be taken into account to assess its professional integrity and impartiality.

Doubts about the fairness and impartiality of the *riba* case started to build up when, a few days before the commencement of hearing on the *riba* case review, the government removed Justice Mohammad Taqi Usmani from the SC bench. During the hearing of the 1999 SC case on *riba* and the government's petition for an extension in June 2001, Justice Mohammad Taqi Usmani was observed very strict on the government over the issue of implementing the Islamic economic and financial system in Pakistan.[83] The religious parties strongly contended that the government imposed early retirement on Justice Mohammad Taqi Usmani in order to pave the way for its continuing with the interest-based economic and financial system in Pakistan.[84]

The appointment of two religious scholars for the hearing on the *riba* case review was highly controversial. Both judges were well-known for holding the personal opinion that bank interest did not fall within the ambit of *riba*, which is prohibited by the holy *Quran* and *Sunnah*. Just a couple of days before the opening of hearing on the *riba* case, Dr. Rashid Ahmed Jullundhari expressed his personal thinking in a favour of bank interest in an interview in one of the daily newspapers of Pakistan.[85] The counsel of the religious parties made the crucial point during the hearing that by giving the aforementioned interview the said judge had prejudged the issue of *riba* and thereby disqualified himself from hearing the *riba* case.[86] Some objections were also raised against the professional integrity of the bench as a whole. For example, while hearing the arguments of the opponents to the government's petition, Chief Justice Munir Sheikh asked the advocates 'whether they had given a thought to the scenario what would happen to people in the absence of an alternative banking instrument'. The Pakistani media placed a question mark over the credibility of the bench in view of this statement.[87]

The counsel of the religious parties did not get a fair chance to contest their case. The Pakistani media registered: 'The hearing of the religious counsel by the judges remained a running battle of wits between the counsel and the bench.'[88] The SC was accused of restricting its hearing on the *riba* review case to a few selected individuals.[89] In the hearing sessions on 21 June 2002, the counsel of *Jamiat-e-Ulema-Pakistan*, Salimullah Khan, argued to the Chief Justice: 'For 15 days you had heard speeches on the negation of Islamic injunctions on interest and now another week will be taken for arguments in their support.'[90] However, the SC wrapped up the review proceedings on 22 June 2002. Earlier, the registrar of the SC had issued a press release announcing that the judgement of the case would be announced after all the concerned parties had been heard in accordance with the rules of the SC.[91]

During the hearing on the *riba* cases at the FSC in 1991 and the SC in 1999, a large number of Islamic scholars and practitioners were invited to present their viewpoints on the subject. In contrast, the hearing of the *riba* review case was conducted under tight security.[92] The court's environments were not too conducive to Islamic scholars and experts appearing and expressing their opinions. The Pakistani media reported that the SC did not allow Dr. Mohammad Tahir, a senior economist of the International Islamic University Islamabad, to present his opinion against bank interest. When he pressed his case before the court for the opportunity to express his opinion on the subject, plain-clothed government security people escorted him from the first bench of the SC.[93] It is notable that, under the chairmanship of Dr. Mohammad Tahir, a research task force had been constituted in May 1997 that prepared the 1998 IIIE Report (see Chapter 7).

During the hearing on the *riba* case at the FSC in 1991, the government counsel were severely criticized by the public and media for defending the government's position in a very casual and tentative manner (see Chapter 7). The government did not take any part at all in the SC hearing on *riba* in 1999. Before delivering its judgement, the SC offered the government's counsel several opportunities to present their opinion before the court or submit it in a written form. The government's counsel did not respond to these repeated invitations. The SC expressed its displeasure to the Attorney General of Pakistan for not representing the government case before the court.[94] However, these were the same counsel of the government who played an active part during the proceedings of the *riba* case review. Even though the judgements of the FSC and the SC on *riba* were not free from criticism, the judgement on the *riba* case review raised very serious doubts about the government's credibility and the professional integrity of the SC in the whole affair. Therefore, it may be argued that the government did all firing and hiring at the SC bench to get the desired verdict.

8.13 Debate over the 2002 SC judgement

The real essence of the points raised by the government and UBL may be explored in the light of Islamic teachings and other established facts. For example, it is a tentative argument that the judiciary of Pakistan has no right to dictate its terms to the government for enacting laws. Articles 203D and F of the 1973 Constitution of Pakistan grant discretionary powers to the FSC and the SC to suggest legislative measures to the government for replacing any law or practice that is opposed to the teachings of Islam as enunciated in the holy *Quran* and *Sunnah* (see Chapter 6).

UBL's contention that bank interest did not constitute *riba* could not be validated from the sources of *Shariah*. The FSC and the SC had thoroughly examined the *riba* controversy, and thereafter resolved that *Shariah* prohibited all forms of interest. The Task Force of the Ministry of Law and Parliamentary Affairs prepared 'Islamization of Financial Transactions Ordinance 2002', which likewise held that any excess on the principal of a loan, including bank interest, was *riba*. The absolute prohibition of *riba* is proved from the holy *Quran* and *Sunnah*, and therefore *Ijma, Ijtehad, Maslahah, Mutashbahat* and the doctrine of necessity cannot be invoked in support of the permissibility of bank interest. The overwhelming majority of the Muslim polity and scholars hold faith that the holy *Quran* and *Sunnah* prohibit all kinds of *riba*, including bank interest (see Chapter 6). On the government's initiatives and backup, UBL tried to revive this old controversy over *riba* so as to create doubts in the minds of credulous people over whether interest fell within the prohibited degree of *riba*.[95] The religious parties accused the government of using its bank as a tool to strengthen its moral stand on the issue and win public support.[96] It may be noted that the government had challenged the 1991 FSC judgement on *riba* by making a plea that bank interest did not constitute *riba* (see Chapter 6). Afterwards, the government approached the SC a couple of times to withdraw this claim.[97] In fact, this claim is not based on any real ground, and the government often used it as a delaying tactic. The SC decided to send back the *riba* case to the FSC for re-examination. It is notable that in July 1997 and February 1999 the same office, though with a different composition of judges, turned down the government's petitions to refer the *riba* case to the FSC by holding that the FSC had already given its final verdict on the matter.[98] The previous SC bench also observed that the *riba* review petition might not effect any material change to the legal standing of the 1999 SC judgement on *riba*, and therefore the government should adopt serious measures to implement the SC orders.[99]

The judgement on the *riba* case review implies that any future decision of the FSC on *riba* would not be taken as comprehensive and valid if it did not give 'definite findings' on all complex matters of the economic system of Pakistan. However, under Article 203D of the 1973 Constitution of Pakistan, the FSC is primarily entrusted with the responsibility to take into account all relevant facts in examining and deciding on the question whether any law or provision of law is repugnant to the injunctions of Islam (see Chapter 6). It may be noted that the FSC and the SC decided in the light of all relevant facts that the prohibition of *riba* was well proven from the holy *Quran*, *Sunnah* and other sources of *Shariah*. Both the courts prescribed basic guidelines for the government in dealing with the practical difficulties involved in eliminating interest from the economy of Pakistan. Time and again, the demands from the FSC to come up with some more 'definite findings' on the *riba* case appear to be only delaying tactics on the part of government of Pakistan. It might have been a fairer and more logical decision if the SC had allowed some reasonable time to the government for undertaking thorough research to find viable remedies to the problems that frustrated the implementation of an Islamic order in the economy of Pakistan.

8.14 Reflection on the government's Islamization efforts

The government submitted that, after making the utmost efforts, it had reached to the conclusion that the parameters prescribed by the SC for transforming the economy on Islamic lines were infeasible. However, it may be noted that the government had supposedly been making efforts to transform the economy on Islamic lines since 1980. Thus, it should have developed a basic foundation over the decades for implementing the 1999 SC judgement on *riba*. It was not the case that the SC demanded abrupt changes in the economic and finance system. In fact, it advised the government to accomplish the decades-old project of the Islamization of the economy within next 3 years. The SC further did a favour to the government by providing a framework of an Islamic economy based on the views of theologians and practitioners of Islamic finance. Therefore, it may be a viable exercise to appraise critically the government's efforts to transform the economy on Islamic lines.

The government's implementation of the SC orders consisted for the most of half-baked plans and some paperwork. In its final 207-page report to the government, the Commission for Transformation presented a model of the Islamic financial system. The given model was based on seven major Islamic instruments, including *Murabaha* (deferred payment sale), *Musawamah* (general sale on stipulated price), *Ijarah* (lease financing), *Mudarabah* (joint venture), *Musharakah* (equity participation), *Bai Salam* (advance payment) and *Bai Istisna* (procurement engagement). The report contained little guidance on how to successfully adopt these Islamic instruments in the existing socio-economic framework of Pakistan. Similarly, the Task Force in the Ministry of Law and Parliamentary Affairs devoted a major part of its efforts to preparing a draft of 'Islamization of Financial Transactions Ordinance, 2002'. The draft was submitted to the government in June 2002, to be effective from 1 July 2002.[100] However, after the outcome of the *riba* case review, there was no urgent need to consider the implementation of the proposed ordinance in Pakistan.

Most often, the government failed to meet the prescribed time limits from the SC for accomplishing different stages of the transformation. For example, the Commission for Transformation in its 'Interim Report of October 2000' insisted on expediting the process of formulating the 'Implementation Action Cell' that may monitor progress on certain important issues, such as the training of bankers, education of clients, public awareness campaigns and establishment of credit rating agencies. The aforementioned activities were supposed to give some solid foundation and shape to the proposed financial set-up. However, it was observed that until April 2001 the government had failed to take practical steps in the light of the given recommendations.[101]

When the government was seeking an extension of the deadline from the SC in June 2001, UBL submitted a comprehensive report on the government's progress on the transformation to establish that the deadline and parameters defined by the SC for enforcing the Islamic economy in Pakistan were unrealistic and unfeasible.[102] The report observed that none of the bodies constituted for the transformation of the financial system was running according to the timetable; for example, the first draft of the '*Riba* Ordinance' that was sent to the Commission for Transformation in November 2000 and revised in January 2001 was still awaiting finalization. The report recorded that legal provisions relating to the Contracts Act, Sale of Goods Act, Company Laws, Income Tax and other legislation needed to be drastically and comprehensively revised. The report claimed that the most serious evidence of the lack of progress was that so far no steps had been taken by the authorities concerned to ensure the smooth transformation of inter-bank government transactions on the basis of *Shariah*.[103]

The government wasted a lot of time due to indecision and a lack of commitment to the transformation. It did not devise any precise strategy or timetable for completing the task of transforming the economy on Islamic lines in steps. The concern showed by international donors further delayed progress.[104] The government even considered declaring a financial emergency in the country to make the SC orders ineffective.[105] The policymakers and experts had no clue about how to deal with the crucial subject of finding Islamic alternatives to domestic and foreign debt, which amounted to more than US$60 billion in the fiscal year 2000–1.[106] During the period December 1999 to December 2000, the government generated liabilities of around US$327 million through selling interest-based government securities.[107] The SC advised the government to find Islamic alternatives to interest-based foreign loans. However, the government constantly assured international donors that Pakistan would honour all international obligations as usual.[108]

There was a general disagreement in the Ministry of Finance and the SBP on the issues of fully implementing the 1999 SC orders on *riba*.[109] All research work and surveys undertaken by these two state institutions led to the same conclusion: that the SC's parameters for enforcing the Islamic economic system were infeasible. It seems that instead of wholeheartedly devoting themselves to completing the transformation, the executive agencies strongly urged the government to continue with the old interest-based financial system and debt management. For example, the Task Force in the Ministry of Finance warned that the modalities of government borrowings from the SBP were redesigned in the 1990s, and any reversal would distort the market and cause major problems in implementing an effective monetary policy.[110] It further resolved that government debt schemes such as prize bonds, defence saving certificates and investment bonds should be made permissible under *Shariah* because such contracts were executed by mutual consent of the parties concerned. Since the interest charged by the SBP on its lending to the government was more of a benchmark rate necessitated by the need to unify the financial system, it should not be construed as conventional interest.[111] The SC, however, resolved in its judgement of 1999 that any voluntary return paid by the government on its interest-based financing schemes was nothing but interest.[112] The foregoing discussion reveals that the government did not make a dedicated effort to follow the SC's prescribed parameters to enforce the Islamic economic and financial system in Pakistan.

8.15 Present and future prospects of IBF in Pakistan

During the hearing on the *riba* case review, the government made strong claims before the SC that it would ensure the parallel development of the IBF system within the conventional banking environments of Pakistan. This would eliminate the risk of any major cost or damage to the economy of Pakistan, and provide a choice to domestic and foreign parties between the two banking and financial systems.[113] However, the real significance of these claims may be explored in the light of a number of facts and findings.

Islamic banks may face serious problems conducting their affairs within the fold of conventional regulations. Indeed, the SBP itself maintained that Pakistani depositors were highly risk averse and so fund-mobilization schemes based on the risk-sharing mechanism could never succeed in the country. In order to attract deposits, Islamic banks would be obliged to offer returns higher than market interest rates, as they did during the so-called IBF period 1981–85 in Pakistan (see Chapter 5). This would oblige Islamic banks to invest in more diversified and innovative projects and thereby take higher risks. However, a big majority of depositors would not approve of Islamic banks taking high risks. Moreover, entrepreneurs with good investment projects would borrow from conventional sources to keep the highest possible returns on their business enterprise to themselves. Clients with risky and bad projects would resort to PLS financing at Islamic banks. This would expose Islamic banks to the risk of non-payments, defaults and losses, leading to their bankruptcy and roll-back (Meenai, 1998; Nienhaus, 1983; Sarker, 1999). Not surprisingly, Islamic banks would follow strongly conservative lending policy by relying heavily on interest-free modes rather than PLS instruments. In the competitive market, where operations were dominated by debt financing, Islamic banks could not avoid determining returns on their investments on the basis of prevailing rates of interest (see Chapter 3). This may create a serious problem for Islamic banks in the event of a rise in interest rates. Islamic banks would not be able to revise their investment portfolios to catch up with higher interest rates, which would erode their profit margins and lower their returns on deposits. This situation would prompt the majority of depositors to withdraw their funds at Islamic banks, so plunging Islamic banks into liquidity crises and credit crunches (ibid). Islamic banks would always receive little benefit from the increasing globalization of business and finance. The government and foreign parties would deal largely with the existing conventional banking system of Pakistan. The 1980 CII Report warned that the real spirit of IBF might be seriously affected in Pakistan if it were adopted under a dual banking system (see Chapters 3 and 4).

It is matter of great interest that so-called IBF has been promoted in the private sector of Pakistan since 2002. Currently there are six fully dedicated Islamic banks, which run their affairs through more than 52 branches established across 16 major cities of Pakistan. They include *Al Baraka* Islamic Bank, Bank Islami Pakistan, Dubai Islamic Bank Pakistan, Emirates Global Islamic Bank, First *Dawood* Islamic Bank and *Meezan* Bank. In addition, nine conventional banks have set up a total 62 fully committed Islamic banking branches across the country (Akhtar, 2006). In 2006, Islamic banking assets were valued at US$1.3 billion, and their operations accounted for 2.2 percent of the overall financial market of Pakistan. Islamic banking deposits are expected to be worth US$13 billion, 10 percent of the total banking deposits in Pakistan, by 2014 (Al-Refai, 2006). Other Islamic financial instruments, including *Sukuks*, Islamic equity funds and *Takaful*, may take root in Pakistan in coming years.

Pakistan is the home of over 165 million people, with Muslim representation of about 97 percent. The IBF industry should experience very promising growth in this overwhelmingly Muslim country. Yet although IBF has a vast potential for growth and development in Pakistan, its operations constitute a meagre share of the countrywide banking market. This is because the majority of people look on existing government-led IBF practice in Pakistan with deep suspicion and contempt. This could be another episode involving political and vested interests, amounting to nothing more than eyewash from the government. Indeed, if the government failed to give an impression that IBF had been prospering under the dual system, it would be abandoning the position it took at the SC in 2002, and would find itself under tremendous pressure from political and public quarters to enforce the Islamic order in the whole economy and financial sector of Pakistan as its foremost constitutional responsibility. The essence of the issue is that the IBF movement has a permanently unpredictable future in Pakistan because it is always being used as a pawn on the political chessboard of the country.

8.16 Summary and conclusions

The SC gave the verdict on 23 December 1999 to uphold the FSC judgement confirming the rejection of the interest-based economy of Pakistan. The SC suggested some measures and parameters to the government for expunging interest from the economy and financial sector of Pakistan by 30 June 2001. The government set up various commissions, tasks forces and working groups to follow the SC parameters for transforming the economy and financial sector of Pakistan on Islamic lines. However, progress was not satisfactory, and therefore the government obtained a time extension until 30 June 2002. Afterwards, the government changed its mind and reshuffled the SC bench. At the beginning of June 2002, the government asked the new SC bench to review its earlier judgement on *riba*.

During the *riba* case review hearing, the government informed the SC that its prescribed parameters for devising an Islamic economic and financial system were unrealistic and harmful to the economy of Pakistan, and so the SC could consider suspending its previous orders on *riba* and approve the government's efforts to promote Islamic financial institutions in Pakistan alongside the existing interest-based financial institutions. UBL strongly supported the government case. It reiterated its stance to the effect that bank interest was permissible in the holy *Quran*, and that the FSC and the SC had been misled by some Islamic scholars over the verses of the holy *Quran* on *riba*. The religious parties in Pakistan opposed the review of the *riba* case. They petitioned the SC to order the government to enforce the Islamic economy under its earlier *riba* judgement of 1999. On 24 June 2002, the SC set aside the judgements of the FSC and the SC on *riba* and asked the FSC to re-examine the *riba* case in order to give 'definite findings' on the points raised by the parties during the review hearing.

There were some grey areas of the *riba* case review that may imply that its outcome was negotiated between the government and the SC bench. Some events pointed to the insincerity of the government in implementing the 1999 SC orders on *riba*. The government remained utterly confused on how to elaborate a systematic plan for the complete transformation of the economy on Islamic lines. The research findings of the government's working groups on the transformation project unanimously resolved that a complete implementation of the 1999 SC orders on *riba* was not possible, and that IBF should therefore be adopted under a dual system. However, IBF practice could not truly succeed in Pakistan while unduly subordinated to political pressures in the country.

9
The Causes of the Failure of Islamic Banking and Finance in Pakistan

9.1 Introduction

The IBF movement, which was launched in Pakistan with high hopes, has repeatedly taken one step forward and two steps back since 1980. Consequently it has lost real significance and appeal in the eyes of the people of Pakistan. This has essentially happened because IBF institutions cannot function as an alien entity in the Muslim polity. They are religious-based bodies, and, therefore, need Islamically imbued socio-political and economic environments to survive and prosper. This very core prerequisite was grossly ignored at the time the IBF system was introduced in Pakistan.

The basic theme of this chapter is captured in Figure 9.1, which shows IBF institutions as an integral part of the entire system. They primarily rely on other state institutions to drive their core objectives, fundamental characteristics and working mechanisms. This chapter appraises the contributions made by the main stakeholders in Pakistan, such as the government machinery, regulators, financial sector, business people, tax and legal and other socio-economic institutions to the success or failure of the IBF system in the country.

9.2 Government machinery

The government is a supreme body whose moral and material support plays a pivotal role in making state institutions succeed. The government in power embarked upon the IBF project in Pakistan, though not with sincere intentions. This section accounts for the role of successive governments and bureaucrats in the failure of the IBF movement in Pakistan.

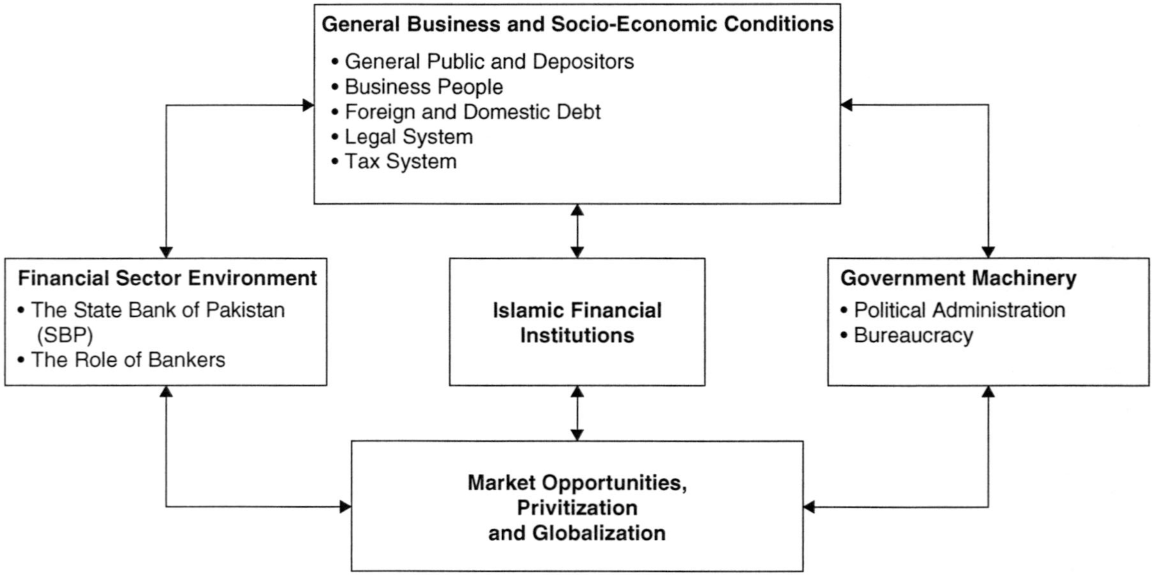

Figure 9.1 Strategic relationship of IBF institutions with other state institutions
Source: Derived from readings on Islamic Economics, for example, M S Husain (1997).

9.2.1 Lack of genuine political support

The early Pakistani political leadership repeatedly stated that the real objective behind the creation of Pakistan was to transform the colonial system of the country in the light of Islamic precepts (Ahmad, J, 1952). However, the newly born country remained bedevilled by the teething problems of post-independence, and therefore no progress was made on the issue of Islamization. Afterwards, the nation's enthusiasm for Islamization lost momentum. The country fell into the hands of leaders who were keen on retaining the existing institutional set-up of Pakistan because it was serving their vested interests. Therefore, they deliberately allowed the capitalist system to put down deeper roots in the economic life of Pakistan (Ahmad, K, 1997).

In the late 1970s, the president of Pakistan, Mohammad Ziaul Haq, was ruling the country as a Chief Martial Law Administrator, and desperately looking for support from religio-political parties to transform his military regime into a democratic one. He adopted certain half-baked Islamic measures in different spheres of the polity to win popularity among those parties and people who had always demanded the enforcement of an Islamic order in Pakistan. His direction to the Council of Islamic Ideology (CII) to prepare a blueprint of Islamic economy had a bearing on his political ambitions. Not surprisingly, his government did not take a genuine interest in adopting the CII's recommendations for establishing an Islamic economy in Pakistan. It placed a 10-year (1980–90) prohibition on the Federal *Shariat* Court (FSC) from issuing a verdict against interest-based government transactions (see Chapter 6).[1] It allowed the SBP to direct financial institutions of Pakistan to invest PLS funds in interest-bearing government securities. During that time banking institutions accepted deposits on a PLS basis and made all interest-based loans under the disguise of mark-up financing (Nomani and Rahnema, 1994; Kennedy, 1996; Rahman, 1997).

After the departure of Ziaul Haq, successive governments likewise made no genuine effort to enforce the IBF system in Pakistan. In 1990, the *Islami Jamhoori Itehad* (IJI) government put transforming the economy of Pakistan on Islamic lines at the top of its agenda. It established the CIE in June 1991 to promote IBF practice in Pakistan. Interestingly, it appealed the FSC's call to immediately enforce Islamic economy in the SC of Pakistan. It did not consider the 1992 CIE Report to revamp the financial sector of Pakistan on Islamic lines. It also delayed the appointment of a full quorum of SC judges for hearing appeals against the 1991 FSC judgement on *riba*. The underlying facts reveal that the IJI government adopted so-called Islamic measures in order to win the support of Islamic elements in its coalition government.[2]

Paradoxically, the existing military-led government manipulated the bench of judges at the SC to obtain a desired verdict on the *riba* case review in June 2002, which negated all the efforts made over the decades to transform the economy of Pakistan on Islamic lines. The developments of IBF in Pakistan under a dual system in recent years are just eyewash, and an attempt by the government to placate Islamic political parties and people. The government cannot uproot the interest-based economy of Pakistan because of its permanent reliance on interest-based borrowings from public and international parties. In truth, the IBF system suffered numerous setbacks in Pakistan due to double standards and lack of political will on the part of the government.

9.2.2 The noncommittal attitude of bureaucrats

Generally speaking, bureaucrats have always enjoyed highly distinguished positions in the administrative set-up of Pakistan. The ruling politicians hugely rely on bureaucratic plans featuring marginal changes to maintain the status quo (Gardezi and Rashid, 1983). In the early 1970s, private banking institutions were nationalized, and consequently came under the exclusive control of government. Pakistani bureaucrats were trained in general administration, without acquiring any deep insight into financial affairs. Therefore, they always followed conservative economic policies and also manipulated market fundamentals for the sake of vested interests. This caused serious damage to the market environment, domestic and foreign investment, and economic growth in Pakistan (Tansi, 1996).[3] Bureaucrats also acquired a strong hold over the flow of bank credit. Eventually, the service-oriented finance sector was transformed into a financial bureaucracy. The government emerged as the biggest borrower in the banking sector of Pakistan due to the extravagance of bureaucrats (Yaqoob, 1995).

The bureaucrats in the Ministry of Finance and SBP were made responsible for overhauling the Pakistani banking sector on an Islamic basis. They found that Islamization worked against their vested interests. Therefore, instead of implementing the IBF system in the spirit and the letter, they devoted all their efforts to practising the conventional banking system under an Islamic label. The CII criticized bureaucrats in the Ministry of Finance and SBP for adopting measures that handicapped the growth and development of IBF in Pakistan.[4]

9.3 The banking and financial sector environments

The SBP and financial institutions resisted radical changes in their functional and operational frameworks as warranted by the IBF system. The overall financial sector's environment in Pakistan is similarly not conducive to IBF. The discussion below delineates these issues.

9.3.1 Lack of professionalism at the SBP

Under the 1956 SBP Act, it is the constitutional responsibility of the SBP to regulate the monetary and credit system of Pakistan and foster its growth in the national interest. Initially, the SBP did reasonably well in pursuing an efficient and impartial regulatory policy. However, the real trouble with its autonomy started after the nationalization of the financial sector in the early 1970s. SBP officers came under the direct control of the Ministry of Finance Pakistan. The government followed the policy of appointing the SBP governor for a 3-year term that was renewable for another term on its approval. It often exploited this provision to use the institution as its tool (Saleem, 1993; Ahmad, S, 1994).[5] Furthermore, it always appointed SBP governors from among senior bureaucrats on the brink of retirement. SBP governors found it hard to introduce radical changes in a short period of three years or to take any risks in working against the government's will. Rather, they fully co-operated with their colleagues in the Ministry of Finance. Thus, for all practical purposes the SBP always acted as a back-room office of the Ministry of Finance of Pakistan (Mullick, 1993).

The SBP has been working under extreme political influence and pressure in recent decades. Lack of tolerance among political parties adversely has affected the professional integrity of the SBP and converted it into a sensitive domain of party politics. The performance of the SBP in managing savings and investments and securing monetary stability and fiscal discipline in the market has most often been far from satisfactory (Mullick, 1993; Saleem, 1993; Yaqoob, 1995). The World Bank Report on *Pakistan-Growth Through Adjustment 1988* stated, 'Unless the SBP can demonstrate intellectual leadership and high professional standards, the pace of financial innovation and deregulation is likely to be slow'. In 1997 increasing pressure from international financial agencies obliged the government of Pakistan to introduce some reforms in its financial sector and restore genuine autonomy to the SBP.[6]

The discussion provides some idea of why the SBP was not in a position to take an independent stand on the issue of IBF. The SBP clearly observed that the government and bureaucrats had no genuine interest in enforcing an Islamic order in the economy. The transformation of the financial sector on Islamic lines was also creating serious institutional and functional problems for the SBP. Therefore, the SBP adopted a casual attitude towards the Islamization of banking and finance operations. It did not establish an internal *Shariah* board for seeking guidance on its Islamization policy. It did not adopt serious measures for providing proper training to bankers on adopting the Islamic financial system. It did not furnish banks with all relevant documents and guidance for practising the approved interest-free modes of financing. Rather, it allowed full freedom to banking institutions to rely exclusively on the interest-like mark-up financing system (see Chapter 6). The SBP was against the IBF movement because it believed that there was no workable Islamic plan, and any premature termination of the existing interest-based system might jeopardize the whole financial set-up in Pakistan. Thus, for its own convenience, as well as to win the appreciation of its bosses, the SBP maintained the status quo in the financial sector of Pakistan.

9.3.2 Lack of Islamic training and education for bankers

Pakistani bankers are trained in the conventional banking and capitalist environment. They have no vision of IBF theory and practice. The nationwide Islamic banking initiative was launched in Pakistan without any proper education and training for the bankers who were supposed to act as traders, businessmen, stockists and lessors in the new set-up. Bankers in Pakistan have a conventional mindset, which holds that lending and borrowing operations cannot be performed on a risk-sharing basis because the announcement of a loss may cause a run on the bank. Therefore, they continued with the same conventional lending, investment and profit distribution operations in the name of Islamic banking. For ostensibly good reasons, they showed purely financial transactions as trade-based activities on paper only. Thus, the bankers did not allow IBF a chance to become established in Pakistan (Rahman, 1997).

9.3.3 Financial mismanagement and incompetence

The IBF practice failed in Pakistan because the existing financial sector of Pakistan lacks proper documentation, transparency, accountability, adequate prudential regulations and supervision.[7] The prevailing characteristics of the Pakistani financial sector are not only undesirable from a market perspective but also strongly opposed to the basic principles and goals of Islamic Economics. These characteristics mainly include non-performing loans and write-offs, the strong hold of an elite on bank

Table 9.1 Loan defaults and write-offs in the financial sector of Pakistan for the period 1985–2002 (Rs in billion)

Year	**Defaults (outstanding)**				**Write-offs**
	Industry	**Agriculture**	**Others**	**Total**	
1985	12.1	1.9	9.5	23.4	0.09
1986	15.1	2.3	10.1	27.5	0.14
1987	17.4	3.2	10.9	31.4	0.20
1988	19.6	4.0	12.9	36.5	0.16
1989	21.8	5.8	14.5	42.1	0.11
1990	22.2	8.9	14.6	45.8	0.33
1991	26.5	8.4	21.2	56.1	0.48
1992	39.3	10.2	28.8	78.4	1.37
1993	50.8	7.7	37.4	95.7	0.98
1994	71.9	9.9	48.9	130.7	1.12
1995	73.3	10.4	61.8	145.4	1.44
1996	92.0	15.1	64.7	171.9	2.27
1997	93.7	17.6	71.3	182.6	7.15
1998	96.3	21.8	66.4	184.4	0.78
2002	NA*	NA*	NA*	279**	NA*
Total					16.60

*NA: not available.
Sources: Karim (1999); ***Business Recorder*, 11 June 2002.

credit and the high cost of banking services for the general public. The discussion below takes stock of these issues to ascertain their negative impacts on the IBF system in Pakistan.

9.3.3.1 Non-performing loans, write-offs and co-operative scandals

The financial sector of Pakistan has been plagued by a high level of non-performing loans. Table 9.1 provides a brief picture of loan defaults for the period 1985–2002 when most of the efforts for adopting the nation-wide IBF system were being made. During the period from 1985 to 1993, bank defaults rose from Rs 23.4 billion to Rs 95.7 billion. They increased further from Rs 130.7 billion in 1994 to Rs 279 billion in June 2002. The write-offs of non-performing loans amounted to Rs 16.60 billion for the period 1985–98. The banking sector allocated Rs 30 billion out of its profits as a provision for unrecoverable loans from 1985 to 1993. The SBP governor pointed out that on average at least 30 percent of the loans of financial institutions of Pakistan had been found to be non-performing during the 1990s (Yaqoob, 1998).[8]

The political misuse of the Pakistani financial sector has been regarded as the major cause of bank defaults. In 1993, an SBP inquiry revealed that bank defaults mostly occurred in cases where top executives of financial institutions were directed by the prime minister's office to distribute loans to its 'close aides and workers' without inspecting the credentials of theirs loan projects and collateral (Mullick, 1993). In 1997, the published list of loan defaulters was largely made up of 5,300 names of top politicians, powerful business tycoons, army generals and other influential people of the country.[9] A review of the list reveals that a large number of defaulters, after defaulting at one bank, successfully applied for fresh loans from other banks in the country. Pakistani banks also made huge advances to many undeserving people under fictitious names.[10] The new media of Pakistan called loan defaulters 'artful dodgers'.[11] Furthermore, in the period 1986–94 the financial sector of Pakistan experienced three major co-operative scandals, which deprived 250,000 depositors over Rs 37 billion of hard-earned money and life savings (Yaqoob, 1995). The administrative crisis and weak regulatory framework of the Pakistani financial sector were the key reasons for all these irregularities (Mahmud, 1995; Khan, A H, 1997).

9.3.3.2 Monopoly on bank credit

The financial institutions of Pakistan do not allow small investors fair and easy access to bank credit. They invariably make huge sums of money by lending to affluent industrialists and businessmen. In 1997 the SBP revealed that 4,327 privileged borrowers utilized Rs 184.8 billion (56 percent) out of total funds of Rs 330 billion deposited by 28.4 million depositors. Furthermore, 26,877 borrowers obtained advances of Rs 72.484 billion. It means that about 31,000 borrowers obtained Rs 257.284 billion or 83 percent of a total of Rs 330 billion in deposits, whereas 42 percent of depositors of less than Rs 100,000 had access to only 4 percent of total banking funds in Pakistan.[12] These figures give some idea of the control of a small group of influential politicians, feudal lords, army officials and businessmen over bank credit in Pakistan.

The affluent class of Pakistan also siphoned national funds from concessionary borrowings and subsidies made available to the Pakistani banking sector exclusively for weak economic groups.[13] In 1993, the SBP governor pointed out that a subsidy of Rs 10 billion was provided on a concessionary loan basis to undeserving borrowers.[14] Furthermore, in the early 1990s, three government-run banks, namely, National Bank Limited of Pakistan, Habib Bank Limited of Pakistan and United Bank

Limited of Pakistan, approved Rs 16 billion in loans at below-market rates under the Prime Minister's Yellow Cab Scheme of self-employment.[15] The SBP later revealed that 87 percent of these loans were made on a political basis to the ruling party's nominees.[16]

9.3.3.3 *Expensive and unpopular financial services*

Financial services in Pakistan are extremely expensive and unpopular because of the high level of bank defaults, substantial provisions for bad debt, concessionary borrowings, subsidies and extravagant spending by bank officials (Yaqoob, 1995). During the 1990s, the average spread between the rate of return on deposits and lending was in a range as wide as 10–11 percent. It was quite contrary to the internationally acceptable level of 2 to 4 percent.[17] More often than not, real rates of return on deposits turned out to be negative in the face of extremely strong inflationary pressures in the economy of Pakistan. Consequently, general depositors in Pakistan did not have any real incentive to save and invest (Saleem, 1994; Sheikh, 1994). The majority of deposit savings in Pakistan come from small savers who commit their funds to banks for necessities such as the education of their children and provision for old age.[18] The expensive and unpopular banking services have aggravated the existing micro and macro economic problems of Pakistan, such as a low level of capital formation and investment, ailing industries, non-performing loans and unsustainable economic growth.

The underlying discussion has provided a deeper insight into the fact that the basic structure of the Pakistani financial sector works against the communal welfare, and cannot be transformed into an ethical-religious mechanism merely by changing its lending and borrowing mechanisms. Indeed, there is an urgent need to truly develop the Islamic infrastructure and norms within the financial sector of Pakistan.

9.4 General socio-economic governance

The general socio-economic set-up of Pakistan mostly works against the idea of implementing the IBF system. General depositors and businessmen in Pakistan are highly reluctant to do business with banks under the PLS principles. The huge burden of internal and foreign loans militates against the plan to transform the economy of Pakistan on Islamic lines. Other socio-economic and moral infrastructures of Pakistan are also against basic Islamic tenets. The discussion below explores some factors that caused the IBF movement in Pakistan to fail.

9.4.1 Risk-averse depositors

General depositors have a risk-averse attitude based on their experience with the banking sector of Pakistan. As explained above, Pakistani banking institutions indulge in unethical and antisocial activities, and so the general public has very little trust in them and do banking only when necessary. The existing banking and market structure of Pakistan has therefore come to be dominated by debt over the years. The number of national saving schemes offering a fixed rate of return has been increasing, while the level of equity investment has drastically fallen (Hook, 1997). General depositors are risk-averse also because most of them are small-time savers. In 2001, small depositors accounted for over 60 percent of a total of Rs 1, 276 billion of deposits in the banking sector of Pakistan. More than 87 percent of investors in interest-based government schemes who invested less than Rs 0.5 million were retired government and private sector functionaries, widows and orphans. These investors always relied on fixed and guaranteed returns on invested funds for their livelihood.[19]

The SBP and Ministry of Finance pointed out that the risk-averse attitude of general depositors was the main obstacle to transforming the economy of Pakistan on Islamic lines. They further argued that any attempt to switch from interest-based modes of deposit-taking to Islamic ones might impose a binding constraint on the investment and growth capacity of the economy of Pakistan, and could destabilize the entire system of financial intermediation in Pakistan.[20] Depositors may be emotionally attached to the cause of Islamization, but real support in terms of committing their funds under the PLS system was in desperately short supply. Thus, the risk-averse attitude of depositors prevented IBF from flourishing in Pakistan.

9.4.2 Cold shoulder from business people

Many business people in Pakistan keep two sets of accounts. They conceal their real income and transfer funds freely from their profit-making enterprises to loss-making enterprises in order to avoid paying tax at exorbitant rates. They declined to enter into a PLS relationship with banks because it required them to share their business profit and their private information with banks. Given this fact, banks found a dearth of honest business people willing to lend under Islamic banking modes. Quite interestingly, business people showed sympathy with the Islamic banking by observing 1 July 2002 as a black day against the continuation of the interest-based finance system in Pakistan.[21] However, they

Table 9.2 Foreign debt in the economy of Pakistan for the period 1955–2006/7: long- and medium-term(US$ million)

Year	Amount of debt	Repayment of principal	Payment of interest	Debt servicing
1955–56	40	1	1	2
1959–60	145	6	5	11
1963–64	661	44	18	62
1967–68	2,099	62	46	108
1971–72	3,766	71	51	122
1975–76	5,755	141	108	249
1979–80	8,658	350	234	584
1983–84	9,469	453	274	727
1987–88	12,913	691	426	1,117
1991–92	17,361	921	592	1,513
1995–96	22,292	1,346	791	2,137
1999–2000	25,359	884	506	1,390
2003–2004	28,900	2,321	657	2,978
2006–07	38,699*	698	417	1,115

Sources: Economic Affair Division, Ministry of Finance of Pakistan, Islamabad;
**Dawn*, 19 August 2007.

also played a significant role in causing the IBF system to fail in Pakistan (Khan, M A, 1992).

9.4.3 Huge burden of foreign and domestic debt

The unsustainable burden of interest-based domestic and foreign loans has been found to be the most serious obstacle to transforming the economy of Pakistan on Islamic lines. Table 9.2 tells a brief story about mounting foreign debt in the economy of Pakistan from 1955 to 2006/7.

Table 9.2 shows that the Pakistani government increased its reliance on long-term foreign debt in the early 1960s in order to industrialize the economy. In 1955, foreign loans amounted to US$40 million, but rose to US$3,766 million in the early 1970s and to US$9,469 at the beginning of 1980s. They climbed further in the next couple of decades, amounted to US$17,361 million in 1991 and US$28,900 million in 2003 respectively. At present, the Pakistani economy bears a foreign debt burden of US$38,699 million. The annual debt-servicing liability (repayment of principal together with interest) also increased due to accumulating debt, rising from US$2 million in 1955 to US$122 million in 1971. It increased from US$727 million in 1983 to 1,513 in 1991, and rose again to US$2,978 million in 2003 before coming down to US$1,115 million in 2006/7 due to substantial debt forgiveness and very substantial grants from the USA.

The government of Pakistan also has a long history of relying on internal public borrowings. Table 9.3 speaks for itself about the spiralling fiscal deficit in the economy of Pakistan for the period 1980–2007. The government of Pakistan sustained an annual fiscal deficit averaging 8.8 percent of Pakistan's GDP in the 1970s and 7 percent during the period from 1980 to 1996 (Khan, AH 1997; Naqvi, 1998; Hussain, I, 1999). However, the fiscal deficit gradually came down to 6.4 percent in the late 1990s and 5.2 percent of GDP in the early 2000s (Hussain, I, 2002).[22] The fiscal deficit amounted to Rs 208.2 billion in 2000 and Rs 373.541 billion in 2007, comprising more or less 4 percent of GDP.[23] Interest payments (on both domestic and foreign debt) also followed the same patterns along with the increasing budget deficit. They amounted to Rs 50 billion in 1991, Rs 249.252 billion in 2001, and Rs 262.285 billion in 2007.

The government of Pakistan did not build up a permanent team of economists and financial managers to ensure that borrowings were backed by assets and put to productive use. Since there was no well-founded foreign debt policy, the government mostly repaid loans along with accrued interest from the proceeds of new loans or rescheduled old loans (Kamal, 1997; Malik, 1997). The government used its banking sector as a captive milch cow to meet its financing needs. Sometimes it resorted to budgetary deficit by printing money against fictitious assets. This malpractice triggered high inflationary pressures, unemployment and increasing poverty (Naseem, 1995). The mounting debt adversely affected the net inflow of capital, monetary policy and sustainable economic growth in Pakistan (Ul Haque, 1997; Naqvi, 1998).

The government did not make any serious attempt to restructure the economy and its borrowings on a risk-sharing basis. In 1990 the government appointed the Prime Minister's Committee on Self-Reliance, which reported in 1991. The report contained a strategy for the elimination of interest from domestic and international government borrowings by using debt–equity swap methods and other interest-free instruments. However, the government ignored this report because it concluded that the goal of self-reliance could not be achieved for Pakistan unless its political and administrative leadership observed a strict financial discipline in its expenditures.[24]

During the hearing of the *riba* case review at the Supreme Court (SC) of Pakistan in June 2002, the government informed the SC that the absence of a viable interest-free alternative to foreign debt was a stumbling block in transforming the economy on Islamic lines.[25] The government always

Table 9.[illegible] Expenditure and budget deficit of the economy of Pakistan for the period 1981–2006/7 (Rs in billion)

Fiscal year	Tax revenue	Total revenue	Total expenditure	Current expenditure	Development expenditure	Interest payments	Fiscal deficit
1981	38.8	49.0	63.6	37.8	25.8	5.9	14.6
1982	43.0	53.8	71.0	44.5	26.5	7.7	17.2
1983	49.0	61.5	87.1	57.7	29.4	11.1	25.7
1984	53.6	74.8	100.0	71.9	28.1	14.1	25.1
1985	61.4	80.0	116.8	83.8	33.0	16.5	36.8
1986	72.4	92.8	134.5	94.7	39.8	19.7	41.6
1987	83.0	105.7	152.4	116.2	36.2	24.0	46.7
1988	93.5	122.8	180.4	133.6	46.7	33.2	57.6
1989	110.3	144.3	201.2	153.1	48.1	38.1	56.9
1990	119.4	158.8	221.6	165.6	56.1	46.7	56.1
1991	129.6	171.8	261.0	195.7	65.3	50.0	89.2
1992	164.3	231.5	321.5	230.1	91.3	62.4	89.9
1993	178.4	241.1	348.7	272.5	76.2	78.8	107.5
1994	208.4	272.7	364.9	293.5	71.5	90.9	92.2
1995	257.9	322.9	428.3	345.9	82.3	97.2	105.4
1996	305.6	380.3	518.1	423.9	94.2	132.5	137.8
1997	324.6	384.3	540.9	455.4	85.5	161.2	156.6
1998	354.8	429.5	634.0	529.9	104.1	202.4	205.0
1999	390.7	468.6	647.8	547.3	100.5	220.1	179.2
2000	406.8	525.4	733.6	645.1	87.7	243.3	208.2
2001	441.600	553.000	717.900	645.700	89.800	249.252	179.700
2002	478.100	624.100	826.250	700.200	126.250	273.894	190.450
2003	555.800	720.800	898.200	791.700	129.200	235.304	180.600
2004	617.899	805.827	940.359	763.077	160.988	226.256	134.532
2005	659.410	900.014	1,116.981	864.500	227.718	219.744	216.967
2006	803.700	1,076.600	1,401.900	1,034.700	356.100	260.021	325.300
2007 (budgeted)	916.100	1,162.700	1,536.241	1,106.200	435.000	262.285	373.541

Source: Pakistan Economic Survey 2006–07, pp. 38–40.

needed to mobilize resources through conventional borrowings so as to meet its financial obligations to domestic and international creditors. Therefore, the changeover to interest-free arrangements could hamper the government's mobilization of funds for paying its outstanding debt, which would seriously handicap the economic and financial set-up of Pakistan.[26] The foregoing discussion demonstrates that the debt problem seriously undermined the prospects of transforming the economy and financial sector of Pakistan on Islamic lines.

9.4.4 Weak and slow legal system

The prevalent legal framework of Pakistan for the recovery of loans is very weak and slow. Pakistani courts normally take 3 to 6 years to make the initial decision on a bank case and then another 5 to 10 years to come up with the final decision on the appeal case. Therefore, financial institutions found it more realistic to waive non-performing or bad loans and to avoid wasting time and money in the courts (Khan, M A, 1997).[27]

The government did not take serious steps to develop more efficient legal systems to safeguard IBF practice against any misuse. Under the 1984 Banking Tribunals Ordinance, the government established ten Special Banking Tribunals in the country with special powers to make ruling on banking cases within 90 days. However, after some time the government ceased supporting the tribunals; as a result the tribunals faced a serious shortage of financial and human resources and became almost defunct. Furthermore, political and bureaucratic influence prevented the tribunals from dealing judicially with banking cases (Akhtar, A R, 1988). On 30 September 1992 more than 33,000 cases were pending before the tribunals, involving the recovery of Rs 2.5 billion of bank loans. At the same time 600 cases were pending in the High Court of Pakistan, involving bank loans of over Rs 5 billion.[28] Thus, due to a weak legal system, financial institutions adopted highly conservative conventional lending polices, which left hardly any scope for IBF practice to succeed in Pakistan.

9.4.5 Rigid and narrowly based tax system

There is a lack of width and elasticity in Pakistan's tax laws. Government revenues (tax, non-tax and surcharges) have been consistently insufficient to finance current expenditures in Pakistan. Fiscal efforts in Pakistan have always fallen far short of expectations. In the early 2000s, the tax to GDP ratio (fiscal effort) averaged around 12 to 14 percent against an average of 18 percent for countries at similar levels of development and income brackets.[29] In 2000–1, total tax revenues comprised only 13 percent of the Pakistan's GDP; there were 1.4 million taxpayers amongst the population of 133 million in Pakistan, whereas the potential was estimated between 5 million and 10 million. The government has introduced tax reforms in recent years, but the tax base still consists of around 1.5 percent of the total citizens of Pakistan (Saeed, 2000; Husain, I, 2005).[30] The agricultural sector always unjustifiably obtained tax relief and concessions that deprived the government's exchequer of revenues worth billions of rupees.

A study conducted by Pakistan Institute of Development Economics showed that on average Rs 88 billion in tax revenues is evaded annually in Pakistan due to collusion between tax collectors and tax evaders (Haq, M Z, 1995). Strong political influence is exerted on the tax administration in Pakistan. A large number of powerful politicians, bureaucrats, industrialists and army officials evade tax. The tax department always grants billions worth of fiscal incentives, such as tax deductions, tax relief, tax holidays and exemptions to influential people in Pakistan. Consequently, the tax base has been constantly eroded, leading to painfully inflated rates of tax. Instead of evolving fair and efficient taxation and revenue collecting systems for meeting its funding needs, the government has always relied heavily on borrowings from internal and external sources for convenience and protecting its vested interests in the existing tax system (Haq, I, 1999).

Ironically, tax officials harass honest business people into meeting their mandatory tax targets, which appear that much more unrealistic and oppressive for the exclusion of the elite from the tax net. The business community has serious grievances against the tax authorities in Pakistan. A large number of business people keep double sets of accounts in order to avoid high tax payments. In this situation, the banking sector alone cannot persuade business people to maintain true records of their business operations so as to procure bank loans under the PLS arrangement. The underlying discussion implies that the arbitrary and unfair tax system in Pakistan tends to develop business conditions that are directly opposed to the basic tenets of Islam and serve as an obstacle to the IBF system in Pakistan.

9.4.6 Malpractices and rampant corruption

Malpractices that are prevalent in the social fabric of Pakistan include bribery, bending of rules and procedures, nepotism, misuse of funds, abuse of power, illegal appointments, hoarding, black marketeering, smuggling, etc. Regular media reports and outcomes of investigations show that a significant number of politicians, top officials and bank executives have been indulging in financial scams and misuse of power. At present, two former prime ministers of Pakistan along with dozens of their parliamentarians have been living in exile since 2000 to avoid arrest on corruption charges. Furthermore, the majority of the business community has been engaged in hoarding, adulteration, bribery and evasion of tax (Nadeem, 1992). A research-based institute – Gallup Institute of Pakistan – conducted a survey in 1992 that revealed that the level of corruption in Pakistan had increased by 50 percent from the 1970s to the 1980s. It was further noted that more than one third of the population attached no stigma to corrupt individuals (Haq, M Z, 1995). Such malpractices have adversely affected the fair and efficient working of market mechanisms in Pakistan. A study conducted by Pakistan Institute of Development Economics found that the size of underground economy during 1991–96 was about 41 percent of total GDP.[31] Dr. Mahbub-ul-Haq, the former Minister of Finance of Pakistan, estimated that corruption accounted for about 2 percent of GNP in 1988, and shot up to 5 percent in 1993 (Fazil, 1997). In 1999, National Accountability Bureau (NAB) was established with high hopes that it would eradicate corruption and other malpractices from Pakistani polity, especially from the top political and administrative ranks. Regrettably, it has become a tool in the hands of government to target political opponents and put them under pressure to join the government's camp or do as directed to get all corruption charges against them dropped (Cheema, 2008).

The SC, during its hearing on the *riba* case in 1999, registered that IBF practice cannot take root in Pakistan without the eradication of rampant malpractices from its polity.[32] In sum, IBF did not prosper in Pakistan because people failed to meet its precondition – adhering to the Islamic character featuring fairness, justice, benevolence, mutual trust and co-operation in socio-economic life.

9.4.7 The exploitative socio-economic set-up

The socio-economic set up of Pakistan is not based on fairness and justice. It is geared towards promoting the welfare of a few social superiors at the expense of the overwhelming majority of people of Pakistan. In the early period of the development of Pakistan, the government utilized the greater part of the country's resources to establish a large-scale capital-intensive industrial sector in urban areas. Consequently, the rural and semi-feudal society of Pakistan was transformed into an urban and industrial society. The government largely neglected devising long-term plans for enforcing economic reforms in the country that could ensure rural and agricultural development, an equitable distribution of wealth and related advantages for the general public (Naseem, 1995).

The former Chief of the Planning Commission of Pakistan, M Haq (1973), pointed out that just 22 family groups controlled 75 percent of the industrial assets, 80 percent of banking and 70 percent of insurance in Pakistan. He added:

> Pakistan's capitalist system is still one of the most primitive in the world. It is a system in which economic feudalism prevails. A handful of people, whether landlords or industrialists or bureaucrats, make all basic decisions because there is an alliance between various vested interests. What Pakistan badly needs today is to broaden the base of its economic and political power.

In the early 1970s, the government nationalized the banking and industrial sectors to eliminate monopoly over the country's resources. However, such measures were not accompanied by rigorous reforms to revamp the entire system of the country. Inevitably, nationalization caused more harm than good to the economy and people of Pakistan (Gardezi and Rashid, 1983).[33] In the early 1990s, the government made a dramatic U-turn to embark upon the privatization and deregulation of the economy and financial sector of Pakistan. The government claimed that these measures would ensure competitiveness and fair dealings in the business and financial spheres. Time and again, the same group of affluent people took out huge loans from financial institutions to purchase the state-owned industrial enterprises. As a result, the public monopolies were largely replaced by private sector monopolies. In 1992, the chairman of the Privatisation Commission of Pakistan warned that, without a complete revamp of the prevalent socio-economic set-up of the country, the process of privatization would further encourage the concentration of wealth in the hands of the country's elites.[34] It is an established fact that the half-baked plans undertaken by the government to promote the welfare of the common people have so far benefited only a small minority of social superiors of Pakistan (Chapra, 1993; Hasan, P, 2004).

The foregoing discussion reveals that economic exploitation is a very complex phenomenon in Pakistan. It involves not only interest but also other gross inequalities in distribution and production systems, which are linked and reinforce each other. Thus, it was hardly possible to enforce the IBF system in the prevalent exploitative socio-political and economic set-up of Pakistan.

9.5 Privatization and globalization of the market economy

The project of Islamic banking was initiated in the early 1980s, when the financial market of Pakistan was mostly regulated and isolated from the mainstream of international financial markets. The financial sector of Pakistan at that time largely consisted of five government-run banks and a few development financial institutions. At beginning of the 1990s, the government adopted a policy of promoting market-oriented banking and finance services to attract foreign capital and investment into the country. The government privatized its two nationalized banks and some non-banking financial institutions, and also granted licences to ten private banks, 90 *Mudarabah* companies, cooperatives and other investment companies in the early 1990s. These developments significantly boosted the competitiveness and global exposure of the Pakistani financial market.

Given the growing pace of privatization and globalization, the project of Islamization of the Pakistani economy and financial market became ever more difficult with the passing years. The top policymakers contended that the country's financial market had become increasingly integrated with international financial markets, and, inevitably, any move towards its Islamization might cause a massive flight of foreign investment and capital from the region. Thus the increasing globalization of business and financial markets gradually diminished the scope for enforcing the IBF system in Pakistan (Khan M M and Bhatti, 2006).

9.6 Summary and conclusions

Ideologically speaking, Islamic financial institutions are ubiquitously integrated into the entire system of Muslim polity. They need genuinely strong support from all state institutions if they are to survive and succeed in their objectives. However, this did not happen in reality when attempts to adopt the nationwide IBF system were undertaken in Pakistan over the decades. The president of Pakistan, General Ziaul Haq, took the initiative of enforcing an Islamic economy in the country, though for the sake of vested interests. His government and all succeeding governments resorted to making merely cosmetic changes to the banking and financial sector of Pakistan. The bureaucrats in the Ministry of Finance did not show any real enthusiasm to implement the IBF system, for their own convenience and vested interests. The SBP did not provide the banking and financial institutions of Pakistan with sufficient resources to learn and practise the Islamic system. It purposefully encouraged the predominant use of conventional mark-up modes in the banking and financial sector of Pakistan. The absence of a fair and expeditious judicial system also discouraged banking and financial institutions in Pakistan from adopting Islamic modes of finance, which run a very high risk of default as compared with conventional lending. The majority of business people in Pakistan rejected bank borrowings on a PLS basis for business privacy as well as tax reasons. General depositors in Pakistan always showed a strong reluctance to bear any real risk on their so-called PLS deposits in Pakistani banks. The glaring socio-economic imbalances in Pakistan, such as the huge burden of domestic and international loans, non-performing loans, lower savings and investments, an inefficient tax system, abject poverty and illiteracy, and moral hazard, duly contributed to defeating the process of the Islamic transformation of the Pakistani economy and financial sector.

10
Summary and Conclusions

Islam envisages economic activities absolutely essential for the material and spiritual growth and prosperity of human beings, within moral and social contexts. Islam clashes seriously with interest, which violates the cardinal principle of fairness and justice by causing the concentration of wealth and social power in the hands of a few. Islamic Economics bans interest along with all other exploitative and anti-social elements. It promotes business and economic dealings based on private ownership, free consent, mutual trust and co-operation, fairness and risk-sharing.

Islamic banking and finance (IBF) is a sub-discipline of Islamic Economics. Its origin, objectives and operative mechanisms are based on *Shariah*. It is mainly an equity-based system that offers a more ethical and efficient alternative to the interest-based conventional system. It conducts its affairs through profit-and-loss-sharing (PLS) instruments, namely, *Mudarabah* (joint venture) and *Musharakah* (equity participation), which ensure the greater availability of venture capital, risk-taking, innovation and entrepreneurship, leading to optimal and sustainable economic growth with communal welfare. IBF seeks greater diversification and flexibility by relying on other secondary alternatives to interest, which include *Murabaha* (deferred payment sale), *Ijarah* (leasing), *Bai Salam* (advance payment) and *Bai Istisna* (procurement engagement).

The conceptual developments of IBF occurred in the late 1940s, and its practice evolved with the emergence of a number of Islamic banks in the Middle East after the mid-1970s. The IBF movement gradually flourished over the decades in the Muslim world. However, it has registered unprecedented growth in recent years due to certain core factors that include consistent high oil prices worldwide, the booming economies of the Middle East, increasing diversification of Islamic banking products, clients and markets, and other changes in the world of politics.

At present IBF successfully operates in 70 countries, with a network of more than 300 institutions across the globe. The Islamic money and capital markets, stock market and insurance market have been the fastest-growing segments of IBF in recent times. An increasing number of regulatory, training, research and accounting institutions are working on developing the IBF infrastructure on a more scientific basis.

The Middle East, South Asia and Southeast Asia have emerged as the main hubs of IBF in modern times. The Middle East provides the most fertile grounds for IBF development and growth. Bahrain is the biggest hub in the IBF world, whereas Iran is the only Muslim country worldwide that has successfully adopted the IBF system at the national level. The growing predominance of IBF in Middle Eastern markets may erode the conventional banking paradigm there in future years so that Islamic banking becomes the basis of the overwhelmingly greater part of business in the Middle East. In South Asia, Pakistan has now allowed six fully dedicated private Islamic banks to operate under a dual system developed after it abandoned its efforts to completely Islamize the economy in 2002. Moreover, Bangladesh hosts six Islamic banks in addition to conventional banks that offer IBF products and services. There is a good chance that IBF will take root in India and Afghanistan in the near future. In Southeast Asia, Malaysia, Indonesia and Singapore are making good headway with IBF. Malaysia is the major contributor to critical developments and innovations in IBF products, systems and regulations. Singapore has recently entered the IBF club and aims to be the top trading centre for *Sukuks*, property and hedge funds. Indonesia has now taken solid steps to gradually increase the share of IBF in its market. Governments of Middle Eastern and Asian countries have been playing a key role in promoting IBF at national and international levels. IBF practice has been revived in Sudan under a parallel system since 2005.

Increasing numbers of Western financial institutions, such as ABN AMRO, Citibank and Goldman Sachs, have been using IBF as an opportunity to add innovation and diversity to their operations and thereby attract funds and investments from Middle East and other Muslim countries. They are becoming partners with Islamic market players to promote IBF products and services in European and Western markets. IBF practice is gaining momentum in the UK, USA, Canada and Australia. These developments have given IBF a window of opportunity to become a truly competitive and integrated part of global financial markets.

While registering impressive progress in the recent times, IBF has been facing following problems and challenges. It needs to improve its liquidity and risk management and corporate governance. It should make major investments in R&D and end its blind imitation of conventional banking. The predominance of *Murabaha* financing should be replaced with PLS financing because it grossly violates the IBF ideology and the Islamic spirit. Furthermore, it should bring its accounting standards and reporting systems up to the international mark. It should work harder to standardize its regulatory frameworks, systems, products and procedures. It is necessary to establish Islamic rating agencies and central *Shariah* boards to improve the market-based discipline and *Shariah*-compliance of IBF across the board. It is highly advisable to establish more IBF training academies to make good the serious shortage of well-qualified *Shariah* and Islamic financial experts. Most importantly, IBF has yet to resolve its identity crisis by adding truly value-added, competitive and diversified products and services to the world of business and finance.

Pakistan embarked upon economic and financial Islamization in the early 1980s, a move that was regarded as the hallmark of the contemporary IBF world. The Council of Islamic Ideology (CII) prescribed a basic framework for restructuring the economy and financial sector of Pakistan on Islamic lines in June 1980. It strongly recommended the PLS system as an ideal replacement of the interest-based system, but then realized that this Islamic system could not work in Pakistan due to moral hazards and lack of institutional support. Therefore, it offered certain secondary modes, such as investment auctioning, *Bai Muajjal*, normal rate of return and time multiple counter-loans to develop an interest-free banking and finance system for a transitional period in Pakistan. Furthermore, it developed the daily product method for transforming the deposit-taking functions of banks on a PLS basis. It also developed the Islamic central banking mechanism, which mainly featured replacing the bank rate tool with the discretionary power of the central bank to fix PLS ratios on its financial assistance to banks and on banks' financings to their clients, and also conducting open market operations on the basis of variable dividend securities instead of interest-based securities. However, it may be noted that the money supply in the Pakistani market could not be regulated with the proposed monetary systems unless the majority of government's borrowings and banking operations were based on the PLS system. In a nutshell, the CII's recommendations were meant to provide a crude foundation for institutionalizing IBF in Pakistan.

At the beginning of 1981, the State Bank Pakistan (SBP) embarked upon implanting the IBF system in Pakistan, though without possessing or seeking any technical or religious guidance. In 1984, the SBP approved 12 Islamic modes to establish a full-fledged IBF system in Pakistan. However, the SBP paved the way for the excessive use of mark-up (*Bai*

Muajjal/Murabaha) at the expense of other approved modes. Eventually, Pakistani banking and finance institutions artificially transformed their money-based operations into trading-based operations under the auspicious of the SBP. They charged a 'mark-up' similar to 'interest' on the price of goods sold to the client on a deferred payment basis. The SBP introduced three major PLS-based schemes, namely, *Musharakah* financing, Participation Terms Certificates (PTCs) and *Mudarabah* companies, which failed due to lack of proper institutional arrangements in Pakistan. Banks mobilized deposits on a PLS basis but largely invested them in interest-based avenues to pay off the fixed rate of returns to their depositors. The IBF movement had lost momentum in Pakistan by the end of the 1980s. In November 1991, the Federal *Shariat* Court (FSC) handed down its judgement that the existing banking and financial system in Pakistan had hitherto been based on interest and that the government should restructure it under *Shariah* by 30 June 1992. This caused a great deal of panic among financial institutions, general depositors, international parties and the government of Pakistan. Eventually, the government and financial institutions in Pakistan challenged the FSC verdict at the Supreme Court (SC).

In July 1991 the government had established the Commission for Islamization of Economy (CIE) to resolve the practical difficulties in the Islamic transformation of the economy of Pakistan. In 1992, the CIE submitted its first report – the 1992 CIE Report – which due to time constraints failed to adopt a comprehensive approach to eliminating interest from the financial sector of Pakistan. Consequently, the report did not provide any fresh impetus to IBF practice in Pakistan. In May 1997 the CIE sought help from the International Institute of Islamic Economics (IIIE), which in July 1998 submitted its final recommendations for effecting the financial Islamization of Pakistan. The IIIE model was primarily based on *Bai Muajjal, Bai Salam, Ijarah, Mudarabah* and *Musharakah*. The IIIE contended that strict legal measures and the mandatory demand for collateral against bank loans could help IBF institutions to operate without requiring a radical shift in the existing conventional banking and socio-economic systems of Pakistan. Moreover, it proposed a large number of interest-free securities for conducting operations in the Islamic inter-money market. It argued that the SBP may trade in these interest-free securities to control the credit supply in the financial market of Pakistan and also provide interest-free financial assistance to the government. However, the IIIE's proposals could not work due to structural imbalances and huge foreign and domestic debt of the economy of Pakistan. The scope for adopting the IIIE's recommendations was overshadowed by the SC judgement on *riba* that was handed down in December 1999.

The SC approved the FSC judgement invalidating the interest-based economy of Pakistan. It set out guidelines for the government to transform the economy and financial sector of Pakistan on Islamic lines by 30 June 2001. The government established high-powered committees in the Ministry of Finance, Ministry of Law and Parliamentary Affairs and SBP to accomplish the Islamic transformation task. However, as the government's progress with the Islamization project was unsatisfactory, the SC put back the date of its completion to 30 June 2002. Later, the government changed its mind and shuffled the judges on the SC bench to get the 1999 orders on *riba* reviewed at the beginning of June 2002. During the *riba* case review, the government raised issues over the SC's exclusive powers, *riba* definition and the impracticability of the SC's prescribed parameters for transforming the economy of Pakistan along Islamic lines. Therefore, it petitioned the SC to suspend its previous judgement on *riba* and instead affirm the government's ongoing efforts to promote Islamic financial institutions parallel to conventional financial institutions in Pakistan. On 24 June 2002, the SC asked the FSC to re-examine the *riba* case by giving a definite finding on the points raised by the parties during the hearing on the *riba* case review. The SC decision on the *riba* case review was clearly political, arbitrary and rather poor. Since 2002, a handful of private Islamic banks have emerged to operate on a limited scale in the financial sector of Pakistan. This is by no means an ideal situation for a country overwhelmingly dominated by Muslims, and constitutionally pledged to eliminate interest from its economy and financial sector.

Several major factors contributed to the failure of the nationwide IBF movement in Pakistan. The political managers and bureaucrats of Pakistan used the move to IBF only to serve their vested interests. They did not make any serious effort to eradicate the deep-rooted conventional system from the economy of Pakistan. The SBP also made ham-fisted attempts to implement IBF conceptual frameworks developed by financial and *Shariah* experts from time to time. Banking and financial institutions in Pakistan did not give a fair opportunity to the IBF system because of moral hazards, accounting problems and the weak judicial framework of the country. Depositors were strongly against the IBF system because of their highly risk-averse attitude and lack of confidence in Pakistan's deposit-taking institutions. The judicial institutions of Pakistan took the matter of implementing the IBF in their hands, but their strict rulings did not work. The inherent macroeconomic instability and administrative crisis in Pakistan denied IBF a fair chance to grow and develop.

Interest-based dealings are prohibited by Islam due to their exploitative nature. This implies that the objective of eliminating interest should be taken as the objective of eliminating all forms of exploitations from the polity. Furthermore, Islam envisages the unification and harmony of all human activities and institutions under *Shariah* principles. The urge to adopt Islamic finance should stem from a conviction that one should follow Islamic ways in all walks of life. Thus, Islamic restructuring of economy and state institutions should take place at the same time in the Muslim polity. It may be noted that Pakistan inherited a very exploitative socio-political and economic nexus from the British colonial era. The people of Pakistan have dreamed about seeking financial independence and prosperity and sharing the benefits of growth widely and equitably among themselves since the dawn of independence in 1947. They unanimously and constitutionally resolved that the objective of economic freedom and prosperity would be pursued through the Islamization of the economy of Pakistan. In the given context, the government of Pakistan was required to adopt the Islamization strategy for the entire system of the country. However, this did not happen; for certain political reasons interest was branded an isolated financial problem in Pakistan, and then billions of dollars of resources were consumed over the decades in the quest for its piecemeal solution, but in vain. One and all conceptual models developed in Pakistan involved a natural reliance on exploitative socio-economic agents, the purpose being to create major loopholes in these models that let interest re-enter by the back door. For example, the 1980 CII Report condemned the system of *Bai Muajjal* (deferred payment sale) but then recommended it to provide bankers with an easy solution to maintain the status quo. The 1992 CIE Report failed to offer a full-fledged plan to deal with the problem of interest within socio-economic contexts. The 1998 IIIE Report openly surrendered to exploitative forces in the Pakistani polity: it asserted that interest was a problem in the financial arena only, and that its solution could be easily sorted out without radically changing the prevailing unjust financial and socio-economic systems of the country.

The bureaucrats and the SBP simply saw these financial models as impracticable in the given socio-political and economic set-up, and thereby maintained their loopholes to preserve the existing interest-based economic and finance system in Pakistan. Moreover, the polity of Pakistan did not reflect the Islamic characteristic to strive as a single entity to adopt the IBF system as one of its virtues, articles of faith and ruling passions. The imposition of the Islamic system by force and in superficial ways is absolutely against its own true spirit. But the government made few efforts to seek the compliance in and participation of the people of Pakistan for the Islamization of the economy through education, awareness raising and moral training. Realistically speaking, the IBF system has yet to be adopted in Pakistan under a truly Islamic and scientific approach. However, the prospects for IBF in Pakistan are highly unpredictable and bleak. The political leadership and financial managers of Pakistan strongly argue that the strategy of promoting IBF within given the conventional set-up of the country is truly mature, market-based and efficient, and highly compatible with contemporary patterns of economic and financial globalization, and has therefore been adopted on a permanent basis. Furthermore, the government of Pakistan has proactively followed the increasingly pro-Western agenda in socio-political and economic institutions of the country in recent years. In view of the Westernized Pakistani political leadership, the liberal-leaning polity and the increasing globalization and integration of economies and financial markets at the present time, the real scope for breakthrough developments in IBF in Pakistan has been shrinking.

Notes

Chapter 2

1. The holy *Quran*: 3:14–15; 4:79; 8:53; 10:44; 17:11; 17:67 and 22:78.
2. The holy *Quran*: 2:86; 2:208; 3:22; 4:134; 6:113; 10:99 and 11:17.
3. Ramonet, I 1998, 'The politics of hunger', *Le Monde Diplomatique*, November, viewed (at Poverty Facts and Stats: Causes) 20 July 2007, <http://www.globalissues.org/TradeRelated/Facts.asp#fact2>.
4. United Nations Development Programme Organization – World Bank, *Human Development Report 1998*, viewed 20 July 2007, <http://hdr.undp.org/reports/global/1998/en/>.
5. It was pointed out by Kofi Annan, former UN Secretary General, in his speech on the International Day for the Eradication of Poverty, 17 October 2000, viewed 20 July 2007, <http://www.un.org/events/poverty2000/messages.htm>.
6. *Global Monitoring Report 2007*, Millennium Development Goals, World Bank, Washington, DC, viewed 20 July 2007, <http://www-wds.worldbank.org/external/default/WDSContentServer/WDSP/IB/2007/04/11/000112742_20070411162802/Rendered/PDF/394730GMR02007.pdf>.
7. Food and Agriculture Organization of the United Nations, *The State of Food Insecurity in the World 2006*; viewed 20 July 2007, <http://www.fao.org/docrep/009/a0750e/a0750e00.htm>.
8. The United Nations World Health Organization, *Micronutrient Deficiencies*, viewed 20 July 2007, <http://www.who.int/nutrition/topics/vad/en/>.
9. United Nations World Food Program, *World Food Program 2006–2007: Facts and Figures, Hunger Facts*, viewed 20 July 2007, <http://www.wfp.org/aboutwfp/facts/hunger_facts.asp#fahaids>.
10. Ibid.
11. Ibid.
12. United Nations World Food Program, *HIV/AIDS Unit 2007*, viewed 20 July 2007, <http://www.wfp.org/aboutwfp/facts/hunger_facts.asp>.
13. Joint United Nations Programme on HIV/AIDS (UNAIDS), *AIDS Epidemic Update December 2006*, viewed 20 July 2007, <http://dta.unaids.org>.
14. *The Jamaica Observer*, 4 February 2005, 'Mandela compares poverty to apartheid, slavery', viewed 20 July 2007, <http://www.jamaicaobserver.com/news/html>.
15. Roy, A 2002, 'Not again, global capitalism is driving us to war', *The Guardian*, 27 September, viewed 24 July 2007, <http://www.guardian.co.uk/g2/story/0,3604,799850,00.html>.
16. Noble Prize Organization, *Interview: Muhammad Yunus, Nobel Peace Prize 2006*, viewed 24 July 2007, <http://nobelprize.org/nobel_prizes/peace/laureates/2006/yunus-telephone.html>.
17. United Nations Millennium Project, *UN Millennium Project Report 2005*, viewed 20 July 2007, <http://www.unmillenniumproject.org/reports/fullreport.htm>.

18. The holy *Quran*: 100:6–7 and 102:1–2.
19. The holy *Quran*: 10:7; 18:103–104; 53:29–37; 59:9 and 64:16.
20. Sachs, J 2002 (Translator), *Nichomachean Ethics, Notes – Aristotle's Nicomachean Ethics (Philosophical Library Series)*, Focus Publishing/R. Pullins Company, Newburyport, MA.
21. Kant, 1797, *Die metaphysik der sitten* (Metaphysics of Morals) (1797); Kant, 1788, *The moral order, kritik der practischen vernunft (Critique of Practical Reason)*, viewed 20 July 2007, <http://www.philosophypages.com/hy/5i.htm#gdwl>.
22. Shirras, G F 1935, 'The Pareto law and the distribution of income', *Economic Journal*: vol. 45, no. 180, pp. 663–681.
23. The holy *Quran*: 2:45; 2:74; 4:162; 30:39 and 64:16.
24. See for example, K Ahmad (1979); Chapra (1979); Z Hasan (1988); Ahmed (1991).
25. Ibid.
26. The holy *Quran*: 9:111.
27. The holy Quran: 4:29; 24:33: 3:11 and 3:103.
28. See for example Islahi (1988).
29. The holy *Quran*: 24:33.
30. The holy *Quran*: 4:12 and 4:176.
31. *Sahih Bukhari*, narrated Abdullah bin Abbas, volume 3, Book 48, number 846.
32. The holy *Quran*: 2:282.
33. The holy *Quran*: 2:195; 5:13 and 7:158; *Sahih Bukhari*, narrated Warrad, volume 9, Book 92, number 395.
34. The holy *Quran*: 48:29; 9:11 and 33:5; *Sahih Bukhari*, narrated An-Nu'man bin Bashir, volume 8, Book 73, number 40.
35. *Sahih Bukhari*, narrated Hakim bin Hizam, volume 8, Book 76, number 448.
36. The holy *Quran*: 3:92 and 15:19.
37. The holy *Quran*: 9:111; 24–25 and 64:16.
38. See, for example, Maududi (1961).
39. Ibid.
40. The holy *Quran*: 9:103; 22:41 and 24:55–56.
41. The holy *Quran*: 2:27; 2:274; 7:31; 7:168; 28:77; 59:7 and 43:32.
42. The holy *Quran*: 9:103 and 22:41.
43. Al-Nasai, Sunan, *Kitab al-Isti adhah, Bab al-Isti adhah min al-dhillah.*
44. The holy *Quran*: 17:27–29; 20:67; 25:67 and 59:7.
45. The holy *Quran*: 3:185; 17:27–29; 34:39; 92:10 and 92:11.
46. The holy *Quran*: 2:143–144.
47. The holy *Quran*: 3:180 and 59:7.
48. *Sahih Bukhari*, narrated Abad, volume 2, Book 24, number 514.
49. The holy *Quran*: 2:188.
50. The holy *Quran*: 83:1–4; 23:2–4 and 83:1–3; see also K Ahmad (1982).
51. The holy *Quran*: 2:219 and 5:90.
52. The holy *Quran*: 2:219.
53. The holy *Quran*: 24:32–33.
54. The holy *Quran*: 30:39; 4:161; 3:130–2 and 2:275–281.
55. *Sahih Bukhari*, narrated Ibn Umar, volume 3, Book 34, number 379.
56. *Muslim*, narrated Jabir, number 2995.
57. OIC Conference 1985; The Federal *Shariat* Court Judgment on *Riba* (Interest) 1991.

58. Matt 6:12.
59. Ps. 112:5.
60. Exodus XXII:25; Leviticus XXV:36–37.
61. Hastings, J 1954 (ed), *Encyclopaedia of Religion and Ethics, Articles on Usury (Hebrew) and Usury (Jewish)*, revised edition, New York.
62. Jowett, B n.d., *Politics by Aristotle 350 BC*, Book 1, Chapter 10, viewed 26 August 2007, <http://www.constitution.org/ari/polit_01.htm>.
63. Global Policy Organization, *UN Millennium Project 2005, Investing in Development*, viewed 20 July 2007, <http://www.globalpolicy.org/socecon/un/2005/02martens.pdf>.
64. Jubilee USA 2007, *Why drop the debt?*, viewed 2 July 2007, <http://www.jubileeusa.org/truth-about-debt/why-drop-the-debt.html>.
65. Ibid.
66. Ibid.
67. Ibid.
68. Jubilee USA 2007, *Debt, Poverty and the MDGs*, Debt and Millennium Development Goals, viewed 20 July 2007, <http://www.jubileeusa.org/truth-about-debt/debt-the-millenium-development-goals.html>.
69. Ibid.
70. Jubilee USA 2007, *Drop the debt, cut the strings*, viewed 3 July 2007, <http://www.jubileeusa.org/truth-about-debt/cut-the-strings.html>.
71. Jubilee USA 2007, *Debt, poverty and the MDGs*, viewed 3 July 2007, <http://www.jubileeusa.org/truth-about-debt/debt-the-millenium-development-goals.html>.
72. Ibid.
73. Jubilee USA 2007, *Getting debt into G-8 Summit conversations*, 31 May, viewed 13 July 2007, <http://jubileeusa.typepad.com/blog_the_debt/2007/05/index.html>.
74. Jubilee USA 2007, *Vulture funds saga needs solutions*, 16 March, viewed 3 July 2007, <http://jubileeusa.typepad.com/blog_the_debt/2007/03/index.html>.
75. Jubilee USA 2007, *Why drop the debt?*, viewed 2 July 2007, <http://www.jubileeusa.org/truth-about-debt/why-drop-the-debt.html>.
76. Jubilee USA 2007, *Delegation meets with Members of Zambia Parliament*, 27 January, viewed 12 July 2007, <http://jubileeusa.typepad.com/blog_the_debt/2007/01/index.html>.
77. The holy *Quran*: 4:135; 5:8; 7:29; 11:85 and 57:25.
78. Sachs, J 2002 (Translator), *Nichomachean Ethics, Notes – Aristotle's Nicomachean Ethics (Philosophical Library Series)*, Focus Publishing/R. Pullins Company, Newburyport, MA.
79. The holy *Quran*: 2:86; 2:102; 3:22; 3:195; 4:134; 6:113 and 19:76.
80. The holy *Quran*: 2:159; 3:148; 6:32; 10:99; 11:17; 16:89; 16:102 and 17:9.
81. *New York Times*, 11 June 2003, 'Camps of terror, often overlooked', viewed 20 July 2007, <http://www.nytimes.com/glogin?>.
82. The holy *Quran*: 43:32.
83. The holy *Quran*: 2:30; 3:66; 9:78 and 10:36.
84. The holy *Quran*: 2:232; 4:26; 4:70; 4:176; 6:59 and 6:71.
85. The holy *Quran*: 2:257; 3:73; 6:90; 6:125; 11:17 and 19:76.
86. The holy *Quran*: 2:102; 3:152; 4:134; 6:32; 12:101; 16:30; 17:21 and 31:5.
87. The holy *Quran*: 14:27; 16:102; 17:9 and 31:3.

88. The holy *Quran*: 2:74; 3:148; 6:32; 10:99; 11:17; 16:89; 16:102 and 30:39.
89. Vladimir Putin remarked, 'Anyone who doesn't regret the passing of the Soviet Union has no heart... Anyone who wants it restored has no brains'. Vladimr Putin Quotes, viewed 20 July 2007, <http://www.paralumun.com/quotesputin.htm>.

Chapter 3

1. See Chapter 4 for a detailed discussion.
2. The Iranian Parliament approved legislation in 1983, which came into force in March 1984, designed to eliminate interest from the nationwide economy and financial markets. See S H Amin (1986) for further details.
3. In 1984 the government of Sudan switched to a full-fledged IBF system economy-wide. See Chapra (2001) for further discussion.
4. *Khaleej Times*, 22 June 2007, '*Sukuks* key to meeting $1.5tr infrastructure needs of ME', viewed 22 August 2007, <http://www.khaleejtimes.com/DisplayArticle.asp?xfile=/data/business/2007/June/bsness_June698.xml&section=business>.
5. Islamic Finance Training, *Managing Islamic funds*, viewed 23 August 2007, <http://www.islamicfinancetraining.com/IslamicFund.php>.
6. *Gulf News*, 16 September 2006, '*Takaful*: a market with great potential', Market watch – special to Gulf news, viewed 16 August 2007, <http://archive.gulfnews.com/articles/06/09/16/10067709.html>.
7. Some Islamic jurists and economists argue that it is against the Islamic spirit to allow the lender or investor to demand collateral or security from the partner as a precondition for investing his funds (Saleh, 1986). However, *Shariah* advisors permit IFIs to demand security or guarantees from clients to cover the risk of negligence and wilful misconduct on their part (Khan, F, 1993).
8. There are two opposite views on the evolution of IBF institutions. One is that IBF has a mostly religious origin (Ahmad, A, 1987). The other argues that the development and growth of IBF reflects petrodollars or oil wealth and economic prosperity in the Middle Eastern world (Presley and Wilson, 1992; Wilson, 1995).
9. It must be noted that the fulfilment of promise is highly valued in Islamic teachings. The holy *Quran* says: 'And fulfil your promise. Verily, you will be answerable for your promise' (The holy *Quran*: I7:34).
10. *Islamic Finance news*, 10 November 2006, 'Meet the Head', vol. 3, no. 40, p. 18.
11. See, for example, Delorenzo Y T (ed) 1999, *A Compendium of Legal Opinions on the Operations of Islamic Banks*, Institute of Islamic Banking Insurance, London, Chapter 1: *Murarabaha*, contract components, *fatwas* nos. 1, 5, 10, 35, 36, 37 and 38.
12. *Islamic Finance News*, 29 September 2006, 'News brief ', vol. 3, no. 34, p. 9.
13. *Islamic Finance News*, 3 November 2006, 'Sukuk-friendly regime for UK?', vol.3, no. 39, p. 6.
14. For detailed information, see the homepage of Dubai International Financial Exchange (DIFX), <http://www.difx.ae/Public/home/home.htm>.

15. *Khaleej Times,* 20 May 2007, 'EGIBL to arrange Dh1.22b *sukuk* in Pakistan', viewed 27 August 2007, <http://www.khaleejtimes.ae/DisplayArticleNew.asp?col=&section=business&xfile=data/business/2007/May/business_May618.xml>.
16. North American Islamic Trust (NAIT), *the Dow Jones*[SM] *Islamic Fund,* viewed 23 August 2007, http://www.investaaa.com/>.
17. Ibid.
18. See the list of Islamic equity funds, <http://www.failaka.com/Library/Articles/Islamic%20Funds%204-2003.PDF>.
19. Institute of Islamic Banking and Insurance London, *Islamic equity funds,* viewed 23 August 2007, <http://www.islamic-banking.com/ibanking/ief.php>.
20. *Gulf News,* 25 April 2007, 'Standard & Poor's launches Islamic equity indices', viewed 23 August, 2007, <http://archive.gulfnews.com/articles/07/04/25/10120619.html>.
21. *Gulf News,* 16 September 2006, 'Takaful: a market with great potential', viewed 16 June 2007, <http://archive.gulfnews.com/articles/06/09/16/10067709.html>.
22. *Islamic Finance News,* 13 April 2007, 'Takaful shapes the future', vol. 4, no. 15, p. 22.
23. *Islamic Finance News,* 20 February 2006, 'Indonesia: *Takaful* market to grow', vol. 3, no. 4, p. 18.
24. *Islamic Finance News,* 10 November 2006, 'Amana *Takaful* Insurance – the growth of *Takaful* in Sri Lanka', vol. 3, no. 40, p. 20.
25. *Khaleej Times,* 7 October 2006, 'GCC Infrastructure expense will exceed US$360b this year', viewed 27 August 2007, <http://www.khaleejtimes.com/DisplayArticleNew.asp?xfile=data/business/2006/October/business_October235.xml&section=business>.
26. *Khaleej Times,* 22 June 2007, '*Sukuks* key to meeting $1.5tr infrastructure needs of ME, Asia', viewed 27 August 2007, <http://www.khaleejtimes.com/DisplayArticleNew.asp?xfile=data/business/2007/June/business_June698.xml&section=business&col=>.
27. *Arab News,* 12 October 2006, 'Bahrain Hopes to Attract More Islamic Businesses', viewed 23 August 2007, <http://www.arabnews.com/?page=6&section=0&article=88100&d=12&m=10&y=2006>.
28. Jordan Islamic Bank, *Annual Report 2006,* viewed 23 August 2007, <http://www.jordanislamicbank.com/annualreport.html>.
29. *Islamic Finance News,* 14 July 2006, 'Kuwait: *Takaful* accounts for 14 percent', vol. 3, no. 23, p. 15.
30. Taib Research 2006, *GCC market report – market commentary,* 6 November, viewed 22 August 2007, <www.taib.com/reports/M01025110606/GCC_06NOV06.pdf>.
31. *Islamic Finance news,* 10 November 2006, 'Qatar: US$700 billion plan for GCC', vol. 3, no 40, p. 6.
32. *Islamic Finance News,* 3 November 2006, 'Badr al Islami Islamic ambitions', vol. 3, no. 39, p. 5.
33. *International Herald Tribune,* 27 March 2007, 'Malaysia relaxes foreign ownership rules for Islamic banks', viewed 21 June 2007, <http://www.iht.com/articles/ap/2007/03/27/business/AS-FIN-Malaysia-Islamic-Banking.php>.

34. Securities Commission, Malaysia 2006, *List of Shariah compliant securities by the Shariah Advisory Council of Securities Commission*, 6 October, viewed 23 August 2007, <http://www.sc.com.my/eng/html/icm/sas/syariahOct06.pdf>.
35. Bank Indonesia, *The Blueprint of Islamic Banking Development in Indonesia 2002*.
36. *Sudan Tribune*, 24 August 2007, 'South Sudan to ban Islamic banking – officials', viewed 25 August 2007, <http://www.sudantribune.com/spip.php?article21559>.
37. *Islamic Finance News*, 26 May 2006, 'Paradigm shift in Islamic banking', vol. 3, no. 16, p. 7.
38. It is pointed out by Majid Dawood, a London-based consultant on *Sharia*-compliance to *Newsweek International Edition:* Matthews, O 2005, 'How the west came to run Islamic banks', *Newsweek International Edition*, 31 October, viewed 25 August 2007, <http://www.msnbc.msn.com/id/9775291/site/newsweek/from/ET/>.
39. For the complete list of the AAOIFI accounting standards, go to the home page of AAOIFI, <http://www.aaoifi.com/>.
40. UAE Intereact 2006, *80 per cent of private wealth in GCC invested outside the region*, 6 September, viewed 24 August 2007, <http://uaeinteract.com/news/rss-news.asp?ID=21981>.
41. *Arab Times*, 13 May 2007, 'Most funds of small projects not utilized: Al-Wuhhaib; Devise long-term strategy for Islamic financial industry', viewed 24 August 2007, <http://www.arabtimesonline.com/arabtimes/kuwait/Viewdet.asp?ID=8121&cat=a>.
42. Islamic Financial Services Board (IFSB), *Guiding Principles on Corporate Goverance for Institutions offering only Islamic Financial Services (Excluding Islamic Insurance(Takaful) Institutions and Islamic Mutual Funds)*, 21 December 2005, viewd 25 August 2007, <http://www.ifsb.org>.
43. Bank Negara Malaysia, IDB, IRTI and IFSB jointly organized the '*Second International Conference on Islamic Banking: Risk Management, Regulation and Supervision*' on 7–8 February 2006, at Kuala Lumpur.

Chapter 4

1. Originally, the Council of Islamic Ideology (CII) was known as the Advisory Council of Islamic Ideology under the 1957 Constitution of Pakistan. It was renamed the Council of Islamic Ideology (CII) in the 1973 Constitution of Pakistan.
2. See the Advisory Council of Islamic Ideology's Resolution on *Riba*, 1964.
3. See the Advisory Council of Islamic Ideology's Resolution on *Riba*, 1969.
4. See comments of Manzer Kahf on the 1980 CII Report, in Ahmed, Z, Iqbal, M & Khan, F M (1983, p. 245).
5. See comments of Mohammad Nejatullah Siddiqi on the 1980 CII Report, in Ahmed, Z, Iqbal, M & Khan, F M (1983, p. 229).
6. See comments of Manzer Kahf on the 1980 CII Report, in in Ahmed, Z, Iqbal, M & Khan, F M (1983, p. 245).
7. If the excess in a loan arising from delay or in term of premium, favour, gift or service as a condition for the loan and in addition to the principal amount

is *riba al-nasi'ah,* which is a common form of interest prohibited by the holy Quran (see Chapra, 1985).

8. See comments of Fahim Khan and Sharafat Ali Hashmi on the 1980 CII Report, in Ahmed, Z, Iqbal, M & Khan, F M (1983, p. 246).
9. See the 1991 FSC Judgement on *riba,* para nos. 163, 168, 160, 161, 162, 163, 182, 211 and 224; The 1999 SC Judgement on *Riba,* para nos. 251–53.
10. See comments of Umer Chapra on the 1980 CII Report, in Ahmed, Z, Iqbal, M & Khan, F M (1983, p. 251).
11. For example see, The International Federation of Accountants (IFAC), *Understanding Financial Statement Audits: A Guide for Financial Statement User 2004,* International Auditing Practice Committee, viewed 27 August 2007, <http://www.ifac.org/Downloads/IFAC_News_01-04.pdf>.
12. *This is cited by M A Khan (1989).*

Chapter 5

1. See names of groups' members in Appendix I-C.
2. See Appendix III. See Zaidi (1987) for the full set of instructions and circulars issued by the SBP for undertaking the phased transformation of the interest-based financial system into the Islamic financial system.
3. Amendment was made on 24 December 1980 by adding new Section 26 A to the 1962 BCO (Zaidi, 1987).
4. Amendment was made on 24 December 1980 by adding new clauses (dd) and (ee) to Section 5 of the 1962 BCO (Zaidi, 1987).
5. Amendment was made on 24 December 1980 by adding a new clause (gg) in Section 5 of the 1962 BCO (Zaidi, 1987).
6. Amendment was made on 24 December 1980 by adding a new paragraph after the third paragraph in Section 5 of the 1962 BCO (Zaidi, 1987).
7. In the 1984 Companies Ordinance, the definition of 'redeemable capital' was included, which allowed financing through PTCs, *Musharakah* Certificates, etc. The new instruments were to become a permanent part of the borrowing companies' equity (Zaidi, 1987).
8. The changes were made on 24 December 1980 by adding new Sections 93A, 93B, 93C and 93D to the 1962 BCO (Zaidi, 1987).
9. See Zaidi (1987) for details on restructuring the banking laws in Pakistan on Islamic lines.
10. BCD Circular No. 26 of the SBP, dated 24.12.1980.
11. Ibid.
12. BCD Circular No. 13 of the SBP, dated 20.6.1982; BCD Circular No.21 of SBP, dated 30.6.1982; BCD Circular No. 37 of the SBP, dated 02.11.1982.
13. BCD Circular No. 13 of 20 June 1984.
14. See Appendix 1-C for the list of members.
15. Ibid.
16. Ibid.
17. Ibid.
18. Cited in Zaidi (1991).

19. It may be noted that the 1992 Report of Commission for Islamization of Economy and The 1999 IIIE Report called the charging of mark-up for 210 days un-Islamic (see Chapter 7).
20. BCD Circular No. 21 of 30 June 1982.
21. See critique of the Daily Product Method in Chapter 4.
22. BCD Circular No. 21 of 30 June 1982; see A J Khan (1984) and Zaidi (1987) for detailed functioning of the *musharakah* financing scheme in the banking sector of Pakistan.
23. The transfer to this reserve account was limited and further qualified through an amendment made on 31.12.1984 to Section 23 of the 1979 Income Tax Ordinance (Zaidi, 1987).
24. BCD Circular No. 27 of 26 November 1984.
25. In the 1990s, the regular tax of 25 percent on *mudarabah* business was still lower than those taxes applicable to other financial institutions and banks (Siddiqui, 1994).
26. *Corporate Authority Report on Mudarabah Accounts 1990–1991*; Jang, 24 January 1991, *'Report on mudarabah accounts 1990–1991'*, pp. 9–10.
27. Ibid.
28. The World Bank and International Monetary Fund, *Pakistan: Technical Note: Conditions of the Banking System 2004*, IMF, Washington, DC.
29. The CII's Consolidated Recommendations; *Economist* (London), 21 March 1981.
30. *Muslim*, 23 February 1985, p. 7.
31. *Muslim*, 20 February 1986; see also S R Khan (1987).
32. *Business Recorder*, 12 January 1981, p. 7; *Pakistan Economist*, 5 February 1981, p. 9; see also Z Ahmed (1987).
33. The CII Meeting, 27 June 1981.
34. *The Muslim*, 17 April 1992, p. 6.
35. The CII's Consolidated Recommendations; *Economist* (London), 21 March 1981.
36. The CII's Consolidated Recommendations, 24 December 1983.
37. The Ministry of Finance, *Pakistan Economic Survey (1984–85)*, The Economic Adviser's Wing, Government of Pakistan, Islamabad, as cited by Siddiqui (1997b).

Chapter 6

1. The 1963 Constitution of Pakistan, Article 203D, the Provision to Article F (1) inserted in 1983, and the Provision to 203D (2) inserted in 1984.
2. See Appendix V.
3. See Appendix V.
4. The Presidential Order No. 14, 1985; the 1991 FSC Judgement on *riba*, para no. 16.
5. See Appendix V.
6. The 1991 FSC Judgement on *riba*, para no. 1; see M A Khan (1994).
7. The 1991 FSC Judgement on *riba*, para no. 104.

8. The 1991 FSC Judgement on *riba*, para nos. 93, 100, 106, 111, 116, 119, 126, 130, 131, 135, 136, 141, 142, 143 and 153; see M A Khan (1994).
9. The 1991 FSC Judgement on *riba*, para nos. 65, 66, 93, 100, 106, 108, 109, 111, 116, 118, 119, 126, 130, 131, 134, 135, 136, 138, 141, 142, 143 and 163.
10. The 1991 FSC Judgement on *riba*, para nos. 249–262, 268 and 383.
11. See Appendix IV-B.
12. The 1991 FSC Judgement on *riba*, para nos. 366 and 368; see M A Khan (1994).
13. The FSC argued that the doctrine of the *Maslahah* in *Shariah* is applicable in cases where religious scholars could find no direct text on the given matter in the holy *Quran* or *Sunnah*. See the 1991 FSC Judgement on *riba*, para nos. 116, 168 and 141–52. It may be noted that the Council of Scholars of Jawa Indonesia had delivered a verdict in the favour of the permissibility of bank interest on the basis of *Maslahah*. The Council categorized bank interest as '*Mutashabat*'. The FSC observed that the application of the doctrine of *Maslahah* in the case of bank interest is inconsistent with the injunctions of the holy *Quran* and *Sunnah* because the absolute prohibition of *riba* and bank interest is proved from the Islamic injunctions beyond any doubt. The FSC undertook rigorous and thorough research on the doctrine of '*Mutashabahat*'. It argued that the holy *Quran*ic injunctions whose meanings are not clear are known as '*Mutashabat*'. For example, the holy *Quran*ic injunctions concerning the Attributes of God, the nature of hell, heaven, etc., fall into the orbit of '*Mutashabihat*', whereas injunctions related to the permission or prohibition of certain acts are crystal clear and fall into the first category, i.e., '*Muhkamat*'. Thus the injunctions concerning the absolute prohibition of *riba* undoubtedly and irrevocably fall into the first category, and therefore the doctrine of *Ijma* or *Ijtehad* or *Maslahah* or necessity cannot be applied or invoked in support of the permissibility of bank interest. See the 1991 FSC Judgement on *riba*, para nos. 130 and 131, for further explanation.
14. See replies of the respondents to question number 2, the 1991 FSC Judgement on *riba*, Appendix A, p. 46.
15. The 1991 FSC Judgement on *riba*, para nos. 46, 116 and 129, and replies of the respondents to question no. 3 at Appendix A, p. 56.
16. The 1991 FSC Judgement on *riba*, para nos. 183 and 193, and replies of the respondents to question no. 5 at Appendix A, p. 66.
17. The 1991 FSC Judgement on *riba*, para nos. 325, 326, 328 and 383, and replies of the respondents to question nos. 9 and 10 at Appendix A, p. 119.
18. The 1991 FSC Judgement on *riba*, para nos. 323 and 383, and replies of the respondents to question no. 8 at Appendix A, p. 111.
19. The 1991 FSC Judgement on *riba*, para nos. 160–3, 168, 182, 211 and 224, and replies of the respondents to question no. 5 at Appendix A, p. 56.
20. These shortcomings in the FSC Judgement on *riba* are pointed out by M A Khan (1994).
21. *Business Recorder*, 14 May 1992.
22. The 1980 CII Report, p. 11, *Business Recorder*, 13 December 1993.
23. The 1991 FSC Judgement on *riba*, para nos. 60–63.
24. *The Muslim*, 13 & 26 March 1992; *Dawn*, 16 April 1992.
25. *The Nation*, 15 March 1992; *Business Recorder*, 15 April 1992.
26. *The Nation*, 23 February 1992.
27. *The Muslim*, 12 August 1992.

28. *Business Recorder*, 23 February 1992.
29. *The Muslim*, 8 August 1992; *The Nation*, 20 October 1992.
30. *The Muslim*, 13 & 20 September 1992.
31. *The News*, 22 March 1992; *Dawn*, 10 May 1992.
32. *The Muslim*, 19 June 1992.

Chapter 8

1. The 1999 SC Judgement on *Riba* was delivered by five judges, namely, Chief Justice Khalil-ur-Rehman Khan, Justice Wahihuddin Ahmad, Justice Mohammad Taqi Usmani, Justice Mahmood Ghazi and Justice Munir.
2. The 1999 SC Judgement on *Riba*, para no. 468.
3. The 1999 SC Judgement on *Riba*, para no. 249.
4. The 1999 SC Judgement on *Riba*, para no. 527; see Auyb (2000).
5. The 1999 SC Judgement on *Riba*, para no. 5.
6. The 1999 SC Judgement on *Riba*, para no. 501.
7. The 1999 SC Judgement on *Riba*, para no. 458.
8. The 1999 SC Judgement on *Riba*, para nos. 23–24 and 476–77.
9. The 1999 SC Judgement on *Riba*, para nos. 477 and 496.
10. The 1999 SC Judgement on *Riba*, para no. 475.
11. The 1999 SC Judgement on *Riba*, para no. 502.
12. The 1999 SC Judgement on *Riba*, para nos. 219 and 501.
13. The 1999 SC Judgement on *Riba*, para no. 78 and 503; see Auyb (2000).
14. The 1999 SC Judgement on *Riba*, para no. 28.
15. The 1999 SC Judgement on *Riba*, para no. 478.
16. The 1999 SC Judgement on *Riba*, para nos. 537 and 480.
17. The 1999 SC Judgement on *Riba*, para nos. 34 and 81; see Auyb (2000).
18. The 1999 SC Judgement on *Riba*, para nos. 36 and 81.
19. The 1999 SC Judgement on *Riba*, para no. 36.
20. The 1999 SC Judgement on *Riba*, para no. 37.
21. The 1999 SC Judgement on *Riba*, para no. 38.
22. The 1999 SC Judgement on *Riba*, para nos. 481–82; see Auyb (2000).
23. The 1999 SC Judgement on *Riba*, para no. 251.
24. The 1999 SC Judgement on *Riba*, para nos. 251–53.
25. The 1999 SC Judgement on *Riba*, para nos. 23, 369 and 473–77; see Auyb (2000).
26. The 1999 SC Judgement on *Riba*, para no. 500.
27. The 1999 SC Judgement on *Riba*, para no. 39.
28. The 1999 SC Judgement on *Riba*, para no. 482.
29. The 1999 SC Judgement on *Riba*, para no. 483; see Auyb (2000).
30. The 1999 SC Judgement on *Riba*, para no. 500.
31. The 1999 SC Judgement on *Riba*, para nos. 513–14.
32. The 1999 SC Judgement on *Riba*, para no. 524; see Auyb (2000).
33. The 1999 SC Judgement on *Riba*, para nos. 49 and 65.
34. The 1999 SC Judgement on *Riba*, para no. 509.
35. The 1999 SC Judgement on *Riba*, para nos. 453–56.
36. The 1999 SC Judgement on *Riba*, para no. 509; see Auyb (2000).
37. The 1999 SC Judgement on *Riba*, para nos. 75 and 499–500.

38. The 1999 SC Judgement on *Riba*, para no. 612.
39. The 1999 SC Judgement on *Riba*, para no. 613; see Auyb (2000).
40. The 1999 SC Judgement on *Riba*, para no. 615.
41. The 1999 SC Judgement on *Riba*, para no. 618.
42. The 1999 SC Judgement on *Riba*, para no. 619; see Auyb (2000).
43. The 1999 SC Judgement on *Riba*, para no. 621.
44. The 1999 SC Judgement on *Riba*, para no. 622.
45. The 1999 SC Judgement on *Riba*, para no. 623.
46. The 1999 SC Judgement on *Riba*, para no. 625; see Auyb (2000).
47. The 1999 SC Judgement on *Riba*, para no. 627.
48. The 1999 SC Judgement on *Riba*, para no. 629.
49. The 1999 SC Judgement on *Riba*, para nos. 513–14; see Auyb (2000).
50. *Dawn*, 15 June 2001.
51. Ibid.
52. Ibid.
53. *The Nation*, 19 June 2001.
54. *The News*, 9 March 2001.
55. *Dawn*, 27 December 2001.
56. *Business Recorder*, 8 January 2002.
57. *The News*, 2 December 2001.
58. *Dawn*, 2 February 2002.
59. See *World Bank Country Assistance Strategy Report, July 2002.*
60. *Dawn*, 25 May 2002.
61. *The News*, 1 June 2002.
62. *Business Recorder*, 7 June 2002.
63. The 2002 SC Judgement on *Riba* Case Review, para no. 21.
64. The 2002 SC Judgement on *Riba* Case Review, para no. 9.
65. The 2002 SC Judgement on *Riba* Case Review, para no. 14.
66. The 2002 SC Judgement on *Riba* Case Review, para no. 10.
67. *The 2002 Task Force Report of Ministry of Finance Pakistan*, Chapter 6.
68. Ibid.
69. See the 98-page SBP Report submitted to SC at hearing on *Riba* Case Review in 2002.
70. *The 2002 Task Force Report of Ministry of Finance Pakistan*, Chapter 6.
71. The 2002 SC Judgement on *Riba* Case Review, para no. 7.
72. Ibid.
73. Ibid.
74. The 2002 SC Judgement on *Riba* Case Review, para no. 6.
75. Ibid.
76. Ibid.
77. *The Nation*, 22 June 2002.
78. *Dawn*, 22 June 2002.
79. Ibid.
80. The 24-page judgement on the *riba* case review was written by Chief Justice Sheikh Riaz Ahmed, and unanimously confirmed by his four colleagues, namely, Justice Munir, Justice Qazi Muhammad Farooq, Dr Allama Khalid Mahmood and Dr Rashid Ahmed Jullundhari.
81. The 2002 SC Judgement on *Riba* Case Review, para no. 18.

82. Ibid.
83. *The Nation*, 21 June 1999; *The News*, 15 June 2001.
84. *Business Recorder*, 6 June 2002.
85. *Business Recorder*, 7 June 2002.
86. Ibid.
87. *Business Recorder*, 22 June 2002.
88. *The News*, 22 June 2002.
89. *The Nation*, 22 June 2002.
90. *Dawn*, 22 June 2002.
91. *The News*, 22 June 2002.
92. *Dawn*, 8 June 2002.
93. *Business Recorder*, 22 June 2002.
94. The 1999 SC Judgement on *Riba*.
95. *The Nation*, 19 May 2001.
96. *The News*, 20 May 2001; *The Nation*, 19 May 2001.
97. *Dawn*, 2 July 1997; *The News*, 22 February 1999.
98. Ibid.
99. *The Nation*, 13 June 2002.
100. *Business Recorder*, 5 June 2002.
101. *Business Recorder*, 12 April 2002.
102. *Dawn*, 17 June 2001; *The News*, 18 June, 2001.
103. Ibid.
104. *Dawn*, 3 June 2001.
105. *The Nation*, 12 June 2002.
106. *Business Recorder*, 12 April 2001.
107. *The News*, 8 June 2001.
108. *Business Recorder*, 13 February 2000.
109. *The Nation*, 19 June 2001.
110. *The 2002 Task Force Report of Ministry of Finance Pakistan*, Chapter 6.
111. Ibid.
112. The 1999 SC Judgement on *Riba*, para no. 457.
113. The 2002 SC Judgement on *Riba* Case Review, para no. 7.

Chapter 9

1. The Presidential Order no. 14, 1985; the 1991 FSC Judgement on *riba*, para no. 16.
2. *The Nation*, 20 March 1999, 'Supreme Court's doubts on government sincerity in enforcing *Shariah*'; *Dawn*, 9 March 1999, '*Riba*-based economy and banking must change now'.
3. *The Prime Minster's Committee Report on Self-Reliance*, Cabinet Report Documents 1991, Government of Pakistan, Islamabad.
4. The CII Meeting, 1981.
5. *Business Recorder*, 15 September 1993, 'SBP autonomy must be real'; *The News*, 29 January 1994, 'Central bank needs transparency of functions'.
6. *The 2002 Task Force Report of Ministry of Finance Pakistan*, Chapter 6; *Business Recorder*, 11 June 2002.
7. Ibid.

8. *The State Bank of Pakistan (SBP)'s Policy Issues 1998.*
9. *Dawn*, 22 January 1997.
10. *Business Week*, 27 January 1997.
11. *The Nation*, 3 September, 1993.
12. *The State Bank of Pakistan News*, 16 June 1997.
13. *Business Recorder*, 21 August 1993, 'Autonomous SBP can stop misuse of the monetary instruments'.
14. *The Business Recorder*, 17 August 1994.
15. *The Muslim*, 28 November 1993.
16. *The Nation*, 22 January 1994.
17. Yaqoob, M 1993, 'The level and structure of mark-up rates in Pakistan', paper presented at the Seminar of Management Association of Pakistan, Karachi, 17 November.
18. *The Nation*, 17 September 1993, 'Crisis in banking'; Yaqoob, M 1998, 'The cancer of loan defaults in Pakistan – major macro economic policy issues in Pakistan', *The 1998 SBP Edition.*
19. *The 2002 Task Force Report of Ministry of Finance Pakistan*, p. 17.
20. Ibid, p. 27.
21. *Dawn*, 2 July 2002.
22. *The 2002 Task Force Report of Ministry of Finance Pakistan*, Chapters 5 and 6; *The Year Book 2004–2005 of Economic Affair Division of Pakistan; Pakistan Economic Survey 2006–007*, viewed 26 August 2007, <http://en.wikipedia.org/wiki/Economy_of_Pakistan>.
23. *Pakistan Economic Survey 2006–007*, viewed 26 August 2007, <http://en.wikipedia.org/wiki/Economy_of_Pakistan>.
24. *The Prime Minster's Committee Report on Self-Reliance*, Cabinet Report Documents 1991, Government of Pakistan, Islamabad, pp. 15–11.
25. *The 2002 Task Force Report of Ministry of Finance Pakistan*, p. 36.
26. Ibid, p. 38.
27. The 1991 FSC Judgement on *riba*, para no. 65.
28. *Dawn*, 12 October 1992.
29. *The 2002 Task Force Report of Ministry of Finance Pakistan*, p. 11.
30. *Dawn*, 9 April 2004, 'World Bank insists on more revenues'.
31. *Business Recorder*, 22 June 2002.
32. *The News*, 26 March 1999.
33. *The Prime Minster's Committee Report on Self-Reliance*, Cabinet Report Documents 1991, Government of Pakistan, Islamabad, p. 17.
34. *The Nation*, 12 December 1992.

References

Abbasi, M B 1994, *Capital Markets in Pakistan*, Feroz Sons Publishers, Karachi.

Abdulmalik, A 2006, 'Islamic finance – rising to the challenge of phenomenal growth', *Arab Banker*, 16 June, viewed 23 August 2007, <http://www.arab-banker.com/dir/1901/1901-IslamicFinance2.asp>.

Abu-Saud, M 1980, 'Money, interest and *qiradh*', in Ahmad K (ed), *Studies in Islamic Economics*, The Islamic Foundation, Leicester, pp. 59–84.

Ahmad, A 1987, *Development and Problems of Islamic Banks*, Islamic Development Bank (IDB), Islamic Research and Training Institute (IRTI), Jeddah.

Ahmad, A, Khan, T & Iqbal, M 1998, *Challenges Facing Islamic Banking*, Islamic Development Bank (IDB), Islamic Research and Training Institute (IRTI), Jeddah.

Ahmad, J (ed) 1952, *Some Recent Speeches and Writings of Mr. Jinnah*, Shaikh Muhammad Ashraf Publishers, Lahore.

Ahmad, K 1997, 'Consensus on *riba*: real hindrance is the lack of will', *Dawn*, 11 August, pp. 7–8.

Ahmad, K 1982, *Public Duties in Islam: The Institution of the Hisba*, The Islamic Foundation, Leicester.

Ahmad, S 1994, 'A central bank without teeth', *Dawn*, 6 January.

Ahmad, S M 1992, *Towards Interest-free Banking*, International Islamic Publishers, New Delhi.

Ahmad, S M 1952, *Economics of Islam – A Comparative Study*, Shaikh Muhammad Ashraf Publishers, Lahore.

Ahmed, Z 1994, 'Islamic banking: state of the art', *Islamic Economic Studies*, vol. 2, no. 1, pp. 1–34.

Ahmed, Z 1991, *Islam, Poverty and Income Distribution*, The Islamic Foundation, Leicester.

Ahmed, Z 1987a, 'Interest-free banking', *Journal of Islamic Banking and Finance*, vol. 4, no. 1, pp. 8–30.

Ahmed, Z 1987b, 'Islamic banking on the crossroads', *Economic Outlook*, vol. 18, no. 10, pp. 9–18.

Ahmed, Z, Iqbal, M & Khan F M (eds) 1983, *Money and Banking in Islam*, International Centre for Research in Islamic Economics, King Abdul-Aziz University, Jeddah.

Akhtar, A R 1988, *The Law and Practice of Interest-free Banking* (*with Banking Tribunals Ordinance*), Mansoor Book House, Lahore.

Akhtar, M R 1996, 'Practice and prospect of *musharakah* financing for small enterprises in Pakistan', *Journal of Islamic Banking and Finance*, vol. 13, no. 3, pp. 7–27.

Akhtar, S 2006, 'The financial sector of Pakistan – the roadmap', *Islamic Finance News*, 26 May, vol. 3, no. 16, pp. 11–12.

Alam, M 2006, 'Islamic finance: going strong', *Oman Economic Review*, 21 June, viewed 22 August 2007, <http://www.oeronline.com/php/2006_june/cover.php>.

Al-Arabi, M A 1966. 'Contemporary banking transactions and Islam's views thereon', *Islamic Review* (London), (May), pp. 10–16.

Aleem, I 1985, Information, uncertainty and rural credit markets in Pakistan, Ph.D. thesis, Oxford University.

Al-Humaidi O 2006, *SABIC offers debut SAR 3 billion sukuk with signing of key documents and underwriting agreement*, media release, SABIC, Riyadh, 24 July, viewed 21 August 2007, <http://www.sabic.com/corporate/en/newsandmediarelations/news/24072006.aspx>.

Al-Omar, F & Abdel-Haq, M 1996, *Islamic Banking: Theory and Practice and Challenges*, Oxford University Press, New Jersey.

Al-Refai, M A 2006, *Unicorn Investment Bank enters Pakistan*, media release, Unicorn Investment Bank, Bahrain, 20 June, viewed 22 August 2007, <http://www.unicorninvestmentbank.com/default.asp?action=article&ID=195>.

Al-Sadr, M B 1974, *Al-bank al-la rabawi fil–Islam* (*Interest-free bank in Islam*), Jami al-Naqi, Kuwait.

Alvi, I 2006, 'The state of the Islamic capital market', paper presented at the IIFM Workshop Sukuk, IIFM, 20 May, viewed 21 August 2007, <http://www.iifm.net/download/Presentations/The%20State%20of%20Islamic%20Capital%20Markets%20and%20Future%20Prospects%20may06.pdf>.

Amacher, R C & Ulbrich, H H 1995, *Economic Principles and Policy*, South-Western College Publishing Company, Cincinnati, Ohio.

Amin, M 2007, 'Facilitating *sukuk* in UK', *Islamic Finance News*, 5 January, vol. 4, no. 1, pp. 10–11.

Amin, S H 1986, *Islamic Banking and Finance: The Experience of Iran*, Vahid Publications, Tehran.

Andrew, G W (ed) 1995, *Waning of the Communist State: Economic Origins of the Political Decline in China & Hungary*, University of California Press, Berkeley.

Anwar, M 1987, *Modelling Interest-free Economy: A Study in Micro Economics and Development*, International Institute of Islamic Thought, Herndon, Virginia.

Applebaum, A 2003, *Gulag: A History*, Broadway Books Publishers, New York.

Archer, S 2006, 'Corporate governance issues', paper presented in a conference on Islamic Finance: Challenges and Opportunities, organized by the World Bank Financial Sector Network and Islamic Financial Services Board (IFSB) at the World Bank headquarters in Washington, DC, 24 April.

Arekat, Z 2006, 'Islamic Finance Forum', *Islamic Finance News*, 6 February, vol. 3, no. 3, p. 19.

Ariff, M 1988, *Islamic Finance and Banking: Theory, Practice and Prospects*, Progressive Publishers, Lahore.

Ashraf, S M 1998, 'Impediments in the Islamization of banks and financial Institutions', *New Horizon*, December, no. 82, pp. 3–5.

Auyb, M 2000, 'An overview of the judgement of Supreme Court on *riba*', *Journal of the Institute of Bankers Pakistan*, vol. 66, no. 4, pp. 27–56.

Bashir, M 1999, 'Risk and profitability measures in Islamic banks: the case study of two Sudanese banks', *Islamic Economic Studies*, vol. 6, no. 2, pp. 1–26.

Bell, D 1976, *The Cultural Contradictions of Capitalism*, Heinemann, London.

Bendjilali, B & Khan, T 1995, *Economics of Diminishing Musharakah*, Islamic Development Bank (IDB), Islamic Research and Training Institute (IRTI), Jeddah.

Berger, A N & Udell G F 1990, 'Collateral loan quality and bank risk', *Journal of Monetary Economics*, vol. 25, (January), pp. 21–42.

Billah, M M 2006, '*Takaful* funds – an overview', *Islamic Finance News*, 27 October, vol. 3, no. 38, pp. 12–14.

Boulding, K E 1973, *A Preface to Grants Economics: The Economics of Love and Fear*, Prager, New York.

Bowden, E V & Bowden, J H 1995, *Economics: The Science of Common Sense*, South-Western College Publishing Company. Cincinnati, Ohio.

Bulow, J & Rogoff, K 1990, 'Cleaning up Third World debt without getting taken to the cleaners', *Journal of Economic Perspective*, vol. 4, no.1, pp. 31–42.

Byrns, R T & Stone, G W 1989, *Economics*, 4th Edition, Scott, Foresman and Co. Glenview, Illinois/London.

Cader, S A 2007, 'The glass has yet to become full', *Islamic Finance News*, 18 May, vol. 4, no. 20, pp. 18–19.

Carens, J 1981, *Equality, Moral Incentives and the Market*, The University of Chicago Press, Chicago.

Chapra, M 2001, 'Islamic banking and finance: the dream and reality', *Journal of Banking and Finance*, vol. 18, no. 2, pp. 7–39.

Chapra, M U 1993, *Islam and Economic Development: A Strategy for Development with Justice and Stability*, International Institute of Islamic Thought, Islamic Research Institute Press, Islamabad.

Chapra, M U 1985, *Towards a Just Monetary System*, The Islamic Foundation, Leicester.

Chapra, M U 1979, *The Islamic Welfare State and its Role in the Economy*, The Islamic Foundation, Leicester.

Cheema, U 2008, 'The man, who rigged 2002 polls, spills the beans', *The News*, 6 March, p. 1.

Chishty, S 1994, 'Terms financial certifications', *Journal of Islamic Banking and Finance*, vol. 11, no. 4, pp. 44–56.

Choudhury, M A 1998, *Studies in Islamic Science and Polity*, Macmillan, London.

Claessens, S 2006, 'Corporate governance of Islamic banks: why is it important, how is it special and what does this imply?', paper presented in the 'Conference on Islamic Finance: Challenges and Opportunities', World Bank Financial Sector Network and Islamic Financial Services Board, World Bank, Washington, DC, 24 April.

Claessens, S & Ishac, D 1991, 'The LDC debt crises: who gains from debt reduction?', *Japan and World Economy*, vol. 3, no. 2, pp. 181–202.

Collard, D 1978, *Altruism and the Economy: A Study in Non-selfish Economics*, Martin Roberson Publishers, Oxford.

Commission of Islamization of Economy (CIE), *Report on Banks and Financial Institutions 1992*, Government of Pakistan, Islamabad.

Council of Islamic Ideology (CII), *Report on the Elimination of Interest from the Economy 1980*, Government of Pakistan, Islamabad.

Croft, J 2007, 'UK banks are catching up', *Gulf News*, 26 January, viewed 22 August 2007, <http://www.gulf-news.com/Business/Business_Feature/10099406.html>.

Darwall, S 2006, *Morality, Respect, and Accountability*, Harvard University Press, Cambridge, Massachusetts.

De Meza, D & Webb, D 1990, 'Risk, adverse selection and capital market failure', *Economic Journal*, vol. 100, no, 399, pp. 206–214.

Edgar, B 2007, *Ending Debt Slavery*, Tampaine.com, 26 March, viewed 3 July 2007, <http://www.tompaine.com/articles/2007/03/26/ending_debt_slavery.php>.

El-Ashker, A 1995, *Profit Index as a Substitute of LIBOR in Islamic Banking Operations*, Islamic Development Bank (IDB), Islamic Research and Training Institute (IRTI), Jeddah.

El-Diwany, T 2006, *Islam Today: Is Islamic Banking Islamic?*, Interactiveislam.com, viewed 23 August 2007, <ttp://www.interactiveislam.com/html/modules.php?name=News&file=article&sid=199>.

El-Gamal, M A 2002, *The Need for Acceptable Sharia Screening of Stocks: A Case Study of Equity REITs*, Failaka International, 24 July, viewed 23 August 2007, <http://www.failaka.com/Library/Articles/IIFF-El-Gamal-REIT.pdf>.

El-Ghazali, A H 1994, *Profit versus Bank Interest in Economic Analysis and Islamic Law*, Islamic Development Bank (IDB), Islamic Research and Training Institute (IRTI), Jeddah.

Elster, J 1985, *Making Sense of Marx*, Cambridge University Press, Cambridge.

Faruqui, J M 1985, *Accepting Bank Interest as riba: A Case of Resistance to Change*, Research Department, United Bank Limited (UBL), Karachi.

Faruqui, J M & Habibullah, S 1983, *Islamization of Banking in Pakistan*, Research Department, United Bank Limited (UBL), Karachi.

Fazil, M S 1997, 'Major Issues and remedies with regard to public debt in Pakistan', *Journal of Islamic Banking and Finance*, vol. 14, no. 4, pp. 42–63.

Federal *Shariat* Court (FSC) of Pakistan, *Judgement on Riba (Interest) 1991*, P.L.D Publishers, Islamabad.

Fisher, I 1945, *100% money*, City Printing, New Haven.

Foley, D K 1971, *Monetary and Fiscal Policy in Growing Economy*, Macmillan, New York.

Friedman, M 1969, *Monetary vs. Fiscal Policy*, Norton, New York.

Fry, M J 1997, *Emancipating the Banking System and Developing Markets for Government Debt*, 3rd Edition, Bank of England, Routledge, London.

Gardezi, H & Rashid J 1983, *Islamic Economic Reforms under the Military Government*, Vanguard Books, Lahore.

Gari, M A 1997, 'A short-term financial industries based on the *salam* contract', in A Ahmad & T Khan (eds), *Islamic Financial Instruments for Public Sector Resource Mobilization*, Islamic Development Bank (IDB), Islamic Research and Training Institute (IRTI), Jeddah, pp. 249–266.

Ghafoor, A L M A 1999, *Islamic Banking and Finance: Another Approach*, Apptec Publications, Toronto.

Ghazi, M A 1993, 'Indexation and inflation, a rejoinder from *Shariah* viewpoint', *Pakistan Banker*, vol. 3, no. 1, pp. 113–117.

Graham, R 2006, '*Shariah* compliance is a riddle – but true riddles always contains the answer', *Islamic Finance News*, 22 September, vol. 4, no. 33, p. 12.

Hakim S, 2002, 'Islamic banking: challenges and corporate governance', paper presented at the LARIBA 2002 Conference Pasadena, CA, 30 March, viewed 24 August 2007, <http://www.lariba.com/knowledge-center/articles/pdf/LARIBA%202002%20-%20Islamic%20Banking%20-%20Challenges.pdf>.

Haq, I 1999, 'Agenda for reform: replacing oppressive tax system', *Business Recorder*, 15 December.

Haq, M 1973, *The Strategy of Economic Planning: A Case Study of Pakistan*, Pakistan Planning Commission, Islamabad.

Haq, M Z 1995, 'Corruption: a national curse', *Economics Review*, vol. 26, no. 11, pp. 11–16.

Haqqani, S A Q 1994, '*Modarabahs* and their operations: Pakistan's experience', *Journal of Islamic Banking and Finance*, vol. 11, no. 2, pp. 16–20.

Harisman 2006, *Indonesia Islamic banking share seen up – central bank*, media release, Bank Indonesia, 10 October, viewed 22 August 2007, <http://www.jogjacity.com/2006/10/10/indonesia-islamic-banking-share-seen-up-central-bank/>.

Haron, S & Ahmad N 2000, 'The effect of conventional interest rate and rate of profit on funds deposited with Islamic banking system in Malaysia', *International Journal of Islamic Services*, vol. 1, no. 4, pp. 1–9.

Harrison, R 2006, 'SAIB launches Islamic banking program', *Arab News*, 26 September, viewed 23 August 2007, <http://www.arabnews.com/?page=6&section=0&article=87203&d=26&m=9&y=2006>.

Hasan, P 2004, 'Poverty and social justice: some challenges for Islamization in Pakistan', in R M Hathaway & W Lee (eds), *Islamization and the Pakistani Economy*, Woodrow Wilson International Centre for Scholars, Washington, DC, pp. 57–65.

Hasan, Z 1988, 'Distributional equity in Islam', in M Iqbal (ed), *Distributive Justice and Need Fulfilment in Islamic Economy*, The Islamic Foundation, Leicester, London, pp. 35–62.

Hasanuz-Zaman, S M 1993, *Indexation of Financial Assets: An Islamic Evaluation*, International Institute of Islamic Thoughts (IIIT), Herndon, VA.

Hayek, F A 1944, *The Road to Serfdom*, University of Chicago, Chicago.

Helfert, E A 1997, *Techniques of Financial Analysis, A Modern Approach*, 9th Edition, Irwin McGraw Hill Publishers, New York.

Higgins, R C 1997, *Analysis for Financial Management*, 5th Edition, Irwin McGraw Hill Publishers, New York.

Hobson, S 2006, 'Project financing – risks underlying *sukuk* structures', *Islamic Finance News*, 8 December, vol. 3, no. 44, p. 15.

Homoud, S H 1994, 'Progress of Islamic banking the aspiration and realities', *Islamic Economic Studies*, vol. 2, no. 1, pp. 71–80.

Hook, A T 1997, *Savings in Pakistan Practice and Policy* (*1981–1996*), State Bank of Pakistan, Karachi.

Howell, D 1981, *Freedom and Capital*, Blackwell, Oxford.

Huda, M N 1964, 'Economics accepting Islam', *World Muslim League* (Singapore), pp. 10–17.

Husain, I 1999, 'Debt and debt servicing reduction program', *Journal of Institute of Bankers Pakistan*, vol. 65, no. 1, pp. 21–43.

Husain, I 2002, 'Strategy for external debt management (1999–2004)', paper presented at the 51st Annual General Meeting of IBP, Karachi, 2 March.

Husain, I 2005 'Economy of Pakistan – an overview', paper presented at the Expo Conference, Karachi, 3 February.

Hussain, H 1994, '*Modarabahs* and their operations: Pakistan's experience', *Journal of Islamic Banking and Finance*, vol. 11, no. 2, pp. 21–32.

Hussain, H Z 2007, 'Ways to curb inflationary pressures', *Dawn*, 29 January, p. 11.

Hussain, M S 1997, 'Islamic banking in the making', *Journal of Islamic Banking and Finance*, vol. 14, no. 3, pp. 53–59.

Ingram, T 1986, 'Islamic banking: a foreign bank's view', *Journal of Islamic Banking and Finance*, vol. 3, no. 2, pp. 19–29.

International Institute of Islamic Economics (IIIE), *Blueprint of Islamic Financial System, including Strategy for Elimination of Riba 1998*, International Islamic University, Islamabad.

Iqbal, M 1998, Islamic banking, in M Kahf (ed), *Lessons in Islamic Economics*, Islamic Development Bank (IDB), Islamic Research and Training Institute (IRTI), Jeddah, pp. 493–524.

Irshad, S A 1964, *Interest-free Banking*, Orient Press of Pakistan, Karachi.

Islahi, A A 1988, *Economic Concepts of Ibn Taimiyah*, The Islamic Foundation, Leicester.

Ismail, S M 1989, *Critical Analysis of Capitalism, Socialism and Islamic Economic Order*, Oriental Publications, Lahore.

Jaidah, S M 2006, 'IIBQ to increase Islamic banking share', *Islamic Finance News*, 10 November, vol. 3, no. 40, p. 7.

Kadir M R A 2006, 'The future direction of the Malaysian *Takaful* industry', *Islamic Finance News*, 15 September, vol. 3, no. 32, pp. 15–16.

Kadri, A 1996, 'Bold venture in Islamic banking', *The News*, 14 August, p. 5.

Kahf, M 1993, *Zakah Management in Some Muslim Societies*, Islamic Development Bank (IDB), Islamic Research and Training Institute (IRTI), Jeddah.

Kahf, M 1978, *The Islamic Economy: Analytical Study of the Functioning of the Islamic Economic System*, American Trust Publication, Indiana.

Kaleem, A & Isa M 2003, 'Causal relationship between Islamic and conventional banking instruments in Malaysia', *International Journal of Financial Services*, vol. 4, no. 4, pp. 1–12.

Kamal, A R 1997, 'Pakistan foreign debt', *Pakistan Banker*, vol. 7, no. 2, pp. 58–65.

Kamil, S 2007, *Islamic rival for World Bank to open in 2008*, Arabianbusiness.com, 3 May, viewed 21 August 2007, <http://www.arabianbusiness.com/index.php?option=com_content&view=article&id=12008>.

Karim, A 1999, 'Bad debt: its cause and cure', *Journal of the Institute of Bankers Pakistan*, vol. 65, no. 3, pp. 21–36.

Karsten, I 1982, 'Islam and financial intermediation', *IMF Staff Papers*, vol. 29, no. 1, pp. 108–142.

Kassim, Z A M 2006, 'The Islamic way to Insurance', *Islamic Finance News*, 21 July, vol. 3, no. 24, pp. 17–18.

Kearl, J R 1993, *Principles of economics*, D. C. Heath Company, Lexington, MA.

Kennedy, C 1996, *Islamization of Law and Economy Cases of Pakistan*, Institute of Policy Studies, The Islamic Foundation, Islamabad.

Keynes, J M 1936, *The General Theory of Employment, Interest and Money*, Macmillan, London.

Khan, A H 1997, *Stabilization Efforts and Structural Reforms in Pakistan*, Institute of Development of Economics, Islamabad.

Khan, A J 1984, 'Elimination of *riba* from the banking system', *Journal of Islamic Banking and Finance*, vol. 1, no. 3, pp. 24–44.

Khan, A J 1991, *Non-interest Banking in Pakistan: Concept, Practice, and Evaluation*, Royal book Company, Karachi.

Khan, F M 1983, Islamic banking as practised now in the world, in Z Ahmed, M Iqbal & F M Khan (eds), *Money and Banking in Islam*, International Centre for Research in Islamic Economics, King Abdul-Aziz University, Jeddah, pp. 259–290.

Khan, G M 1992, 'Islamic financing and income tax', *Pakistan Banker*, vol. 2, no. 1, pp. 7–15.

Khan, M A 1985, 'Islamic banking in Pakistan', *International Journal of Islamic and Arabic Studies*, vol. 2, no. 2, pp. 21–34.

Khan, M A 1989, 'A survey of critical literature on interest-free banking', *Journal of Islamic Banking and Finance*, vol. 6, no. 1, pp. 7–28.

Khan, M A 1992, *Islamic Banking in Pakistan: The Future Path*, All Pakistan Islamic Education Congress, Lahore.

Khan, M A 1994, 'Review of the Federal Shariat Court (FSC) judgement on *riba*', in K Ahmad (ed), *Elimination of riba from the Economy*, Institute of Policy Studies, Islamabad, pp. 11–26.

Khan, M A 1997, 'Performance auditing for Islamic banks', *Islamic Economic Studies*, vol. 5, nos. 1 & 2, pp. 23–36.

Khan, M M & Bhatti, M I, 2006, 'Why Interest-Free Banking and Finance Movement Failed in Pakistan, with Bhatti, MI, *Humanomics*, vol. 23, 3, 4, pp. 145–161.

Khan, M M & Bhatti, M I, 2008a, 'Development in Islamic Banking: A Financial Risk-allocation Approach', *The Journal of Risk Finance*, vol. 9, Issue, 1, pp. 40–51.

Khan, M M & Bhati, M I 2008b, 'Islamic Banking and Finance: On its Way to Globalization', with Bhatti, M I, accepted in *Journal of Managerial Finance, Special Issue on Interest-Free Banking*, vol. 34, Issue 9 and 10.

Khan, M M 2003, 'Interest-Free Finance: The Interest-Free Banking and Finance Movement in Pakistan, unpublished PhD thesis, Swinburne University of Technology, Melbourne, Australia.

Khan, M M 2008c, 'Main Features of the Interest-free Banking Movement in Pakistan (1980–2006), accepted in *Journal of Managerial Finance, Special Issue on Interest-Free Banking*, vol. 34, Issue 9 and 10.

Khan, S K & Mirakhor A 1987, *Theoretical Studies in Islamic Banking and Finance*, Book Distribution Centre, Houston.

Khan, S R 1987, *Profit and Loss Sharing: An Islamic Experiment in Finance and Banking*, Oxford University Press, New York.

Khan, T 1996, *Practices and Performance of Modaraba Companies: A Case Study of Pakistan's Experience*, Islamic Development Bank (IDB), Islamic Research and Training Institute (IRTI), Jeddah.

Khan, T 1995, 'Demand for and supply of mark-up and PLS funds in Islamic banking: some alternative explanations', *Islamic Economic Studies*, vol. 3, no. 1, pp. 39–78.

Khojah, I 2006, 'Kuwait leads global Islamic finance', *Islamic Finance News*, 2 June, vol. 3, no. 17, p. 3.

Laffont, J J & Tirole, J A 1993, *A Theory of Incentives in Procurement and Regulation*, MIT Press, London.

Lashkar, H 1991, 'Bungling in contract documents distort Pakistan's Islamic banking', *The News*, 15 December, p. 7.

Lassard D R & Walliamson, J 1985, *Financial Intermediation Beyond the Debt Crisis*, Institute for International Economics, Washington, DC.

McAfee, R P & McMillan, J 1987, 'Auctions and bidding', *Journal of Economic Literature*, vol. 25, no. 2, pp. 24–37.

McConnell, C R & Brue, S L 1996, *Economics: Principles, Problems, and Policies*, 5th Edition, Cambridge University Press, New York.

Macfarlane, B 2006, '*Shariah* compliant insurance products – *Takaful* in the UK', *Islamic Finance News*, 9 June, vol. 3, no. 18, pp. 18–19.

Mahmud, S K 1995, 'Pakistan's administration crises', *Pakistan Banker*, vol. 5, no. 2, pp. 29–34.

Malik, M H 1997, 'Some new evidence on the incident of poverty in Pakistan', *Pakistan Development Review*, vol. 27, no. 4, pp. 507–515.

Mannan, M A 1970, *Islamic Economics: Theory and Practice (Comparative Study)*, Ashraf Printing Press, Lahore.

Maududi, S A A 1961, *Interest*, Islamic Publications, Lahore.

Meenai, A A 1998, 'Islamic banking – where are we going wrong?', *New Horizon*, February, no. 72, pp. 3–5.

Ministry of Finance of Pakistan, *Task Force Report 2002*, Government of Pakistan, Islamabad.

Mirakhor, A M 1988, The progress of Islamic banking: the case of Iran and Pakistan, in C Mallat (ed), *Islamic Law and Finance*, Graham and Trotman, London, pp. 91–116.

Mudawi, A Y 2005, 'The experience of Islamic banks in Sudan', *in Encyclopaedia of Islamic Banking*, The Islamic Foundation, London, pp. 26–37.

Mullick, M A H 1993, 'SBP: struggling to assert its autonomous character', *The Nation*, 14 August.

Nacpil, L 2007, *Stop vulture debt bondage*, BLOG THE DEBT, Jubilee USA, 28 February, viewed 22 August 2007, <http://jubileeusa.typepad.com/blog_the_debt/2007/02/index.html>.

Nadeem, A H 1992, 'Corruption at the top: an appraisal', *Pakistan Banker*, vol. 2, no. 1, pp. 117–120.

Naqvi, S N H 1998, 'The quest for macro economic stability – Pakistan case', *Journal of Islamic Banking Finance*, vol. 15, no. 2, pp. 20–29.

Naqvi, S N H 1982, *Ethics and Economics: An Islamic Synthesis*, The Islamic Foundation, Leicester.

Narveson, J (ed) 1983, *Moral Issues*, Oxford University Press, New York.

Naseem, S M 1995, 'Mass poverty in Pakistan, some preliminary findings', *Pakistan Development Review*, vol. 13, no. 4. pp. 12–26.

Nicholas, J 2006, *Oregonian takes drive to World Bank*, Oregonlive.com, viewed 22 August 2007, <http://www.oregonlive.com/news/oregonian/index.ssf?/base/news>.

Nielsen, K 1979, 'Radical egalitarian justice: justice as equality', *Social Theory and Practice*, vol. 5, pp. 209–226.

Nienhaus, V 1983, Profitability of Islamic PLS banks competing with interest banks: problems and prospects, *Journal of Research in Islamic Economics* (Jeddah), vol.1, no. 1, pp. 37–47.

Nomani, F & Rahnema, A 1994, *Islamic Economic Systems*, Zed Books Ltd, London.

Obaidullah, M 2005, *Rating of Islamic Financial Institutions: Some Methodological Suggestions*, Scientific Publishing Centre, King Abdualaziz University, Jeddah.

Othman, Z 2006, 'Interview with the Chief Executive Officer of *Takaful* Re', *Islamic Finance News*, 20 October, vol. 3, no. 37, p. 20.

Parker, M 2006, 'Islamic banking gains momentum in Lebanon', *Arab News*, 4 April, viewed 22 August 2007, <http://www.arabnews.com/?page=6&section=0&article=80256&d=4&m=4&y=2006>.

Perlman, R 1976, *The Economics of Poverty*, McGraw Hill, London.

Persson, T & Tabellini, G E 1994, *Monetary and Fiscal Policy*, MIT Press, Cambridge.

Presley, J R & Wilson, R 1992, *Banking in the Arab Gulf*, Macmillan, London.

Prime Minister's Committee Report on Self-Reliance 1991, Cabinet Report Document 1991, Government of Pakistan, Islamabad.

Quershi, A 1946, *Islam and the Theory of Interest*, Shaikh Muhammad Ashraf Publishers, Lahore.

Qureshi, D M 1984, 'Islamization of financial institutions in Pakistan: assessment', *Journal of Islamic Banking and Finance*, vol. 1, no. 1, pp. 58–71.

Qureshi, D M 2005, 'Vision table: questions and answers session', in *Proceedings of the First Pakistan Islamic Banking and Money Market Conference*, 14–15 September, Karachi, pp. 15–22.

Rahman, T 1997, 'Interest-free banking in Pakistan: an appraisal', *Journal of Islamic Banking and Finance*, vol. 14, no. 4, pp. 6–10.

Ramsey, F P 1928, 'A mathematical theory of saving', *Economic Journal*, vol. 38, no. 152, pp. 543–559.

Rana, F H 2006, 'Growing business prospect of Islamic banking', *The Daily Star*, 28 August, viewed 22 August 2007, <http://www.thedailystar.net/2006/08/28/d608281503138.htm>.

Ranzini, S L 2007, 'Islamic finance (finally) taking roots in North America', *Islamic Finance News*, 30 March, vol. 4, no.13, pp. 10–11.

Rawls, J 1993, *Political Liberalism*, Columbia University Press, New York.

Rawls, J 1971, *A Theory of Justice*, Harvard University Press, Cambridge.

Razak, S A 2006a, *Millennium Finance Corporation launches USD1 billion Global Energy Fund and USD1 billion TMT Fund managed by Millennium Private Equity*, media release, Dubai Islamic Bank, United Arab Emirates, 14 November, viewed 22 August 2007, <http://www.dib.ae/en/art_130.htm>.

Razak, S A 2006b, *DIB breaks another world record in Sukuk*, media release, Dubai Islamic Bank, United Arab Emirates, 9 December, viewed 22 June 2007, <http://www.dib.ae/en/art_136.htm>.

Robertson, D H 1937, 'Alternative theories of the rate of interest: three rejoinders', *Economic Journal*, (December), pp. 47–59.

Saadullah, R 1994, 'Concept of time and Islamic economics', *Islamic Economic Studies*, vol. 2, no. 1, pp. 81–102.

Saeed, K A 2000, *Economy of Pakistan*, New Fine Printing Press, Lahore.

Saleem, F 1993, 'How long can an independent state bank last?', *The Business Recorder*, 27 October.

Saleem, F 1994, 'Promoting the interest of banks deposits', *The Business Recorder*, 4 May.

Saleh, A N 1986, *Unlawful Gain and Legitimate Profit in Islamic Law: riba, gharar, and Islamic Banking*, Cambridge University Press, Cambridge.

Salim, N 2006, 'Wealth management', *Islamic Finance News*, 24 November 2006, vol. 3, no. 42, pp. 8–9.

Sarker, M A 1999, 'Agency problems and its nature, characteristics and relevance with the Islamic modes of contracts', *New Horizon*, February, no. 84, pp. 9–11.

Scharf, T W 1983, *Arab and Islamic Banks: New Business Partners for Developing Countries*, Development Centre Studies of the Organization for Economic Co-Operation and Development (OECD), Paris.

Schultz, B 2004, *Henry Sidgwick: Eye of the Universe – An Intellectual Biography*, Cambridge University Press, Cambridge.

Sen, A 1987, *On Ethics and Economics*, Basil Blackwell, New York.

Shafi, M M 1998, *Distribution of Wealth in Islam*, Dawah Academy, Karachi.

Shah, 2007, *Third World debt undermines development*, globalissues.org, June, viewed 20 August 2007, <http://www.globalissues.org/TradeRelated/Debt.asp>.

Sharif, Z M 2006, 'Islamic finance in Australia', *Islamic Finance News*, 2 May, vol. 3, no.14, pp. 11–12.

Sheikh, A 1994, 'Devising a new banking order', *The News*, 27 April 27.

Siddiqi, M N 1983, *Banking without Interest* (revised English edition), The Islamic Foundation, Leicester.

Siddiqi, M N 1981, *Muslim Economic Thinking: Survey of Contemporary Literature*, The Islamic Foundation, Leicester.

Siddiqi, M N 1967, *Banking without Interest* (Urdu), Islamic Publication, Lahore.

Siddiqi, N 1948, 'Islami usul par banking (Banking according to Islamic Principles)', *Chiragh-e-Rah* (Karachi), vol. 1, nos. 11 & 12, pp. 24–28 and 60–64.

Siddiqui, S H 1997a, *Mudarabah Finance in the Contemporary World: An Overview of mudarabah of Pakistan*, All Pakistan Islamic Education Congress, Lahore.

Siddiqui, S H 1997b, 'Islamization of banking system: Pakistan's experience', *Journal of Islamic Banking and Finance*, vol. 14, no. 4, pp. 11–22.

Siddiqui, S H 1994, *Islamic Banking*, Royal Book Company, Karachi.

Simons, H 1948, *Economic Policy for Free Society*, University of Chicago Press, Chicago.

Smith, A 1776, *An Enquiry into the Nature and Causes of the Wealth of Nations*, edited by Edwin Cannan (1904), Methuen, London.

Smith, J W 2005, *Economic Democracy: The Political Struggle of the 21st Century*, Democracy Press, W. Camden.

Smyth, M J 2006, 'Islamic funds come of age', *Middle East Banker*, November, pp. 28–30.

Stapleton, K 2006, 'New Mutual Funds observe Islamic law, Deutsche Bank introduces Sharia-compliant funds', *Investment Advisor*, viewed 23 August 2007, <http://www.investmentadvisor.com/article.php?article=7317>.

Stein, M S 2006, *Distributive Justice and Disability, Utilitarianism and Egalitarianism*, Yale University Press, New Haven, Connecticut.

Sultan, S A B M 2006, 'An overview of accounting standards for Islamic financial institutions', *Islamic Finance News*, 14 & 21 April, vol. 3, nos. 10 & 11, pp. 10–11 & 12–13.

Sundararajan, V & Errico, L 2002, 'Islamic financial institutions and products in the global financial system: key issues in risk management and challenges ahead', *Working Paper no. 02/192*, International Monetary Fund (IMF), Washington, DC, viewed 25 August 2007, <http://www.imf.org/external/pubs/ft/wp/2002/wp02192.pdf>.

Supreme Court of Pakistan, *Shariah* Appellate Bench (SAB), *Judgment on* Riba 1999, *Shariat* Law Reports, Lahore.

Supreme Court of Pakistan, *Shariah* Appellate Bench (SAB), *Judgment on Riba Case Review 2002, Shariat* Law Reports, Lahore.

Tansi, V 1990, *Fiscal Policy in Open Developing Economies*, International Monetary Fund (IMF), Washington, DC.

Tansi, V 1996, 'Corruption, governmental activities and markets', *Business Recorder*, 9 June.

Tett, G 2006, 'Banks seek Islamic scholars versed in finance', *Financial Times*, 19 May, viewed 25 August 2007, <http://www.ft.com/cms/s/81425438-e75f-11da-9046-0000779e2340.html>.

The Prime Minister's Committee Report on Self-Reliance 1991, Cabinet Report Documents, Government of Pakistan, Islamabad.

Tolefat, A 2006, '*Takaful*: mixed model is the best approach', *Islamic Finance News*, 29 September, vol. 3, no. 34, p. 16.
Udovitch, A L 1970, *Partnership and Profit in Medieval Islam*, Princeton University Press, Princeton, New Jersey.
Ul Haque, N 1997, 'Financial market reform in Pakistan', *Pakistan Development Review*, vol. 36, no. 4, pp. 839–854.
Usmani, M T 1996, 'Developing an interest-free economy', *Albalagh International*, (February–March), pp. 12–23.
Uzair, M 1997, 'Interest, inflation and Islam', *Dawn*, 11 November, p. 8.
Uzair, M 1978, *Interest Free Banking*, Royal Book Company, Karachi.
Uzair, M 1955, *An Outline of Interestless Banking*, Raihan Publications, Karachi.
Vallentyne, H & Steiner, Y 2000, *The Origins of Left-libertarianism – An Anthology of Historical Writings*, Macmillan, London.
Varley, R 2006, 'The evolving Middle East private equity market', *Islamic Finance news*, 14 April, vol. 3, no. 23, p. 11.
Venardos, A 2006, 'Banking in Singapore', *Islamic Finance News*, 24 November, vol. 3, no. 42, pp. 10–12.
Vogel, F E & Hayes S L 1998, *Islamic Law and Finance, Religion, Risk and Return*, Kluwer Law International, London.
Walzer, M & David, M 1995, *Pluralism, Justice and Equality*, Oxford University Press, Oxford.
Warde, I 2000, *Islamic Finance in the Global Economy*, Edinburgh University Press, Edinburgh.
Watkins, N 2007, *Will vultures be allowed to undermine the G-8 Summit?*, CommonDreams.org, 31 May, viewed 23 August 2007, <http://www.commondreams.org/archive/2007/05/29/1559/>.
Weber, M 1958, *The Protestant Ethic and the Spirit of Capitalism*, Charles Scribner's Sons, New York.
Welch, C 2000, *A world in chains – developing countries and debt*, findarticles.com, 4 September, viewed 30 August 2007, <http://findarticles.com/p/articles/mi_m2465/is_6_30/ai_65653648?lstpn=article_result>.
Wilson, R 1997, 'Islamic finance and ethical investment', *International Journal of Social Economics*, vol. 24, no. 11, pp. 1325–1342.
Wilson, R 1995, *Economic Development in the Middle East*, Routledge, London.
Wilson, R 1994, 'Development of financial instruments in an Islamic framework', *Islamic Economic Studies*, vol. 2, no. 1, pp. 103–115.
Yaqoob, M 1998, 'The cancer of loan defaults in Pakistan – major macro economic policy issues in Pakistan', State Bank of Pakistan (SBP), Karachi.
Yaqoob, M 1995, 'Who should control money', *Pakistan Banker*, vol. 5, no. 2, pp. 7–10.
Yaqoob, M 1993, 'The level and structure of mark-up rates in Pakistan', paper presented at the Seminar of Management Association of Pakistan, 17 November, Karachi.
Zaidi, N A 1991, *State of Islamization of Pakistan Economy*, Royal Book Company, Karachi.
Zaidi, N A 1987, *Eliminating Interest from Banks in Pakistan*, Royal Book Company, Karachi.
Zarqa, M A 1983, 'Stability in an interest-free Islamic economy: a note', *Pakistan Journal of Applied Economics*, vol. 2, (winter), pp. 181–88.

Appendices

Appendix I

The Composition of Committees Constituted by the Government of Pakistan from 1980 to 2002 for Working on the Islamization of Economy and Financial Sector of Pakistan

I-A List of Members of the Council of Islamic Ideology (CII) (as on 15.6.1980)

Chairman

Justice Dr. Tanzil-ur-Rahman

Members

1. Mawlana Zafar Ahmad Ansari
2. Mr. Khalid M Ishaque
3. Mufti Sayyahuddin Kakakhel
4. Khawaja Qamruddin Siyalvi
5. Mawlana Muhammad Taqi Usmani
6. Mawlana Muhammad Hanif Nadvi
7. Dr. Ziauddin Ahmed
8. Allama Syed Muhammad Razi
9. Mawlana Shamsul Haq Afghani
10. Dr. Mrs. Khawar Khan Chisti
11. Fazlur Rahman Khan

I-B Members of the Panel of Economists and Bankers Appointed by the Council of Islamic Ideology in November 1977

Chairman

Dr. Ehsan Rashid
Professor of Economics and Director
Applied Economic Research Centre
University of Karachi, Pakistan.

Members

1. Dr. Rafiq Ahmed
   Pro-Vice Chancellor
   University of Punjab
   Lahore, Pakistan
2. Sheikh Mahmood Ahmad
   Lahore, Pakistan
3. Mr. Abdul Jabbar Khan
   President Habib Bank Limited
   Karachi, Pakistan
4. Dr. Nurul Islam Mian
   Director, Institute of Economic Studies
   University of Peshawar
   Peshawar, Pakistan
5. Dr. Syed Nawab Haider Naqvi
   Director
   Pakistan Institute of Development Economics
   Islamabad, Pakistan
6. Dr. Mian M Nazeer
   Professor of Economics
   University of Peshawar
   Peshawar, Pakistan
7. Mr. D M Qureshi
   Managing Director
   Banker's Equity Limited
   Karachi, Pakistan
8. Professor Shakrullah
   Head of the Economics Department
   Baluchistan University
   Quetta, Pakistan
9. Dr. A H Siddiqi
   Director of Studies
   Administrative Staff College
   Lahore, Pakistan
10. Mr. Khadim Hosain Siddiqui
    Member of Pakistan Banking Council
    Karachi, Pakistan

11. Mr. A K Sumar
    Karachi, Pakistan
12. Mr. Abdu Wasay
    Bank of Credit and Commerce International
    Karachi, Pakistan
13. Dr. S M Hasan-uz-Zaman
    Chief, Islamic Economics Division
    Research Department
    State Bank of Pakistan
    Karachi, Pakistan

Convenor

Dr. Ziauddin Ahmad
Deputy Governor
State Bank of Pakistan

I-C Members of the Committees Appointed by the State Bank of Pakistan and Pakistan Banking Council in 1977, 1980 and 1984 to Develop the Legal and Institutional Frameworks for the Implementation of an Islamic Banking System

The Panel of Bankers and Economists appointed by the Council of Islamic Ideology in 1977

1. Mr. Abdul Jabbar Khan	Pakistan Banking Council
2. Mr. M A Wasay	Muslim Commercial Bank of Pakistan
3. Mr. Khadim Hussain Siddiqui	Allied Bank of Pakistan

The Superior Task Force Formed by the Pakistan Banking Council in 1980

1. Mr. Muhammad Usman	National Bank of Pakistan
2. Mr. A A Sherkoti	National Bank of Pakistan
3. Mr. Mufti Muhammad Sabir	United Bank Limited
4. Mr. Ashiq Hussain Farooqui	United Bank Limited
5. Mr. Sardar Ahmed Mirza	Muslim Commercial Bank
6. Mr. Alamdar Hussain	Allied Bank Limited

Four Special Committees Constituted by the Pakistan Banking Council in 1984

(1) Documentation Committee

1. Mr. Mehr A Barlas	National Bank of Pakistan
2. Mr. S Nasim Ahmed	Habib Bank Limited
3. Mr. A Majid Khan	United Bank Limited

4. Mr. Inam Ilahi	Allied Bank Limited
5. Mr. S A Shaikh	American Express Bank

Co-opted Members

1. Mr. Nawazish Ali Zaidi	United Bank Limited
2. Mr. Azizuddin Khan	Muslim Commercial Bank
3. Mr. S Imtiaz Hussain	Habib Bank Limited
4. Mr. Zamir A Siddiqui	National Bank of Pakistan

(2) System and Accounting Committee

1. Mr. Sheik Lal Jani	Pakistan Banking Council
2. Mr. Khalid S Hassan	National Bank of Pakistan
3. Mr. M Ashfaq Ali	Habib Bank Limited
4. Mr. A Raziq Siddiq	United Bank Limited
5. Mr. A Razzaq Adam	Muslim Commercial Bank
6. Mr. Aziz Patel	Allied Bank Limited
7. Mr. Shaukat Tareen	Citi Bank

(3) Legal Committee

1. Mr. Tahir Ali Tayyebi	Habib Bank Limited
2. M. Jameel Sheikh	National Bank of Pakistan
3. Mr. B K Sayani	United Bank Limited
4. Mr. Azizuddin	Muslim Commercial Bank
5. Mr. Baqi Mohomedally	Grindlays Bank

Co-opted Members

1. Mr. K R Chagla	Habib Bank Limited
2. Mr. Naseem Rizvi	Allied Bank Limited

(4) Training Committee

1. Mr. A H Zubairi	Allied Bank Limited
2. Mr. Kh Rashidullah	National Bank of Pakistan
3. Mr. Nawazish Ali Zaidi	United Bank Limited
4. Mr. I A Magoon	Habib Bank Limited
5. Mr. SA Mirza	Muslim Commercial Bank
6. Mr. Mahfooz Ali	Middle East Bank

I-D Members of the Commission for Islamization of Economy Appointed by the Government of Pakistan in July 1991

Chairman

Mr. I A Hanfi
Governor
State Bank of Pakistan

Members

1. Senator Abdur Rahim Mandokhel
2. Arbab Jahangir Khan
   Member, Natioanl Assembly
3. Ch. Abdul Ghafoor
   Member, National Assembly
4. Justice Muhammad Taqi Usmani
   Judge, Shariah appellate Bench
   Supreme Court of Pakistan
5. Mr. Khalid M Ishaque
   Advocate, Supreme Court
   Karachi
6. Mr. Mukhtar Masood
   Former Federal Secretary
7. Dr. Ziauddin Ahmed
   Former Director General
   International Institute of Islamic Economics
   International Islamic University
   Islamabad
8. Mr. Abdul Jabbar Khan
   Former President
   National Bank of Pakistan
9. Dr. Rafiq Ahmed Khan
   Former Vice-Chancellor
   Punjab University
10. Mr. Ebrahim Sidat
    Chartered Accountant
    Karachi

Member/Secretary

Mr. Nawazish Ali Zaidi
Former Executive Vice President
United Bank Limited

I-E Members of the International Institute of Islamic Economics (as on May 15, 1997)

Chairman

Prof. Dr. Sayyid Tahir

Members

1. Prof. Dr. Mohammad Ramzan Akhter
2. Dr. Nasim Shah Shirazi
3. Dr. Syed Zahid Ali
4. Dr. Mazhar Iqbal
5. Mr. Atiquzzafar (Member, Drafting Committee)
6. Dr. Qazi Najeeb Rehman
7. Dr. Salman Syed Ali (Member, Drafting Committee)
8. Dr. Mahboob Ahmed
9. Mr. Abdul Jabbar
10. Mr. Muhammad Iqbal Anjum
11. Mr. Muhammad Ayub Siddiqui
12. Mr. Ghulam Mustafa Sajid
13. Mr. Atif Waheed (Member/ Secretary, Drafting Committee).

I-F Members of the Commission on Transformation of the Financial System Constituted in the State Bank of Pakistan to Transform the Banking Financial System of Pakistan on Islamic Lines Under the 1999 Supreme Court Orders on *Riba* (Interest)

Chairman

A Hanfi, the former Governor of SBP

Members

1. Muhammad Younous Khan, the former Additional Secretary Finance Division. Securities and Exchange Commission of Pakistan
2. M Ashraf Janjua, the former Chief Economic Advisor of the State Bank of Pakistan
3. Slaman Shah, the former Senior Economist of State Bank of Pakistan
4. Dr. Pervez Hasan, Senior Advocate
5. Mawlana Muhammad, Religious Scholar
6. Mohammad Taqi Usmani, Religious Scholar
7. Zakir Mehmood, President of Habib Bank of Pakistan
8. Amar Zafar Khan, President of United Bank Limited
9. S Muhmmad Hussain, Senior Chartered Accountant
10. Dr. Fahim Khan, Senior Banker and Head of the Islamic Research and Training Institute Islamic Development Bank Jeddah Saudi Arabia

I-G Task Force in the Ministry of Law and Parliamentary Affairs Constituted to Formulate New Laws on Islamic Lines Under the 1999 Supreme Court (SC) Orders on Riba (Interest)

Chairman

1. Dr Mamood Gazi, The Minster of Religious Affairs

Members

1. Dr. Tariq Hassan
2. Zafar Ali Khan
3. Zafar Hussain

Extenuation in the Task Forces

4. I A Hanfi
5. Mohammad Younas Khan
6. Mohammad Ashraf Janjoaa
7. Salman Shah
8. Dr. Pervez Hassan
9. Molana Taqi Usmani
10. Zakir Mehmood
11. Amar Zafar Khan
12. S Muhammad Hussain
13. Mohammad Fahim Khan

Changes Made in the Task Force

14. Mohammad Taqi Usmani Replaced by Muhammad Rafi Usmani
15. Muhammad Hussain Replaced by Muhammad Saadat
16. Muhammd Javed Zafar also became member committee but soon left the Task Force

I-H Task Force in the Ministry of Finance Constituted to Transform the Economy of Pakistan on Islamic Lines Under the 1999 Supreme Court (SC) Orders on Riba (Interest)

Chairman

Jawed Ahmed Noel, Ministry of Finance, Pakistan

Members

1. Dr Tariq Hassan, Adviser to Finance Minister
2. Dr Mushtaq A Khan, Economic Adviser to the State Bank of Pakistan
3. Syed Muhammad Hussain, Chartered Accountant
4. Dr Khalid Zaheer, Assistant Professor, LUMS
5. Dr Ashfaque Hassan Khan, Economic Adviser, Finance Ministry

Appendix II

Guidelines Provided by the Council of Islamic Ideology in its 1980 Report for Financing Different Sectors of the Economy of Pakistan on the Basis of its Approved Profit and Loss Sharing and Interest-Free Modes of Financing

Term of Finance	*Type of Finance*	*The Proposed Mode of Financing*	*The Basic Criteria for Judgement*
1 Industry			
Long-term	Fixed Investment	PLS	The parties maintain the certified books of account
		Hire-Purchase or *Bai Muajjal* or Leasing	The parties do not maintain the certified books of account
	Bridge Financing	'Firm Commitment' by banks, i.e., the banks to purchase equity at a negotiated price which can be below the face value of the shares (Company's Act to be amended)	The parties maintain the certified books of account
	Debenture Financing	Participation Term Certificates (PTCs)	—ditto–
	Working Capital	PLS on commission basis	The parties maintain the certified books of account
	Cash Credit, Over Draft and Demand Loan	PLS on daily product basis	–ditto–
	Bills of Exchange	Commission basis: Variable according to amount of bills but not according to period	–ditto–

Short-term	Working Capital	Normal Rate of Return or *Bai Muajjal*	The parties do not maintain the certified books of account
2 Agriculture			
Short-term	Purchase of inputs: Seeds, fertilizers, pesticides etc.	Interest-free loan under 'Special Loan Facility'	The holdings of the farmers are up to Subsistence level (12.5 acres of farms)
		Bai Muajjal or *Bai Salam*	The holdings of the farmers are above subsistence level (12.5 acres of farms)
Medium-term	Purchase of plough, cattle etc.	Interest-free loan under ' Special Loan Facility'	The holdings of the farmers are up to subsistence level (12.5 acres of farms)
		Bai Muajjal	The holdings of the farmers are above subsistence level (12.5 acres of farms)
		Interest-free loans up to Rs. 10,000/-	Small farmers (small farmers to be defined by the SBP later on)
	Dairy and poultry farming	PLS or Normal Rate of Return	Medium- and large- size farmers (medium and large-size farmers to be decided by the SBP later on)
		Interest-free loan under 'Special Loan Facility'	The holdings of the farmers are up to subsistence level (12.5 acres of farms)
Long-term	Land improvement and development	PLS or Normal Rate of Return	The farmers holding farms above subsistence level (12.5 acre of farm)
	Purchase of tractors, installation of tube wells.	PLS or *Bai Muajjal* or Hire-Purchase	All types of farmers

(*Continued*)

Term of Finance	*Type of Finance*	*The Proposed Mode of Financing*	*The Basic Criteria for Judgement*
3 Commerce			
Short-term	Working capital: Cash Credit Overdraft Demand Loan, Discounting of Bills etc.	*Bai Muajjal* or Special Loan Facility	Small retailers who do not maintain the certified books of account
		PLS	Large borrowers who maintain the certified books of account
	Letter of Credit (LCs)	Commission or Service Charge	All clients
4 Construction			
Medium- and long- term	Fixed Investment for house construction	PLS	Individual borrowers
	Fixed and working capital	PLS	Construction companies
5 Transport			
Medium- and long- term	Purchase of trucks, buses, taxes, vans etc.	Hire-purchase or *Bai Muajjal*	All borrowers
6 Other Sectors			
Medium- and long- term	Mining, quarrying electricity etc.	PLS	All borrowers
	Purchase of capital goods and machinery	*Bai Muajjal* or Investment Auctioning	All borrowers
7 Personal Loans			
Medium- and long- term	For consumer durable	*Bai Muajjal* or Hire-Purchase	Individuals
	Financing higher studies and relief in case of calamity etc.	Loans without interest. The funds of *Zakah* with the government.	Individuals

Source: Faruqui, J M (1985).

Appendix III

The Banking and Control Department of the State Bank of Pakistan Issued the Following Circulars From Time to Time for Eliminating interest From the Banking Sector of Pakistan Under the Phased Programme

BCD/BPRD Circular/Cir: Letter

S. No.	*Subject*	*No.*	*Date*
1.	Separate Accounting for PLS Deposits	26	24.12.1980
2.	Investment of PLS deposits in Government Transactions	26	24.12.1980
3.	Investment avenues for PLS Funds	21	30.6.1982
4.	Investment avenues for PLS Funds	37	02.11.1982
5.	Elimination of *Riba* from the Banking System	32	05.6.1984
6.	Rate of Service Charge Recoverable on Finances Provided by Way of Lending Other Than *'Qard-e-Hasanah'*	26	06.11.1984
7.	Elimination of *Riba* from the Banking System – Rates of Return in the Case of Trade-Related Modes of Financing	27	26.11.1984
8.	Elimination of *Riba* from the Banking System – Rates of Return in the Case of Investment Type Modes of Financing	28	26.11.1984
9.	Elimination of *Riba* from the Banking System – Making of PLS Term Deposits by Banks/DFIs With the State Bank of Pakistan	31	6.11.1984
10.	Bank Charges	32	26.11.1984
11.	Finances Provided by the State Bank of Pakistan to Banks and DFIs for Meeting Temporary Liquidity Difficulties (Including T.T. Discounting Facilities)	33	26.11.1984
12.	Determination of Rates of Profit on Various Types of PLS Liabilities of the Banks and DFIs	34	26.11.1984

(*Continued*)

S. No.	*Subject*	*No.*	*Date*
13.	Rates of Profit in Case of Trade Related Modes of Financing Rates of Profit in Case of Investment Type Modes of Financing	38	10.12.1984
14.	Scheme for Financing Locally Manufactured Machinery	39	10.12.1984
15.	Export Finance Scheme	40	10.12.1984
16.	Classification of Accounts in the Weekly Statement of Position Hire-Purchase	3	5.1.1985
17.	Determination of Rates of Profit on Various Types of PLS Liabilities of Banks and DFIs	7	11.2.1985
18.	Provision of Finance by Banks and DFIs to Their Employees For Various Purposes Under Rules Framed by Them	8	1.2.1985
19.	Scales of Fines for Defaults by Exporter/Suppliers-Export Finance Scheme	9	12.2.1985
20.	Determination of Rates of Profit on Various Types of PLS Liabilities of the Banks and DFIs – Certificate from the External Auditors of Correctness of Information Provided to the State Bank of Pakistan	10	20.2.1985
21.	Penalty for Defaults in Maintenance of Cash Reserve and Liquid Assets by the Banks	19	7.5.1985
22.	Rates of Profit in Case of Trade-Related Modes of Financing	23	25.5.1985
23.	Rates of Profit in the Case of Investment Type Modes of Financing	24	25.5.1985
24.	Rate of Service Charge Recoverable on Finances Provided by Way of Lending Other Than '*Qard-e-Hasana*' – Total Asset	27	8.6.1985
25.	Determination of Rates of Profit on Various Types of PLS Liabilities of Banks and DFIs – Reserves	28	8.6.1985
26.	Elimination of *Riba* From the Banking System Payment of Profit on PLS/Savings	29	12.6.1985
27.	Bank Accounts – Benefit of the Return For the Preceding Half Year	1	15.1.1986
28.	Determination of Rates of Profit on Various Types of PLS Liabilities of the Banks and DFIs – Export Refinance	2	16.1.1986
29.	Elimination of *Riba* From the Banking – New System of Fines – Export Finance Scheme	4	12.7.1985
30.	Elimination of *Riba* From the Banking System Determination of Rates of Profit on Various Types of PLS Liabilities of the Banks and DFIs	6	12.7.1987
31.	Elimination of *Riba* From the Banking System Determination of Rates of Profit on Various Types of PLS Liabilities of the Banks and DFIs	8	20.6.1989

32.	Elimination of *Riba* From the Banking System Rates of Profit in Case of Trade Related Modes of Financing	6	15.8.1993
33.	Elimination of *Riba* From the Banking System Determination of Rates of Profit on Various Types of PLS Liabilities of the Banks and DFIs	18	20.6.1989
34.	Terms and Conditions for Grant of Financing Facilities by State Bank	4	1.3.1994
35.	Rates of Profit Under Trade Related Modes of Finance	5	1.3.1994
36.	Rates of Profit Under Trade Related Modes of Finance	16	13.11.1994
37.	Elimination of *Riba* from the Banking System Rates of Profit in the Case of Investment Type Modes of Financing	17	13.11.1994
38.	Rates Not Applicable in the Case of Finances Provided For Fixed industrial Investment	18	22.12.1994
39.	Rates of Profit under Trade Related and Investment Type Modes of Finance	12	20.12.1994
40.	Rate of Profit Under Trade Related Modes of Financing	2	17.1.1995
41.	Rate of Profit Under Trade Related Modes of Financing	4	26.3.1995
42.	Elimination of *Riba* From the Banking System – Rates of Profit in the Case of Investment Type Modes of Financing	5	26.3.1995
43.	Rates of Profit Under Trade Related/Investment Type of Finance	12	31.5.1995
44.	Cap of Lending Rate Removed	13	6.6.1995

Appendix IV

115 Petitions and Three *Shariat* Suo Moto Notices Filed by Different Parties With the Federal *Shariat* Court Between June 30 to October 24, 1991 to Challenge a Host of Banking and Fiscal Laws of Pakistan on Grounds that they Contain Interest Provisions

IV-A List of *Shariat* Position/L

Shariat Petition Nos. 30/I, 21/L, 27/L, 8/K, 31/I, 21/L, 27/L, 16/I, 16/L, 17/I, 14/I, 19/I, 17/L, 68/L, 72/I, 33/L, 18/L, 18/I, 21/I, 20/I, 12/L, 7/K, 27/I, 73/I, 13/L of 1990, 1/K, 4/K, 32/I, 48/L, 68/L, 71/L, 56/I, 16-C/I, 17-C/I, 74/I, 33/I, 42/I, 69/L, 70/L, 35/I, 16-A/I, 17-A/I, 2/I, 2/L, 24/L, 25/L, 17/I, 31/I, 45/I, 16/I, 72/L, 74/L, 57/I, 3/I, 1/L, 27/I, 28/I, 30/I, 85/L, 51/I, 64/I, 65/I, 66/I, 67/I, 13/L, 27/L, 34/L, 36/L, 39/L, 22/L, 39/I, 33/L, 41/L, 44/I, 60/L, 46/I, 46/L, 47/I, 48/I, 62/L, 54/I, 79/L, 68/I, 102/L, 17/L, 18/L, 26/L, 29/L, 30/L, 31/L, 32/L, 26/I, 28/L, 43/I, 42/L, 21/L, 49/L, 67/L, 73/L, 76/L, 50/I, 89/L, 90/L, 66/L, 91/L, 93/L, 58/I, 16-B/I, 17-B/I 101/L, 73/I of 1991 and *Shariat* Suo Motu No. 4/I of 1991, heard on 9 June, 1991.

1. By *Shariat* Petition Nos. 30/I, 21/L, 27/L, 8/K of 1990, 1/K, 4/K, 32/I, 48/L, 71/I, 56/I, 16-C//I, and 17-C/I of 1991, The 1938 Interest Act, which contains only one section, has been challenged.
2. By *Shariat* Petition Nos. 31/I, of 1990, Section 8 of The 1873 Government Savings Banks Act has been challenged.
3. By *Shariat* Petition Nos. 21/L, 27/L of 1990, 33/I, 42/I, 69/L, 70/L, 35/I, 16-A/I, 17-A/I, of 1991 and S.S.M. No.2/I pf 1991, sections 78, 79 and 80 of The 1881 Negotiable Instruments Act have been challenged.
4. By *Shariat* Petition No. 2/L of 1991, section 34 of The 1984 Land Acquisition Act has been challenged.

IV-B The Federal *Shariat* Court Judgement of 1991 on *Riba* (Interest)

The Federal *Shariat* Court adjudged the following 20 banking and fiscal laws that contained various provisions of interest on November 14, 1991.

1. The 1839 Interest Act
2. The 1873 Government Savings Banks Act
3. The 1881 Negotiable Instruments Act
4. The 1894 Land Acquisition Act
5. The 1908 Code of Civil Procedure
6. The 1925 Cooperative Societies Act

7. The 1927 Cooperative Societies Rules
8. The 1938 Insurance Act
9. The 1956 State Bank of Pakistan Act
10. The 1965 West Pakistan Money-Lenders Ordinance
11. The 1965 West Pakistan Money-Lenders Rules
12. The 1960 Punjab Money-Lenders Ordinance
13. The 1960 Sindh Money-Lenders Ordinance
14. The 1960 N.W.F.P Money-Lenders Ordinance
15. The 1960 Balochistan Money Lenders Ordinance
16. The 1961 Agricultural Development Bank of Pakistan Rules
17. The 1962 Banking Companies Ordinance
18. The 1963 Banking Companies Rules
19. The 1974 Banks (Nationalization) (Payment of Compensation) Rules
20. The 1979 Banking Companies (Recovery of Loans), Ordinance

IV-C The Supreme Court (SC) Judgement of 1991 on *Riba* (Interest)

The Supreme Court adjudged the following main banking, fiscal laws and other laws that contained various provisions of interest in its Judgement on riba (interest) on December 23, 1999.

1. The 1839 Interest Act
2. The 1960 West Pakistan Money Lenders Ordinance
3. The 1965 West Pakistan Money Lenders Rules
4. The 1960 Punjab Money Lenders Ordinance
5. The 1960 Sindh Money Lenders Ordinance
6. The 1960 NWFP Money Lenders Ordinance
7. The 1960 Balochistan Money Lenders Ordinance
8. The 1962 Banking Companies Ordinance, Section 9

Appendix V

The Federal *Shariat* Court's Questionnaire on *Riba* (Interest) and its Respondents (The 1991 FSC Judgement)

The Federal *Shariat* Court prepared a questionnaire relating to the impugned banking and fiscal laws and distributed it among Islamic scholars, bankers and economists, seeking their opinions on the said questions. The contents of the questionnaire and the names of the respondents are given below.

Question No. 1: What is the definition of *riba* according to the holy *Quran* and the *Sunnah* of the holy Prophet Mohammad (pbuh)? Does it cover the simple and compound interest existing in the present financial system?

Respondents:
Maulana Gawhar Rahman
Maulana Muhammad Rafi Osmani
Dr. Saidullah Qazi
Maulana Syed Ma'ruf Shah Shirazi
Dr. Nejatullah Siddiqi
Dr. S M Hasanuzzaman
Dr. M Ramazan Akhtar
Prof. Dr. Ala'addin Kharofa
Mr. Nawazish Ali Zaidi
Mr. Ziaul Haq
Mr. M Arshad Javed
Mr. Imtiaz Pervez

Question No. 2: If banking were based on interest-free transactions, what would be its basic practical shape in conformity with the injunctions of Islam?

Respondents:
Maulana Gawhar Rahman
Maulana Muhammad Rafi Osmani
Dr. Saidullah Qazi
Maulana Syed Ma'ruf Shah Shirazi
Dr. Nejatullah Siddiqi
Dr. S M Hasanuzzaman
Dr. M Ramazan Akhtar
Prof. Dr. Ala'addin Kharofa
Mr. Nawazish Ali Zaidi
Mr. Ziaul Haq
Mr. M Arshad Javed

Question No.3:

I. Can capital, according to the injunctions of Islam, be regarded as an agent of production, thus requiring remuneration for its use?
II. Does devaluation of the currency affect the payment of loans taken out before such devaluation?
III. Can inflation causing a rise in the cost/value of gold and consumer goods in term of currency have any effect on the sum borrowed?

Respondents: Maulana Gawhar Rahman
Maulana Muhammad Rafi Osmani
Dr. Saidullah Qazi
Maulana Syed Ma'ruf Shah Shirazi
Dr. Nejatullah Siddiqi
Dr. S M Hasanuzzaman
Dr. M Ramazan Akhtar
Prof. Dr. Ala'addin Kharofa
Mr. Nawazish Ali Zaidi
Mr. Ziaul Haq
Mr. M. Arshad Javed
Prof. Sayyid Tahir

Question No. 4: What would be the alternatives in the context of present-day economic conditions for carrying on domestic and foreign trade efficiently without resorting to banking facilities based on interest?

Respondents: Maulana Gawhar Rahman
Dr. Saidullah Qazi
Maulana Syed Ma'ruf Shah Shirazi
Dr. Nejatullah Siddiqi
Dr. S M Hasanuzzaman
Dr. M Ramazan Akhtar
Prof. Dr. Ala'addin Kharofa
Mr. Nawazish Ali Zaidi
Mr. M Arshad Javed

Question No 5: Is interest permissible on the transactions between two *Muslim states* or a *Muslim* state and *non-Muslim* state?

Respondents: Maulana Gawhar Rahman
Dr. Saidullah Qazi
Maulana Syed Ma'ruf Shah Shirazi
Dr. Nejatullah Siddiqi

	Dr. S M Hasanuzzaman Dr. M Ramazan Akhtar Prof. Dr. Ala'addin Kharofa Mr. Nawazish Ali Zaidi Mr. Ziaul Haq Mr. M Arshad Javed
Question No. 6:	Is it possible to carry on insurance business otherwise than on the basis of interest?
Respondents:	Maulana Gawhar Rahman Dr. Saidullah Qazi Maulana Syed Ma'ruf Shah Shirazi Dr. Nejatullah Siddiqi Dr. S M Hasanuzzaman Dr. M Ramazan Akhtar Prof. Dr. Ala'addin Kharofa Mr. Nawazish Ali Zaidi Mr. Ziaul Haq Mr. M Arshad Javed
Question No. 7:	Does interest accruing on the Provident Fund come under *riba*?
Respondents:	Maulana Gawhar Rahman Maulana Muhammad Rafi Osmani Dr. Saidullah Qazi Maulana Syed Ma'ruf Shah Shirazi Dr. Nejatullah Siddiqi Dr. S M Hasanuzzaman Dr. M Ramazan Akhtar Prof. Dr. Ala'addin Kharofa Mr. Nawazish Ali Zaidi Mr. Ziaul Haq Mr. M Arshad Javed
Question No. 8:	Can the payment of prize money on Prize Bonds or Savings Bank Accounts or other similar schemes be regarded as *riba*?
Respondents:	Maulana Gawhar Rahman Maulana Muhammad Rafi Osmani Dr. Saidullah Qazi Maulana Syed Ma'ruf Shah Shirazi Dr. Nejatullah Siddiqi Dr. S M Hasanuzzaman

Dr. M. Ramazan Akhtar
Prof. Dr. Ala'addin Kharofa
Mr. Nawazish Ali Zaidi
Mr. Ziaul Haq
Mr. M Arshad Javed

Question No. 9: Would it be lawful under Islamic law to differentiate between business loans on which interest may be charged and consumption loans which should be free of interest?

Respondents:
Maulana Gawhar Rahman
Maulana Muhammad Rafi Osmani
Dr. Saidullah Qazi
Maulana Syed Ma'ruf Shah Shirazi
Dr. Nejatullah Siddiqi
Dr. S M Hasanuzzaman
Dr. M Ramazan Akhtar
Prof. Dr. Ala'addin Kharofa
Mr. Nawazish Ali Zaidi
Mr. Ziaul Haq
Mr. M Arshad Javed

Question No. 10: If interest were completely abolished, what would be the inducements in an Islamic economic system to save and to economize on the use of capital?

Respondents:
Maulana Gawhar Rahman
Maulana Muhammad Rafi Osmani
Dr. Saidullah Qazi
Maulana Syed Ma'ruf Shah Shirazi
Dr. Nejatullah Siddiqi
Dr. S M Hasanuzzaman
Dr. M Ramazan Akhtar
Prof. Dr. Ala'addin Kharofa
Mr. Nawazish Ali Zaidi
Mr. Ziaul Haq

Apart from above respondents, the following experts on Islamic banking presented their viewpoints on the *riba* case before the Federal *Shariat* Court (FSC) in 1991.

1. Mr. Mansoor Ahmad Khan, Advocate, Karachi, Pakistan
2. Mr. Khadim Hussain Siddiqui, Former President, Allied Bank Limited, Karachi, Pakistan

3. Dr. Hasanuzzaman, Chief of Islamic Banking Division, State Bank of Pakistan, Karachi, Pakistan
4. Dr. Muhammad Uzair, Economic Advisor, National Development Finance Corporation of Pakistan, Karachi, Pakistan
5. Dr. Muhammad Hussain, Director, International Islamic University, Islamabad, Pakistan
6. Dr. Faiz Muhammad, Director-General, International Institute of Islamic Economics, International Islamic University, Islamabad, Pakistan

Appendix VI

The Supreme Court (SC)'s Questionnaire on *Riba* (Interest) and its Respondents (The 1999 SC Judgement)

The Supreme Court (SC) prepared the questionnaire and distributed it to Islamic jurists, scholars and experts on Islamic banking, seeking their advice on the *riba* case. The contents of the questionnaire were as follows.

Question No. 1: The holy Quran has prohibited 'riba'. What is meant by this term? What is its true definition and connotation in the light of the holy Quran and Sunnah of the holy Prophet (pbuh)?

Question No. 2: What is the true scope of the transactions to which the ban on *riba* is applicable? Can the term *riba* also be applied to the commercial or productive loans advanced by banking and financial institutions and to the interest charged thereon?

Question No. 3: Pakistani banks and some financial institution finance their clients on the basis of a buyback on mark-up agreements. According to this method the client of the bank purports to sell a particular commodity to the bank, and simultaneously buys it back at a high price on deferred payment basis. A certain rate of mark-up (percent per annum) is applied to the second sale. Does this arrangement fall within the ambit of *riba*?

Question No. 4: Is there any difference between a Muslim and a non-Muslim in the matter of prohibition of *riba*? Can the prohibition of *riba* be extended to the loans obtained from non-Muslim, or for that matter, from Muslim foreign countries whose laws and national policies, together with international monetary laws and policies, are not within the control of the State of Pakistan?

Question No. 5: The Government of Pakistan and some institutions under its control acquire loans by issuing bonds and certificates, etc. and pay a fixed period-wise 'profit' to the holders of such securities. Does this profit fall within the definition of *riba*?

Question No. 6: It is evident that the value of the paper currency has a tendency to decrease in an inflationary situation. If a debtor who has borrowed a particular amount of paper currency repays the same amount to his creditor after a substantial time, the creditor can suffer the effects of inflation. If he demands that his debtor pay more in order to compensate him for loss of value he has suffered, can this demand be treated as a demand for *riba*?

Question No. 7: If all the forms of interest or mark-up are held to be repugnant to the Islamic injunctions, what modes of financing do you suggest for: (a) financing trade and industry; (b) financing the budget deficit; (c) acquiring foreign loans; and (d) other such needs and purposes?

Question No. 8: If you are of the view that all the forms of interest are prohibited by the Islamic *Shariah,* then what procedure would you suggest for eliminating it from the economy? If you prefer a gradual process, what strategy do you suggest for the purpose that may fulfil the requirements of the holy *Quran* and *Sunnah*?

Question No. 9: If all the transactions based on interest are held to violate the Islamic injunctions, what will be the treatment of the past transactions and agreements? Especially, what procedure should the government adopt with regard to previous foreign loans?

The Supreme Court considered the views of the Islamic scholars, bankers and economists in deciding on the *riba* (interest) case in 1999.

The following *ulema,* scholars and economists, amongst others, submitted written answers to the questionnaire issued by the Supreme Court:

1. Mr. Sartaj Aziz, Minister for Finance and Economic Affairs, Government of Pakistan. Islamic Development Bank, Jeddah
2. Prof. Khurshid Ahmad, Institute of Policy Studies
3. Dr. Ziauddin Ahmed, Karachi, Pakistan
4. Mr. Zafar Ishaque Ansari, Director General Islamic Research Institute, International Islamic University, Islamabad, Pakistan
5. Dr. Nawazish Li Zaidi, Rawalpindi, Pakistan
6. Dr. Arshad Zaman, Karachi, Pakistan
7. Mr. Abdur Rauf Sheikh, Lahore, Pakistan

8. Prof. Dr. Muhammad Najatullah Siddiqui, International Islamic Economics Centre, Malik Abdul Aziz University, Jeddah
9. Mr. Alsiddique Muhammad al-Amin, Teachers, Al-Shariah Al–islamia Law Department, Khartoom University, Sudan
10. Syed Maroof Shah Shirazi, Shariah Academy, International Islamic University, Islamabad, Pakistan
11. Mr. Anwar Ahmad Minai, Karachi, Pakistan
12. Syed Naseeb Ali Shah, Nazim Majlis-e-Fiqhi, Jamiat Ulami Pakistan
13. Mr. G M Saleem, Advocate, Karachi, Pakistan
14. Mr. Mehmood Ashraf, Chartered Management Accountant, Karachi
15. Mr. Abdul Moin Ansari, Latifabad, Hyderabad, Pakistan
16. Prof. Dr. Muhammad Tahir ul Qadri, Lahore, Pakistan
17. Dr. Attaullah Khan Niazi, Economic Expert
18. Mr. Abdul Hafeez Khokhar, Advocate
19. Mr. Aqdas Ali Kazmi, Chief/Director Tax Policy, Central Board of Revenue, Islamabad, Pakistan
20. Mr. Aurangzeb Haque
21. Prof. Ziauddin Ahmad

Besides learned counsel for the parties, the following scholars, economists and bankers appeared and made their submissions to the Supreme Court:

1. Dr. Syed Muhammad Tahir, International Islamic University, Pakistan
2. Dr. Waqar Masood Khan, Director General (Planning), international Islamic University, Islamabad, Pakistan
3. Mr. Abdul Jabbar Khan, former President National Bank of Pakistan
4. Dr. Umar Chapra, Jeddah
5. Mr. Ibrahim Sidat
6. Dr. S Muhammad Hussain
7. Dr. Irshad Zaman, Accountants/Economists
8. Mr. Maqbool Soomroo
9. Dr. Shahid Hasan Siddiqui, Economist
10. Mr. Abdul Wadood Khan
11. Hafiz Abdul Rehman Madni, Chairman, Islamic Research Council, Lahore, Pakistan
12. Dr. Aslam Khaki, Advocate, Islamabad, Pakistan
13. Prof. Khurshid Ahmad, IPS, Pakistan
14. Mr. H U Beg. (Retired Finance Secretary, Government of Pakistan)

15. Prof. Syed Nawaz Haider Naqvi
16. Mr. Muhammad Yahya (Deputy Secretary General, Mutahida *Ulema* Council of Pakistan)
17. Maulana Gauhar Rehman
18. Mr. Iqbal Khan (Foreign Expert-Managing Director Global Islamic Finance; HSBC Investment Bank PLC, United Kingdom.
19. Dr. Ahmad Muhammad Ali (President, Islamic Development Bank, Jeddah) along with his delegation namely, Mr. Muad Ali, Umar (Vice President, IDB), Dr. M Alfatah (Legal Adviser IDB), Mr. D M Qureshi (Adviser Treasury, IDB), Mr. Muhhad Al-Jehri(Director, IDB), Dr. Hussain Hassan (Head of Shariah Board, Dubai Islamic Bank) and Mr. Adnan Al Bahr, Managing Director and Chairman, International Investment Company Kuwait)
20. Mr. Ismail Qureshi, ASC
21. Mr. Faheem Ahmad (Marketing Coordinator, Financial Research and Analysis, Credit Rating Company Ltd., Pakistan, Karachi)

Index

Note: Page numbers in *italics* denote tables/figures.